WOMAN

IN THE

NINETEENTH CENTURY,

AND KINDRED PAPERS RELATING TO THE

SPHERE, CONDITION, AND DUTIES
OF WOMAN.

BY

MARGARET FULLER OSSOLI

EDITED BY HER BROTHER, ARTHUR B. FULLER.

New and Complete Edition,
WITH AN INTRODUCTION BY HORACE GREELEY.

GREENWOOD PRESS, PUBLISHERS
WESTPORT, CONNECTICUT

PREFACE.

It has been thought desirable that such papers of Margaret Fuller Ossoli as pertained to the condition, sphere and duties of Woman, should be collected and published together. The present volume contains not only her " Woman in the Nineteenth Century,"— which has been before published, but for some years out of print, and inaccessible to readers who have sought it,— but also several other papers, which have appeared at various times in the *Tribune* and elsewhere, and yet more which have never till now been published.

My free access to her private manuscripts has given to me many papers, relating to Woman, never intended for publication, which yet seem needful to this volume, in order to present a complete and harmonious view of her thoughts on this important theme. I have preferred to publish them without alteration, as most just to her views and to the reader ; though, doubtless, she would have varied their expression and form before giving them to the press.

It seems right here to remark, in order to avoid any misapprehension, that Margaret Ossoli's thoughts were not directed so exclusively to the subject of the present volume as have been the minds of some others. As to the movement for the emancipation of Woman from the unjust burdens and disabilities to which she has been subject even in our own land, my sister could neither remain indifferent nor silent ; yet she preferred, as in respect to every other reform, to act independently and to speak independently from her own stand-point, and never to merge her individuality in any existing organization. This she did, not as condemning such organizations, nor yet as judging them wholly unwise or uncalled for, but because she believed she could herself accomplish more for their true and high objects, unfettered by such organizations, than if a member of them. The opinions avowed throughout this volume, and wherever expressed, will, then, be found, whether consonant with the reader's or no, in all cases honestly and heartily her own,— the result of her own thought and faith. She never speaks, never did speak, for any clique or sect, but as her individual judgment, her reason and conscience, her observation and experience, taught her to speak.

I could have wished that some one other than a brother should have spoken a few fitting words of Margaret Fuller, as a woman, to form a brief but proper accompaniment to this volume, which may reach some who have never read her "Memoirs," recently published, or have never known her in personal life. This seemed the more desirable, because the strictest verity in speaking of her must seem, to such as knew her not, to be eulogy. But, after several disappointments as to the editorship of the volume, the duty, at last, has seemed to devolve upon me ; and I have no reason to shrink from it but a sense of inadequacy.

It is often supposed that literary women, and those who are active and earnest in promoting great intellectual, philanthropic, or religious movements, must of necessity neglect the domestic concerns of life. It may be that this is sometimes so, nor can such neglect be too severely reprehended ; yet this is by no means a necessary result. Some of the most devoted mothers the world has ever known, and whose homes were the abode of every domestic virtue, themselves the embodiment of all these, have been women whose minds were highly cultured, who loved and devoted both thought and time to literature, and were active in philanthropic and diffusive efforts for the welfare of the race.

The letter to M., which is published on page 345, is inserted chiefly as showing the integrity and wisdom with which Margaret advised her friends ; the frankness with which she pointed out to every young woman who asked counsel any deficiencies of character, and the duties of life ; and that among these latter she gave due place to the humblest which serve to make home attractive and happy. It is but simple justice for me to bear, in conjunction with many others, my tribute to her domestic virtues and fidelity to all home duties. That her mind found chief delight in the lowest forms of these duties may not be true, and it would be sad if it were ; but it is strictly true that none, however humble, were either slighted or shunned.

In common with a younger sister and brother, I shared her care in my early instruction, and found ever one of the truest counsellors in a sister who scorned not the youngest mind nor the simplest intellectual wants in her love for communion, through converse or the silent page, with the minds of the greatest and most gifted.

During a lingering illness, in childhood, well do I remember her as the angel of the sick-chamber, reading much to me from books useful and appropriate, and telling many a narrative not only fitted to wile away the pain of disease and the weariness of long confinement, but to elevate the mind and heart, and to direct them to all things noble and holy ; ever ready to watch while I slept, and to perform every gentle and kindly office. But her care of the sick — that she did not neglect, but was eminent in that sphere of womanly duty, even when no tie of kindred claimed this of her, Mr. Cass's letter abundantly shows ; and also that this gentleness was united to a heroism which most call manly, but which, I believe, may as justly be called truly womanly. Mr Cass's letter is inserted because it arrived too late to find a place in her " Memoirs," and yet more because it bears much on Margaret Ossoli's characteristics as a woman.

A few also of her private letters and papers, not bearing, save, indirectly, on the subject of this volume, are yet inserted in it, as further illustrative of her thought, feeling and action, in life's various relations. It is believed that nothing which exhibits a true woman, especially in her relations to others as friend, sister, daughter, wife, or mother, can fail to interest and be of value to her sex, indeed to all who are interested in human welfare and advancement, since these latter so much depend on the fidelity of Woman. Nor will anything pertaining to the education and care of children be deemed irrelevant, especially by mothers, upon whom these duties must always largely devolve.

Of the intellectual gifts and wide culture of Margaret Fuller there is no need that I should speak, nor is it wise that one standing in my relation to her should. Those who knew her personally feel that no words ever flowed from her pen equalling the eloquent utterances of her lips; yet her works, though not always a clear expression of her thoughts, are the evidences to which the world will look as proof of her mental greatness.

On one point, however, I do wish to bear testimony — not needed with those who knew her well, but interesting, perhaps, to some readers into whose hands this volume may fall. It is on a subject which one who knew her from his childhood up — at *home*, where best the *heart* and *soul* can be known, — in the unrestrained hours of domestic life, — in various scenes, and not for a few days, nor under any peculiar circumstances — can speak with confidence, because he speaks what he "doth know, and testifieth what he hath seen." It relates to her Christian faith and hope. "With all her intellectual gifts, with all her high, moral, and noble characteristics," there are some who will ask, "was her intellectual power sanctified by Christian faith as its basis? Were her moral qualities, her beneficent life, the results of a renewed heart?" I feel no hesitation here, nor would think it worth while to answer such questions at all, were her life to be read and known by all who read this volume, and were I not influenced also, in some degree, by the tone which has characterized a few sectarian reviews of her works, chiefly in foreign periodicals. Surely, if the Saviour's test, "By their fruits ye shall know them," be the true one, Margaret Ossoli was pre-eminently a Christian. If a life of constant self-sacrifice, — if devotion to the welfare of kindred and the race, — if conformity to what she believed God's law, so that her life seemed ever tne truest form of prayer, active obedience to the Deity, — in fine, if carrying Christianity into all the departments of action, so far as human infirmity allows, — if these be the proofs of a Christian, then whoever has read her "Memoirs" thoughtfully, and without sectarian prejudice or the use of sectarian standards of judgment, must feel her to have been a Christian. But not alone in outward life, in mind and heart, too, was she a Christian. The being brought into frequent and intimate contact with religious persons has been one of the chief privileges of my vocation, but never yet have I met with any person whose reverence for holy things was deeper than hers. Abhorring, as all honest minds must, every species of cant, she respected true religious thought and feeling, by whomsoever cherished. God seemed nearer to her than to any person I have ever known. In the influences of His Holy Spirit upon the heart she fully believed, and in experience realized them. Jesus, the friend of man, can never have been more truly loved and honored than she loved and honored him. I am aware that this is strong language, but strength of language cannot equal the strength of my conviction on a point where I have had the best opportunities of judgment. Rich as is the religion of Jesus in its list of holy confessors, yet it can spare and would exclude none who in heart, mind and life, confessed and reverenced him as did she. Among my earliest recollections, is her devoting much time to a thorough examination of the evidences of Christianity, and ultimately declaring that to her, better than all arguments or usual processes of proof, was the soul's want of a divine religion, and the voice within that soul which declared the teachings of Christ to be true and from God ; and one of my most cherished possessions is that Bible which she so diligently and thoughtfully read, and which bears, in her own handwriting, so many proofs of discriminating and prayerful perusal. As in regard to reformatory movements so here, she joined no organized body of believers, sympathizing with all of them whose views were noble and Christian ; deploring and bearing faithful testimony against anything she deemed narrowness or perversion in theology or life.

This volume from her hand is now before the reader. The fact that a large share of it was never written or revised by its authoress for publication will be kept in view, as explaining any inaccuracy of expression or repetition of thought, should such occur in its pages. Nor will it be deemed surprising, if, in papers written by so progressive a person, at so various periods of life, and under widely-varied circumstances, there should not always be found perfect unison as to every expressed opinion.

It is probable that this will soon be followed by another volume, containing a republication of " Summer on the Lakes," and also the " Letters from Europe," by the same hand.

In the preparation of this volume much valuable assistance has been afforded by Mr. Greeley, of the New York *Tribune*, who has been earnest in his desire and efforts for the diffusion of what Margaret has written.

A. B. F.

BOSTON, *May* 10*th* 1855.

INTRODUCTION.

THE problem of Woman's position, or " sphere," — of her duties, responsibilities, rights and immunities *as* Woman, — fitly attracts a large and still-increasing measure of attention from the thinkers and agitators of our time. The legislators, so called, — those who ultimately enact into statutes what the really governing class (to wit, the thinkers) have originated, matured and gradually commended to the popular comprehension and acceptance, — are not as yet much occupied with this problem, only fitfully worried and more or less consciously puzzled by it. More commonly they merely echo the mob's shallow retort to the petition of any strong-minded daughter or sister, who demands that she be allowed a voice in disposing of the money wrenched from her hard earnings by inexorable taxation, or in shaping the laws by which she is ruled, judged, and is liable to be sentenced to prison or to death, " It is a woman's business to obey her husband, keep his home tidy, and nourish and train his children." But when she rejoins to this, " Very true ; but suppose I choose not to have a husband, or am not chosen for a wife — what then ? I am still subject to your laws. Why am I not entitled, as a rational human being, to a voice in shaping them ? I have physical needs, and must somehow earn a living. Why should I not be at liberty to earn it in any honest and useful calling ? " — the mob's flout is hushed, and the legislator is struck dumb also. They were already at the end of their scanty resources of logic, and it would be cruel for woman to ask further : " Suppose me a wife, and my husband a drunken prodigal — what am I to do then ? May I not earn food for my babes without being exposed to have it snatched from their mouths to replenish the rumseller's till, and

aggravate my husband's madness? If some sympathizing relative
sees fit to leave me a bequest wherewith to keep my little ones
together, why may I not be legally enabled to secure this to their
use and benefit? In short, why am I not regarded by the law as
a *soul*, responsible for my acts to God and humanity, and not as a
mere body, devoted to the unreasoning service of my husband? "
The state gives no answer, and the champions of her policy evince
wisdom in imitating her silence.

The writer of the following pages was one of the earliest as well
as ablest among American women, to demand for her sex equality
before the law with her titular lord and master. Her writings on
this subject have the force which springs from the ripening of profound reflection into assured conviction. She wrote as one who had
observed, and who deeply felt what she deliberately uttered. Others have since spoken more fluently, more variously, with a greater
affluence of illustration; but none, it is believed, more earnestly
or more forcibly. It is due to her memory, as well as to the great
and living cause of which she was so eminent and so fearless an
advocate, that what she thought and said with regard to the position of her sex and its limitations, should be fully and fairly placed
before the public. For several years past her principal essay on
" Woman," here given, has not been purchasable at any price,
and has only with great difficulty been accessible to the general
reader. To place it within the reach of those who need and require it, is the main impulse to the publication of this volume;
but the accompanying essays and papers will be found equally
worthy of thoughtful consideration.

H. GREELEY.

CONTENTS.

PART I.

PART II.

PART III.

PART IV.

PREFACE

TO

WOMAN IN THE NINETEENTH CENTURY.

THE following essay is a reproduction, modified and expanded, of an article published in "The Dial, Boston, July, 1843," under the title of "The Great Lawsuit. — Man *versus* Men; Woman *versus* Women."

This article excited a good deal of sympathy, and still more interest. It is in compliance with wishes expressed from many quarters that it is prepared for publication in its present form.

Objections having been made to the former title, as not sufficiently easy to be understood, the present has been substituted as expressive of the main purpose of the essay; though, by myself, the other is preferred, partly for the reason others do not like it,— that is, that it requires some thought to see what it means, and might thus prepare the reader to meet me on my own ground. Besides, it offers a larger scope, and is, in that way, more just to my desire. I meant by that title to intimate the fact that, while it is the destiny of Man, in the course of the ages, to ascertain and fulfil the law of his being, so that his life shall be seen, as a whole, to be that of an angel or messenger, the action of prejudices and passions which attend, in the day, the growth of the individual, is continually obstructing the holy work that is to make the earth a part of heaven. By Man I mean both man and woman; these are the two halves of one thought. I lay no especial stress on the welfare of either. I believe that the development of the one cannot be effected without that of the other. My highest wish is that this truth should be distinctly and rationally apprehended, and the conditions of life and freedom recognized as the same for the daughters and the sons of time ; twin exponents of a divine thought.

I solicit a sincere and patient attention from those who open the following pages at all. I solicit of women that they will lay it to heart to ascertain what is for them the liberty of law. It is for this, and not for any, the largest, extension of partial privileges that I seek. I ask them, if interested by these suggestions, to search their own experience and intuitions for better, and fill up with fit materials the trenches that hedge them in. From men I ask a noble and earnest attention to anything that can be offered on this great and still obscure subject, such as I have met from many with whom I stand in private relations.

And may truth, unpolluted by prejudice, vanity or selfishness, be granted daily more and more as the due of inheritance, and only valuable conquest for us all !

November, 1844.

WOMAN

IN THE

NINETEENTH CENTURY.

" Frailty, thy name is WOMAN."
" The Earth waits for her Queen."

THE connection between these quotations may not be
obvious, but it is strict. Yet would any contradict us,
if we made them applicable to the other side, and began
also,

Frailty, thy name is MAN.
The Earth waits for its King?

Yet Man, if not yet fully installed in his powers, has
given much earnest of his claims. Frail he is indeed,—
how frail! how impure! Yet often has the vein of gold
displayed itself amid the baser ores, and Man has appeared before us in princely promise worthy of his future.

If, oftentimes, we see the prodigal son feeding on the
husks in the fair field no more his own, anon we raise
the eyelids, heavy from bitter tears, to behold in him the
radiant apparition of genius and love, demanding not
less than the all of goodness, power and beauty. We
see that in him the largest claim finds a due foundation.

That claim is for no partial sway, no exclusive posses-sion. He cannot be satisfied with any one gift of life, any one department of knowledge or telescopic peep at the heavens. He feels himself called to understand and aid Nature, that she may, through his intelligence, be raised and interpreted; to be a student of, and servant to, the universe-spirit; and king of his planet, that, as an angelic minister, he may bring it into conscious harmony with the law of that spirit.

In clear, triumphant moments, many times, has rung through the spheres the prophecy of his jubilee; and those moments, though past in time, have been translated into eternity by thought; the bright signs they left hang in the heavens, as single stars or constellations, and, already, a thickly sown radiance consoles the wanderer in the darkest night. Other heroes since Hercules have fulfilled the zodiac of beneficent labors, and then given up their mortal part to the fire without a murmur; while no God dared deny that they should have their reward,

> Siquis tamen, Hercule, siquis
> Forte Deo doliturus erit, data præmia nollet,
> Sed meruise dari sciet, invitus que probabit,
> Assensere Dei.

Sages and lawgivers have bent their whole nature to the search for truth, and thought themselves happy if they could buy, with the sacrifice of all temporal ease and pleasure, one seed for the future Eden. Poets and priests have strung the lyre with the heart-strings, poured out their best blood upon the altar, which, reared anew

from age to age, shall at last sustain the flame pure
enough to rise to highest heaven.   Shall we not name
with as deep a benediction those who, if not so immediately, or so consciously, in connection with the eternal
truth, yet, led and fashioned by a divine instinct, serve
no less to develop and interpret the open secret of love
passing into life, energy creating for the purpose of happiness; the artist whose hand, drawn by a preëxistent
harmony to a certain medium, moulds it to forms of life
more highly and completely organized than are seen elsewhere, and, by carrying out the intention of nature,
reveals her meaning to those who are not yet wise enough
to divine it; the philosopher who listens steadily for
laws and causes, and from those obvious infers those yet
unknown; the historian who, in faith that all events
must have their reason and their aim, records them, and
thus fills archives from which the youth of prophets may
be fed; the man of science dissecting the statements,
testing the facts and demonstrating order, even where he
cannot its purpose?

Lives, too, which bear none of these names, have
yielded tones of no less significance.   The candlestick
set in a low place has given light as faithfully, where it
was needed, as that upon the hill.   In close alleys, in
dismal nooks, the Word has been read as distinctly, as
when shown by angels to holy men in the dark prison
Those who till a spot of earth scarcely larger than is
wanted for a grave, have deserved that the sun should
shine upon its sod till violets answer.

So great has been, from time to time, the promise,

that, in all ages, men have said the gods themselves came down to dwell with them; that the All-Creating wandered on the earth to taste, in a limited nature, the sweetness of virtue; that the All-Sustaining incarnated himself to guard, in space and time, the destinies of this world; that heavenly genius dwelt among the shepherds, to sing to them and teach them how to sing. Indeed,

" Der stets den Hirten gnadig sich bewies."

"He has constantly shown himself favorable to shepherds."

And the dwellers in green pastures and natural students of the stars were selected to hail, first among men, the holy child, whose life and death were to present the type of excellence, which has sustained the heart of so large a portion of mankind in these later generations.

Such marks have been made by the footsteps of *man* (still, alas! to be spoken of as the *ideal* man), wherever he has passed through the wilderness of *men*, and whenever the pigmies stepped in one of those, they felt dilate within the breast somewhat that promised nobler stature and purer blood. They were impelled to forsake their evil ways of decrepit scepticism and covetousness of corruptible possessions. Convictions flowed in upon them. They, too, raised the cry: God is living, now, to-day; and all beings are brothers, for they are his children. Simple words enough, yet which only angelic natures can use or hear in their full, free sense.

These were the triumphant moments; but soon the lower nature took its turn, and the era of a truly human life was postponed.

Thus is man still a stranger to his inheritance, still a pleader, still a pilgrim. Yet his happiness is secure in the end. And now, no more a glimmering consciousness, but assurance begins to be felt and spoken, that the highest ideal Man can form of his own powers is that which he is destined to attain. Whatever the soul knows how to seek, it cannot fail to obtain. This is the Law and the Prophets. Knock and it shall be opened; seek and ye shall find. It is demonstrated; it is a maxim. Man no longer paints his proper nature in some form, and says, "Prometheus had it; it is God-like;" but "Man must have it; it is human." However disputed by many, however ignorantly used, or falsified by those who do receive it, the fact of an universal, unceasing revelation has been too clearly stated in words to be lost sight of in thought; and sermons preached from the text, "Be ye perfect," are the only sermons of a pervasive and deep-searching influence.

But, among those who meditate upon this text, there is a great difference of view as to the way in which perfection shall be sought.

"Through the intellect," say some. "Gather from every growth of life its seed of thought; look behind every symbol for its law; if thou canst see clearly, the rest will follow."

"Through the life," say others. "Do the best thou knowest to-day. Shrink not from frequent error in this gradual, fragmentary state. Follow thy light for as much as it will show thee; be faithful as far as thou canst, in hope that faith presently will lead to sight Help others, without blaming their need of thy help. Love much, and be forgiven."

"It needs not intellect, needs not experience," says a third. "If you took the true way, your destiny would be accomplished in a purer and more natural order. You would not learn through facts of thought or action, but express through them the certainties of wisdom. In quietness yield thy soul to the causal soul. Do not disturb thy apprenticeship by premature effort; neither check the tide of instruction by methods of thy own. Be still; seek not, but wait in obedience. Thy commission will be given."

Could we indeed say what we want, could we give a description of the child that is lost, he would be found. As soon as the soul can affirm clearly that a certain demonstration is wanted, it is at hand. When the Jewish prophet described the Lamb, as the expression of what was required by the coming era, the time drew nigh. But we say not, see not as yet, clearly, what we would. Those who call for a more triumphant expression of love, a love that cannot be crucified, show not a perfect sense of what has already been given. Love has already been expressed, that made all things new, that gave the worm its place and ministry as well as the eagle; a love to which it was alike to descend into the depths of hell, or to sit at the right hand of the Father.

Yet, no doubt, a new manifestation is at hand, a new hour in the day of Man. We cannot expect to see any one sample of completed being, when the mass of men still lie engaged in the sod, or use the freedom of their limbs only with wolfish energy. The tree cannot come to flower till its root be free from the cankering worm, and its whole growth open to air and light. While any one is base, none can be entirely free and noble. Yet something new shall presently be shown of the life of man, for hearts crave, if minds do not know how to ask it.

Among the strains of prophecy, the following, by an earnest mind of a foreign land, written some thirty years ago, is not yet outgrown ; and it has the merit of being a positive appeal from the heart, instead of a critical declaration what Man should *not* do.

" The ministry of Man implies that he must be filled from the divine fountains which are being engendered through all eternity, so that, at the mere name of his master, he may be able to cast all his enemies into the abyss ; that he may deliver all parts of nature from the barriers that imprison them ; that he may purge the ter-restrial atmosphere from the poisons that infect it ; that he may preserve the bodies of men from the corrupt influ-ences that surround, and the maladies that afflict them ; still more, that he may keep their souls pure from the malignant insinuations which pollute, and the gloomy images that obscure them ; that he may restore its serenity to the Word, which false words of men fill with mourning and sadness; that he may satisfy the desires of the angels, who await from him the development of the marvels of nature ; that, in fine, his world may be filled with God, as eternity is."*

Another attempt we will give, by an obscure observer

* St. Martin.

of our own day and country, to draw some lines of the desired image. It was suggested by seeing the design of Crawford's Orpheus, and connecting with the circumstance of the American, in his garret at Rome, making choice of this subject, that of Americans here at home showing such ambition to represent the character, by calling their prose and verse " Orphic sayings " — " Orphics." We wish we could add that they have shown that musical apprehension of the progress of Nature through her ascending gradations which entitled them so to do, but their attempts are frigid, though sometimes grand ; in their strain we are not warmed by the fire which fertilized the soil of Greece.

Orpheus was a lawgiver by theocratic commission. He understood nature, and made her forms move to his music. He told her secrets in the form of hymns, Nature as seen in the mind of God. His soul went forth toward all beings, yet could remain sternly faithful to a chosen type of excellence. Seeking what he loved, he feared not death nor hell ; neither could any shape of dread daunt his faith in the power of the celestial harmony that filled his soul.

It seemed significant of the state of things in this country, that the sculptor should have represented the seer at the moment when he was obliged with his hand to shade his eyes.

Each Orpheus must to the depths descend ;
For only thus the Poet can be wise ;
Must make the sad Persephone his friend,
And buried love to second life arise ;

> Again his love must lose through too much love,
>   Must lose his life by living life too true,
> For what he sought below is passed above,
>   Already done is all that he would do ;
> Must tune all being with his single lyre,
>   Must melt all rocks free from their primal pain,
> Must search all nature with his one soul's fire,
>   Must bind anew all forms in heavenly chain.
> If he already sees what he must do,
> Well may he shade his eyes from the far-shining view

A better comment could not be made on what is required to perfect Man, and place him in that superior
position for which he was designed, than by the interpretation of Bacon upon the legends of the Syren coast.
"When the wise Ulysses passed," says he, " he caused
his mariners to stop their ears with wax, knowing there
was in them no power to resist the lure of that voluptuous
song. But he, the much experienced man, who wished
to be experienced in all, and use all to the service of
wisdom, desired to hear the song that he might understand its meaning. Yet, distrusting his own power to be
firm in his better purpose, he caused himself to be bound
to the mast, that he might be kept secure against his
own weakness. But Orpheus passed unfettered, so absorbed in singing hymns to the gods that he could not
even hear those sounds of degrading enchantment."

Meanwhile, not a few believe, and men themselves
have expressed the opinion, that the time is come when
Eurydice is to call for an Orpheus, rather than Orpheus
for Eurydice ; that the idea of Man, however imperfectly
brought out, has been far more so than that of Woman :

that she, the other half of the same thought, the other chamber of the heart of life, needs now take her turn in the full pulsation, and that improvement in the daughters will best aid in the reformation of the sons of this age.

It should be remarked that, as the principle of liberty is better understood, and more nobly interpreted, a broader protest is made in behalf of Woman. As men become aware that few men have had a fair chance, they are inclined to say that no women have had a fair chance. The French Revolution, that strangely disguised angel, bore witness in favor of Woman, but interpreted her claims no less ignorantly than those of Man. Its idea of happiness did not rise beyond outward enjoyment, unobstructed by the tyranny of others. The title it gave was " citoyen," " citoyenne ; " and it is not unimportant to Woman that even this species of equality was awarded her. Before, she could be condemned to perish on the scaffold for treason, not as a citizen, but as a subject. The right with which this title then invested a human being was that of bloodshed and license. The Goddess of Liberty was impure. As we read the poem addressed to her, not long since, by Beranger, we can scarcely refrain from tears as painful as the tears of blood that flowed when " such crimes were committed in her name." Yes ! Man, born to purify and animate the unintelligent and the cold, can, in his madness, degrade and pollute no less the fair and the chaste. Yet truth was prophesied in the ravings of that hideous fever, caused by long ignorance and abuse. Europe is conning a valued lesson from the blood-stained page. The same tendencies, further unfolded, will bear good fruit in this country.

Yet, by men in this country, as by the Jews, when Moses was leading them to the promised land, everything has been done that inherited depravity could do, to hinder the promise of Heaven from its fulfilment. The cross, here as elsewhere, has been planted only to be blasphemed by cruelty and fraud. The name of the Prince of Peace has been profaned by all kinds of injustice toward the Gentile whom he said he came to save. But I need not speak of what has been done towards the Red Man, the Black Man. Those deeds are the scoff of the world ; and they have been accompanied by such pious words that the gentlest would not dare to intercede with " Father, forgive them, for they know not what they do."

Here, as elsewhere, the gain of creation consists always in the growth of individual minds, which live and aspire, as flowers bloom and birds sing, in the midst of morasses; and in the continual development of that thought, the thought of human destiny, which is given to eternity adequately to express, and which ages of failure only seemingly impede. Only seemingly ; and whatever seems to the contrary, this country is as surely destined to elucidate a great moral law, as Europe was to promote the mental culture of Man.

Though the national independence be blurred by the servility of individuals ; though freedom and equality have been proclaimed only to leave room for a monstrous display of slave-dealing and slave-keeping ; though the

free American so often feels himself free, like the Roman, only to pamper his appetites and his indolence
through the misery of his fellow-beings ; still it is not in
vain that the verbal statement has been made, " All men
are born free and equal." There it stands, a golden certainty wherewith to encourage the good, to shame the
bad. The New World may be called clearly to perceive
that it incurs the utmost penalty if it reject or oppress
the sorrowful brother. And, if men are deaf, the angels
hear. But men cannot be deaf. It is inevitable that an
external freedom, an independence of the encroachments
of other men, such as has been achieved for the nation,
should be so also for every member of it. That which
has once been clearly conceived in the intelligence cannot fail, sooner or later, to be acted out. It has become
a law as irrevocable as that of the Medes in their ancient
dominion ; men will privately sin against it, but the law,
as expressed by a leading mind of the age,

" Tutti fatti a sembianza d'un Solo,
　Figli tutti d'un solo riscatto,
　In qual'ora, in qual parte del suolo
　Trascorriamo quest' aura vital,
　Siam fratelli, siam stretti ad un patto :
　Maladetto colui che lo infrange,
　Che s'innalza sul fiacco che piange
　Che contrista uno spirto immortal." *

" All made in the likeness of the One,
　All children of one ransom,
　In whatever hour, in whatever part of the soil,
　We draw this vital air,

* Manzoni.

We are brothers ; we must be bound by one compact ;
  Accursed he who infringes it,
Who raises himself upon the weak who weep,
  Who saddens an immortal spirit.''

This law cannot fail of universal recognition. Accursed be he who willingly saddens an immortal spirit —
doomed to infamy in later, wiser ages, doomed in future
stages of his own being to deadly penance, only short of
death. Accursed be he who sins in ignorance, if that
ignorance be caused by sloth.

We sicken no less at the pomp than the strife of
words. We feel that never were lungs so puffed with
the wind of declamation, on moral and religious subjects, as now. We are tempted to implore these
'' word-heroes,'' these word-Catos, word-Christs, to beware of cant* above all things ; to remember that hypocrisy is the most hopeless as well as the meanest of
crimes, and that those must surely be polluted by it, who
do not reserve a part of their morality and religion for
private use. Landor says that he cannot have a great
deal of mind who cannot afford to let the larger part of
it lie fallow ; and what is true of genius is not less so of
virtue. The tongue is a valuable member, but should
appropriate but a small part of the vital juices that are
needful all over the body. We feel that the mind may

---

* Dr. Johnson's one piece of advice should be written on every
door : '' Clear your mind of cant.'' But Byron, to whom it was so
acceptable, in clearing away the noxious vine, shook down the build
ing. Sterling's emendation is worthy of honor :

   '' Realize your cant, not cast it off.''

" grow black and rancid in the smoke " even " of altars."
We start up from the harangue to go into our closet and
shut the door. There inquires the spirit, " Is this rhetoric the bloom of healthy blood, or a false pigment art-
fully laid on?" And yet again we know where is so
much smoke, must be some fire; with so much talk about
virtue and freedom, must be mingled some desire for
them; that it cannot be in vain that such have become
the common topics of conversation among men, rather than
schemes for tyranny and plunder, that the very newspapers see it best to proclaim themselves " Pilgrims,"
" Puritans," " Heralds of Holiness." The king that
maintains so costly a retinue cannot be a mere boast, or
Carabbas fiction. We have waited here long in the dust;
we are tired and hungry; but the triumphal procession
must appear at last.

Of all its banners, none has been more steadily upheld, and under none have more valor and willingness for
real sacrifices been shown, than that of the champions
of the enslaved African. And this band it is, which,
partly from a natural following out of principles, partly
because many women have been prominent in that cause,
makes, just now, the warmest appeal in behalf of Woman.

Though there has been a growing liberality on this
subject, yet society at large is not so prepared for the
demands of this party, but that its members are, and will
be for some time, coldly regarded as the Jacobins of their
day.

" Is it not enough," cries the irritated trader, " that
you have done all you could to break up the national

union, and thus destroy the prosperity of our country, but now you must be trying to break up family union, to take my wife away from the cradle and the kitchen-hearth to vote at polls, and preach from a pulpit? Of course, if she does such things, she cannot attend to those of her own sphere. She is happy enough as she is. She has more leisure than I have,— every means of improvement, every indulgence."

" Have you asked her whether she was satisfied with these *indulgences?* "

" No, but I know she is. She is too amiable to desire what would make me unhappy, and too judicious to wish to step beyond the sphere of her sex. I will never consent to have our peace disturbed by any such discussions."

" ' Consent — you?' it is not consent from you that is in question — it is assent from your wife."

" Am not I the head of my house?"

" You are not the head of your wife. God has given her a mind of her own."

" I am the head, and she the heart."

" God grant you play true to one another, then! I suppose I am to be grateful that you did not say she was only the hand. If the head represses no natural pulse of the heart, there can be no question as to your giving your consent. Both will be of one accord, and there needs but to present any question to get a full and true answer. There is no need of precaution, of indulgence, nor consent. But our doubt is whether the heart *does* consent with the head, or only obeys its decrees with a passiveness that precludes the exercise of its natural

powers, or a repugnance that turns sweet qualities to
bitter, or a doubt that lays waste the fair occasions of
life. It is to ascertain the truth that we propose some
liberating measures."

Thus vaguely are these questions proposed and discussed at present. But their being proposed at all implies much thought, and suggests more. Many women
are considering within themselves what they need that
they have not, and what they can have if they find they
need it. Many men are considering whether women are
capable of being and having more than they are and
have, *and* whether, if so, it will be best to consent to
improvement in their condition.

This morning, I open the Boston "Daily Mail," and
find in its " poet's corner " a translation of Schiller's
" Dignity of Woman." In the advertisement of a book
on America, I see in the table of contents this sequence,
" Republican Institutions. American Slavery. American Ladies."

I open the " *Deutsche Schnellpost*," published in
New York, and find at the head of a column, *Judenund
Frauen-emancipation in Ungarn* — " Emancipation
of Jews and Women in Hungary."

The past year has seen action in the Rhode Island
legislature, to secure married women rights over their
own property, where men showed that a very little examination of the subject could teach them much; an
article in the Democratic Review on the same subject
more largely considered, written by a woman, impelled,
it is said, by glaring wrong to a distinguished friend, hav-

ing shown the defects in the existing laws, and the state of opinion from which they spring; and an answer from the revered old man, J. Q. Adams, in some respects the Phocion of his time, to an address made him by some ladies. To this last I shall again advert in another place.

These symptoms of the times have come under my view quite accidentally : one who seeks, may, each month or week, collect more.

The numerous party, whose opinions are already labeled and adjusted too much to their mind to admit of any new light, strive, by lectures on some model-woman of bride-like beauty and gentleness, by writing and lending little treatises, intended to mark out with precision the limits of Woman's sphere, and Woman's mission, to prevent other than the rightful shepherd from climbing the wall, or the flock from using any chance to go astray.

Without enrolling ourselves at once on either side, let us look upon the subject from the best point of view which to-day offers ; no better, it is to be feared, than a high house-top. A high hill-top, or at least a cathedral-spire, would be desirable.

It may well be an Anti-Slavery party that pleads for Woman, if we consider merely that she does not hold property on equal terms with men; so that, if a husband dies without making a will, the wife, instead of taking at once his place as head of the family, inherits only a part of his fortune, often brought him by herself, as if she were a child, or ward only, not an equal partner.

We will not speak of the innumerable instances in

which profligate and idle men live upon the earnings of industrious wives; or if the wives leave them, and take with them the children, to perform the double duty of mother and father, follow from place to place, and threaten to rob them of the children, if deprived of the rights of a husband, as they call them, planting themselves in their poor lodgings, frightening them into paying tribute by taking from them the children, running into debt at the expense of these otherwise so overtasked helots. Such instances count up by scores within my own memory. I have seen the husband who had stained himself by a long course of low vice, till his wife was wearied from her heroic forgiveness, by finding that his treachery made it useless, and that if she would provide bread for herself and her children, she must be separate from his ill fame — I have known this man come to install himself in the chamber of a woman who loathed him, and say she should never take food without his company. I have known these men steal their children, whom they knew they had no means to maintain, take them into dissolute company, expose them to bodily danger, to frighten the poor woman, to whom, it seems, the fact that she alone had borne the pangs of their birth, and nourished their infancy, does not give an equal right to them. I do believe that this mode of kidnapping — and it is frequent enough in all classes of society — will be by the next age viewed as it is by Heaven now, and that the man who avails himself of the shelter of men's laws to steal from a mother her own children, or arrogate any superior right in them, save that of superior virtue, will bear the stigma he deserves, in common with him who steals grown men from their mother-land, their hopes, and their homes.

I said, we will not speak of this now; yet I *have* spoken, for the subject makes me feel too much. I could give instances that would startle the most vulgar and callous; but I will not, for the public opinion of their own sex is already against such men, and where cases of extreme tyranny are made known, there is private action in the wife's favor. But she ought not to need this, nor, I think, can she long. Men must soon see that as, on their own ground, Woman is the weaker party, she ought to have legal protection, which would make such oppression impossible. But I would not deal with "atrocious instances," except in the way of illustration, neither demand from men a partial redress in some one matter, but go to the root of the whole. If principles could be established, particulars would adjust themselves aright. Ascertain the true destiny of Woman; give her legitimate hopes, and a standard within herself; marriage and all other relations would by degrees be harmonized with these.

But to return to the historical progress of this matter. Knowing that there exists in the minds of men a tone of feeling toward women as toward slaves, such as is expressed in the common phrase, "Tell that to women and children;" that the infinite soul can only work through them in already ascertained limits; that the gift of reason, Man's highest prerogative, is allotted to them in much lower degree; that they must be kept from mischief and melancholy by being constantly engaged in active labor, which is to be furnished and directed by those better able to think, &c., &c.,— we need not multiply instances, for who can review the experience of last week without recalling words which imply, whether in jest or earnest, these views, or views like these,— knowing this, can we wonder that many reformers· think that measures are not likely to be taken in behalf of women, unless their wishes could be publicly represented by women?

"That can never be necessary," cry the other side. "All men are privately influenced by women; each has his wife, sister, or female friends, and is too much biased by these relations to fail of representing their interests; and, if this is not enough, let them propose and enforce their wishes with the pen. The beauty of home would be destroyed, the delicacy of the sex be violated, the dignity of halls of legislation degraded, by an attempt to introduce them there. Such duties are inconsistent with those of a mother;" and then we have ludicrous pictures of ladies in hysterics at the polls, and senate-chambers filled with cradles.

But if, in reply, we admit as truth that Woman seems destined by nature rather for the inner circle, we must add that the arrangements of civilized life have not been, as yet, such as to secure it to her. Her circle, if the duller, is not the quieter. If kept from "excitement," she is not from drudgery. Not only the Indian squaw carries the burdens of the camp, but the favorites of Louis XIV. accompany him in his journeys, and the washerwoman stands at her tub, and carries home her work at all seasons, and in all states of health. Those who think the physical circumstances of Woman would make a part in the affairs of national government unsuitable, are by no means those who think it impossible for negresses to endure field-work, even during pregnancy, or for sempstresses to go through their killing labors.

As to the use of the pen, there was quite as much opposition to Woman's possessing herself of that help to free agency as there is now to her seizing on the rostrum or the desk; and she is likely to draw, from a permission to plead her cause that way, opposite inferences to what might be wished by those who now grant it.

As to the possibility of her filling with grace and dignity any such position, we should think those who had seen the great actresses, and heard the Quaker preachers of modern times, would not doubt that Woman can express publicly the fulness of thought and creation, without losing any of the peculiar beauty of her sex. What can pollute and tarnish is to act thus from any motive except that something needs to be said or done. Woman could take part in the processions, the songs, the dances of old religion; no one fancied her delicacy was impaired by appearing in public for such a cause.

As to her home, she is not likely to leave it more than she now does for balls, theatres, meetings for promoting missions, revival meetings, and others to which she flies, in hope of an animation for her existence commensurate with what she sees enjoyed by men. Governors of ladies'-fairs are no less engrossed by such a charge, than the governor of a state by his; presidents of Washingtonian societies no less away from home than presidents of conventions. If men look straitly to it, they will find that, unless their lives are domestic, those ot the women will not be. A house is no home unless it contain food and fire for the mind as well as for the body. The female Greek, of our day, is as much in the street as the male to cry, "What news?" We doubt not it was the same in Athens of old. The women, shut out from the market-place, made up for it at the religious festivals. For human beings are not so constituted that they can live without expansion. If they do not get it in one way, they must in another, or perish.

As to men's representing women fairly at present, while we hear from men who owe to their wives not only all that is comfortable or graceful, but all that is wise, in the arrangement of their lives, the frequent remark, "You cannot reason with a woman,"— when from those of delicacy, nobleness, and poetic culture, falls the contemptuous phrase "women and children," and that in no light sally of the hour, but in works intended to give a permanent statement of the best experiences,— when not one man, in the million, shall I say? no, not in the hundred million, can rise above the belief that Woman was made *for Man*,— when such traits as these are daily forced upon the attention, can we feel that Man will always do justice to the interests of Woman? Can we think that he takes a sufficiently discerning and religious view of her office and destiny *ever* to do her justice, except when prompted by sentiment,— accidentally or transiently, that is, for the sentiment will vary according to the relations in which he is placed? The lover, the poet, the artist, are likely to view her nobly. The father and the philosopher have some chance of liberality ; the man of the world, the legislator for expediency, none.

Under these circumstances, without attaching importance, in themselves, to the changes demanded by the champions of Woman, we hail them as signs of the times. We would have every arbitrary barrier thrown down. We would have every path laid open to Woman as freely as to Man. Were this done, and a slight temporary fermentation allowed to subside, we should see crystallizations more pure and of more various beauty. We believe the divine energy would pervade nature to a degree unknown in the history of former ages, and that no discordant collision, but a ravishing harmony of the spheres, would ensue.

Yet, then and only then will mankind be ripe for this, when inward and outward freedom for Woman as much as for Man shall be acknowledged as a *right*, not yielded as a concession. As the friend of the negro assumes that one man cannot by right hold another in bondage, so should the friend of Woman assume that Man cannot by right lay even well-meant restrictions on Woman. If the negro be a soul, if the woman be a soul, apparelled in flesh, to one Master only are they accountable. There is but one law for souls, and, if there is to be an interpreter of it, he must come not as man, or son of man, but as son of God.

Were thought and feeling once so far elevated that

Man should esteem himself the brother and friend, but nowise the lord and tutor, of Woman,— were he really bound with her in equal worship,— arrangements as to function and employment would be of no consequence. What Woman needs is not as a woman to act or rule, but as a nature to grow, as an intellect to discern, as a soul to live freely and unimpeded, to unfold such powers as were given her when we left our common home. If fewer talents were given her, yet if allowed the free and full employment of these, so that she may render back to the giver his own with usury, she will not complain; nay, I dare to say she will bless and rejoice in her earthly birth-place, her earthly lot. Let us consider what obstructions impede this good era, and what signs give reason to hope that it draws near.

I was talking on this subject with Miranda, a woman, who, if any in the world could, might speak without heat and bitterness of the position of her sex. Her father was a man who cherished no sentimental reverence for Woman, but a firm belief in the equality of the sexes. She was his eldest child, and came to him at an age when he needed a companion. From the time she could speak and go alone, he addressed her not as a plaything, but as a living mind. Among the few verses he ever wrote was a copy addressed to this child, when the first locks were cut from her head; and the reverence expressed on this occasion for that cherished head, he never belied. It was to him the temple of immortal intellect. He respected his child, however, too much to be an indulgent parent. He called on her for clear judgment, for courage, for

honor and fidelity; in short, for such virtues as he knew.
In so far as he possessed the keys to the wonders of this
universe, he allowed free use of them to her, and, by the
incentive of a high expectation, he forbade, so far as
possible, that she should let the privilege lie idle.

Thus this child was early led to feel herself a child of
the spirit. She took her place easily, not only in the
world of organized being, but in the world of mind. A
dignified sense of self-dependence was given as all her
portion, and she found it a sure anchor. Herself securely
anchored, her relations with others were established with
equal security. She was fortunate in a total absence of
those charms which might have drawn to her bewildering
flatteries, and in a strong electric nature, which repelled
those who did not belong to her, and attracted those who
did. With men and women her relations were noble,—
affectionate without passion, intellectual without coldness.
The world was free to her, and she lived freely in it.
Outward adversity came, and inward conflict; but that
faith and self-respect had early been awakened which
must always lead, at last, to an outward serenity and an
inward peace.

Of Miranda I had always thought as an example, that
the restraints upon the sex were insuperable only to
those who think them so, or who noisily strive to break
them. She had taken a course of her own, and no man
stood in her way. Many of her acts had been unusual,
but excited no uproar. Few helped, but none checked
her; and the many men who knew her mind and her
life, showed to her confidence as to a brother, gentleness

as to a sister. And not only refined, but very coarse men approved and aided one in whom they saw resolution and clearness of design. Her mind was often the leading one, always effective.

When I talked with her upon these matters, and had said very much what I have written, she smilingly replied : "And yet we must admit that I have been fortunate, and this should not be. My good father's early trust gave the first bias, and the rest followed, of course. It is true that I have had less outward aid, in after years, than most women ; but that is of little consequence. Religion was early awakened in my soul,— a sense that what the soul is capable to ask it must attain, and that, though I might be aided and instructed by others, I must depend on myself as the only constant friend. This self-dependence, which was honored in me, is deprecated as a fault in most women. They are taught to learn their rule from without, not to unfold it from within.

"This is the fault of Man, who is still vain, and wishes to be more important to Woman than, by right, he should be."

"Men have not shown this disposition toward you," I said.

"No; because the position I early was enabled to take was one of self-reliance. And were all women as sure of their wants as I was, the result would be the same. But they are so overloaded with precepts by guardians, who think that nothing is so much to be dreaded for a woman as originality of thought or char-

acter, that their minds are impeded by doubts till they
lose their chance of fair, free proportions. The difficulty
is to get them to the point from which they shall naturally develop self-respect, and learn self-help.

" Once I thought that men would help to forward this
state of things more than I do now. I saw so many of
them wretched in the connections they had formed in
weakness and vanity. They seemed so glad to esteem
women whenever they could.

" ' The soft arms of affection,' said one of the most
discerning spirits, ' will not suffice for me, unless on
them I see the steel bracelets of strength.'

" But early I perceived that men never, in any extreme of despair, wished to be women. On the contrary,
they were ever ready to taunt one another, at any sign
of weakness, with,

" ' Art thou not like the women, who,' —

The passage ends various ways, according to the occasion and rhetoric of the speaker. When they admired
any woman, they were inclined to speak of her as ' above
her sex.' Silently I observed this, and feared it argued
a rooted scepticism, which for ages had been fastening on
the heart, and which only an age of miracles could eradicate. Ever I have been treated with great sincerity;
and I look upon it as a signal instance of this, that an
intimate friend of the other sex said, in a fervent moment, that I ' deserved in some star to be a man.' He
was much surprised when I disclosed my view of my
position and hopes, when I declared my faith that the

feminine side, the side of love, of beauty, of holiness, was now to have its full chance, and that, if either were better, it was better now to be a woman ; for even the slightest achievement of good was furthering an especial work of our time.   He smiled incredulously.   ' She makes the best she can of it,' thought he.   ' Let Jews believe the pride of Jewry, but I am of the better sort, and know better.'

" Another used as highest praise, in speaking of a character in literature, the words ' a manly woman.'

" So in the noble passage of Ben Jonson :

> ' I meant the day-star should not brighter ride,
>   Nor shed like influence from its lucent seat ;
> I meant she should be courteous, facile, sweet,
>   Free from that solemn vice of greatness, pride ;
> I meant each softest virtue there should meet,
>   Fit in that softer bosom to abide,
> Only a learned and a *manly* soul
>   I purposed her, that should with even powers
> The rock, the spindle, and the shears control
>   Of destiny, and spin her own free hours.' "

" Methinks," said I, " you are too fastidious in objecting to this.   Jonson, in using the word ' manly,' only meant to heighten the picture of this, the true, the intelligent fate, with one of the deeper colors."

" And yet," said she, " so invariable is the use of this word where a heroic quality is to be described, and I feel so sure that persistence and courage are the most womanly no less than the most manly qualities, that I would exchange these words for others of a larger sense, at the risk of marring the fine tissue of the verse.

Read, ' A heavenward and instructed soul,' and I should be satisfied.   Let it not be said, wherever there is energy or creative genius, ' She has a masculine mind.' "

This by no means argues a willing want of generosity toward Woman.   Man is as generous towards her as he knows how to be.

Wherever she has herself arisen in national or private history, and nobly shone forth in any form of excellence, men have received her, not only willingly, but with triumph.   Their encomiums, indeed, are always, in some sense, mortifying ; they show too much surprise.   " Can this be you ? " he cries to the transfigured Cinderella ; " well, I should never have thought it, but I am very glad.   We will tell every one that you have ' *surpassed your sex.*' "

In every-day life, the feelings of the many are stained with vanity.   Each wishes to be lord in a little world, to be superior at least over one ; and he does not feel strong enough to retain a life-long ascendency over a strong nature.   Only a Theseus could conquer before he wed the Amazonian queen.   Hercules wished rather to rest with Dejanira, and received the poisoned robe as a fit guerdon.   The tale should be interpreted to all those who seek repose with the weak.

But not only is Man vain and fond of power, but the same want of development, which thus affects him morally, prevents his intellectually discerning the destiny of Woman.   The boy wants no woman, but only a girl to play ball with him, and mark his pocket handkerchief.

Thus, in Schiller's Dignity of Woman, beautiful as the poem is, there is no " grave and perfect man," but only a great boy to be softened and restrained by the influence of girls.   Poets — the elder ˙brothers of their race — have usually seen further ; but what can you expect of every-day men, if Schiller was not more prophetic as to what women must be ?   Even with Richter, one foremost thought about a wife was that she would " cook him something good."   But as this is a delicate subject, and we are in constant danger of being accused of slighting what are called " the functions," let me say, in behalf of Miranda and myself, that we have high respect for those who " cook something good," who create and preserve fair order in houses, and prepare therein the shining raiment for worthy inmates, worthy guests.   Only these " functions " must not be a drudgery, or enforced necessity, but a part of life.   Let Ulysses drive the beeves home, while Penelope there piles up the fragrant loaves; they are both well employed if these be done in thought and love, willingly. But Penelope is no more meant for a baker or weaver solely, than Ulysses for a cattle-herd.

The sexes should not only correspond to and appreciate, but prophesy to one another.   In individual instances this happens.   Two persons love in one another the future good which they aid one another to unfold.   This is imperfectly or rarely done in the general life.   Man has gone but little way ; now he is waiting to see whether Woman can keep step with him ; but, instead of calling out, like a good brother, " You can do it, if you only think so," or impersonally, "Any one can do what he tries to do;" he often discourages with school-boy brag: "Girls can't do that; girls can't play ball." But let any one defy their taunts, break through and be brave and secure, they rend the air with shouts.

This fluctuation was obvious in a narrative I have lately seen, the story of the life of Countess Emily Plater, the heroine of the last revolution in Poland. The dignity, the purity, the concentrated resolve, the calm, deep enthusiasm, which yet could, when occasion called, sparkle up a holy, an indignant fire, make of this young maiden the figure I want for my frontispiece. Her portrait is to be seen in the book, a gentle shadow of her soul. Short was the career. Like the Maid of Orleans, she only did enough to verify her credentials, and then passed from a scene on which she was, probably, a premature apparition.

When the young girl joined the army, where the report of her exploits had preceded her, she was received in a manner that marks the usual state of feeling. Some of the officers were disappointed at her quiet manners; that she had not the air and tone of a stage-heroine. They thought she could not have acted heroically unless in buskins; had no idea that such deeds only showed the habit of her mind. Others talked of the delicacy of her sex, advised her to withdraw from perils and dangers, and had no comprehension of the feelings within her breast that made this impossible. The gentle irony of her reply to these self-constituted tutors (not one of whom showed himself her equal in conduct or reason), is as good as her indignant reproof at a later period to the general, whose perfidy ruined all.

But though, to the mass of these men, she was an embarrassment and a puzzle, the nobler sort viewed her with a tender enthusiasm worthy of her. "Her name," said her biographer, "is known throughout Europe. I paint her character that she may be as widely loved."

With pride, he shows her freedom from all personal affections; that, though tender and gentle in an uncommon degree, there was no room for a private love in her consecrated life. She inspired those who knew her with a simple energy of feeling like her own. "We have seen," they felt, "a woman worthy the name, capable of all sweet affections, capable of stern virtue."

It is a fact worthy of remark, that all these revolutions in favor of liberty have produced female champions that share the same traits, but Emily alone has found a biographer. Only a near friend could have performed for her this task, for the flower was reared in feminine seclusion, and the few and simple traits of her history before her appearance in the field could only have been known to the domestic circle. Her biographer has gathered them up with a brotherly devotion.

No! Man is not willingly ungenerous. He wants faith and love, because he is not yet himself an elevated being. He cries, with sneering scepticism, "Give us a sign." But if the sign appears, his eyes glisten, and he offers not merely approval, but homage.

The severe nation which taught that the happiness of the race was forfeited through the fault of a Woman, and

showed its thought of what sort of regard Man owed her,
by making him accuse her on the first question to his
God, — who gave her to the patriarch as a handmaid,
and, by the Mosaical law, bound her to allegiance like a
serf, — even they greeted, with solemn rapture, all
great and holy women as heroines, prophetesses, judges
in Israel; and, if they made Eve listen to the serpent,
gave Mary as a bride to the Holy Spirit. In other
nations it has been the same down to our day. To
the Woman who could conquer a triumph was awarded.
And not only those whose strength was recommended to
the heart by association with goodness and beauty, but
those who were bad, if they were steadfast and strong,
had their claims allowed. In any age a Semiramis, an
Elizabeth of England, a Catharine of Russia, makes her
place good, whether in a large or small circle. How
has a little wit, a little genius, been celebrated in a
Woman! What an intellectual triumph was that of the
lonely Aspasia, and how heartily acknowledged! She,
indeed, met a Pericles. But what annalist, the rudest
of men, the most plebeian of husbands, will spare from
his page one of the few anecdotes of Roman women —
Sappho! Eloisa! The names are of threadbare celebrity. Indeed, they were not more suitably met in·their
own time than the Countess Colonel Plater on her first
joining the army. They had much to mourn, and their
great impulses did not find due scope. But with time
enough, space enough, their kindred appear on the
scene. Across the ages, forms lean, trying to touch the
hem of their retreating robes. The youth here by my

side cannot be weary of the fragments from the life of
Sappho. He will not believe they are not addressed to
himself, or that he to whom they were addressed could
be ungrateful. A recluse of high powers devotes himself to understand and explain the thought of Eloisa;
he asserts her vast superiority in soul and genius to her
master; he curses the fate that casts his lot in another
age than hers. He could have understood her; he would
have been to her a friend, such as Abelard never could.
And this one Woman he could have loved and reverenced,
and she, alas! lay cold in her grave hundreds of years
ago. His sorrow is truly pathetic. These responses,
that come too late to give joy, are as tragic as anything
we know, and yet the tears of later ages glitter as they
fall on Tasso's prison bars. And we know how elevating
to the captive is the security that somewhere an intelligence must answer to his.

The Man habitually most narrow towards Woman will
be flushed, as by the worst assault on Christianity, if you
say it has made no improvement in her condition. Indeed, those most opposed to new acts in her favor, are
jealous of the reputation of those which have been
done.

We will not speak of the enthusiasm excited by actresses, improvisatrici, female singers, — for here mingles
the charm of beauty and grace, — but female authors, even
learned women, if not insufferably ugly and slovenly,
from the Italian professor's daughter who taught behind
the curtain, down to Mrs. Carter and Madame Dacier,
are sure of an admiring audience, and, what is far bet-

ter, chance to use what they have learned, and to learn
more, if they can once get a platform on which to stand.

But how to get this platform, or how to make it of
reasonably easy access, is the difficulty. Plants of great
vigor will almost always struggle into blossom, despite
impediments. But there should be encouragement, and
a free genial atmosphere for those of more timid sort,
fair play for each in its own kind. Some are like the
little, delicate flowers which love to hide in the dripping
mosses, by the sides of mountain torrents, or in the shade
of tall trees. But others require an open field, a rich
and loosened soil, or they never show their proper
hues.

It may be said that Man does not have his fair play
either; his energies are repressed and distorted by the
interposition of artificial obstacles. Ay, but he himself
has put them there; they have grown out of his own
imperfections. If there *is* a misfortune in Woman's lot,
it is in obstacles being interposed by men, which do *not*
mark her state; and, if they express her past ignorance,
do not her present needs. As every Man is of Woman
born, she has slow but sure means of redress; yet the
sooner a general justness of thought makes smooth the
path, the better.

Man is of Woman born, and her face bends over him
in infancy with an expression he can never quite forget.
Eminent men have delighted to pay tribute to this image,
and it is an hackneyed observation, that most men of
genius boast some remarkable development in the mother.
The rudest tar brushes off a tear with his coat-sleeve at

the hallowed name. The other day, I met a decrepit old man of seventy, on a journey, who challenged the stage company to guess where he was going. They guessed aright, "To see your mother." "Yes," said he, "she is ninety-two, but has good eyesight still, they say. I have not seen her these forty years, and I thought I could not die in peace without." I should have liked his picture painted as a companion-piece to that of a boisterous little boy, whom I saw attempt to declaim at a school exhibition —

> " O that those lips had language ! Life has passed
> With me but roughly since I heard thee last."

He got but very little way before sudden tears shamed him from the stage.

Some gleams of the same expression which shone down upon his infancy, angelically pure and benign, visit Man again with hopes of pure love, of a holy marriage. Or, if not before, in the eyes of the mother of his child they again are seen, and dim fancies pass before his mind, that Woman may not have been born for him alone, but have come from heaven, a commissioned soul, a messenger of truth and love ; that she can only make for him a home in which he may lawfully repose, in so far as she is

> " True to the kindred points of Heaven and home."

In gleams, in dim fancies, this thought visits the mind of common men. It is soon obscured by the mists of sensuality, the dust of routine, and he thinks it was only some meteor or ignis fatuus that shone. But, as ?

Rosicrucian lamp, it burns unwearied, though condemned to the solitude of tombs ; and to its permanent life, as to every truth, each age has in some form borne witness. For the truths, which visit the minds of careless men only in fitful gleams, shine with radiant clearness into those of the poet, the priest, and the artist.

Whatever may have been the domestic manners of the ancients, the idea of Woman was nobly manifested in their mythologies and poems, where she appears as Sita in the Ramayana, a form of tender purity ; as the Egyptian Isis,* of divine wisdom never yet surpassed. In Egypt, too, the Sphynx, walking the earth with lion tread, looked out upon its marvels in the calm, inscrutable beauty of a virgin's face, and the Greek could only add wings to the great emblem. In Greece, Ceres and Proserpine, significantly termed " the great goddesses," were seen seated side by side. They needed not to rise for any worshipper or any change; they were prepared for all things, as those initiated to their mysteries knew. More obvious is the meaning of these three forms, the Diana, Minerva, and Vesta. Unlike in the expression of their beauty, but alike in this,— that each was self-sufficing. Other forms were only accessories and illustrations, none the complement to one like these. Another might, indeed, be the companion, and the Apollo and Diana set off one another's beauty. Of the Vesta, it is to be observed, that not only deep-eyed, deep-discerning Greece, but ruder Rome, who represents the only form of good man (the always busy warrior) that could be

---

* For an adequate description of the Isis, see Appendix A.

indifferent to Woman, confided the permanence of its glory
to a tutelary goddess, and her wisest legislator spoke of
meditation as a nymph.

Perhaps in Rome the neglect of Woman was a reaction
on the manners of Etruria, where the priestess Queen,
warrior Queen, would seem to have been so usual a character.

An instance of the noble Roman marriage, where the
stern and calm nobleness of the nation was common to
both, we see in the historic page through the little that
is told us of Brutus and Portia.   Shakspeare has
seized on the relation in its native lineaments, harmoniz-
ing the particular with the universal; and, while it is
conjugal love, and no other, making it unlike the same
relation as seen in Cymbeline, or Othello, even as one
star differeth from another in glory.

> " By that great vow
> Which did incorporate and make us one,
> Unfold to me, yourself, your other half,
> Why you are heavy. *   *   *
> Dwell I but in the suburbs
> Of your good pleasure ?   If it be no more,
> Portia is Brutus' harlot, not his wife."

Mark the sad majesty of his tone in answer.   Who
would not have lent a life-long credence to that voice of
honor ?

> " You are my true and honorable wife ;
> As dear to me as are the ruddy drops
> That visit this sad heart."

It is the same voice that tells the moral of his life in
the last words —

> " Countrymen,
> My heart doth joy, that, yet in all my life,
> I found no man but he was true to me."

It was not wonderful that it should be so.

Shakspeare, however, was not content to let Portia rest her plea for confidence on the essential nature of the marriage bond :

> "I grant I am a woman ; but withal,
> A woman that lord Brutus took to wife.
> I grant I am a woman : but withal,
> A woman well reputed — Cato's daughter.
> Think you I am *no stronger than my sex*,
> Being so fathered and so husbanded ? "

And afterward in the very scene where Brutus is suffering under that " insupportable and touching loss," the death of his wife, Cassius pleads —

> " Have you not love enough to bear with me,
> When that rash humor which my mother gave me
> Makes me forgetful ?
> *Brutus.* — Yes, Cassius, and henceforth,
> When you are over-earnest with your Brutus,
> He'll think your mother chides, and leaves you so."

As indeed it was a frequent belief among the ancients, as with our Indians, that the *body* was inherited from the mother, the *soul* from the father. As in that noble passage of Ovid, already quoted, where Jupiter, as his divine synod are looking down on the funeral pyre of Hercules, thus triumphs —

> " Nec nisi *maternâ* Vulcanum parte potentem,
> Sentiet. Aeternum est, à me quod traxit, et expers

Atque immune necis, nullaque domabile flamma
Idque ego defunctum terrâ cœlestibus oris
Accipiam, cunctisque meum lætabile factum
Dis fore confido.

" The part alone of gross *maternal* frame
Fire shall devour ; while that from me he drew
Shall live immortal and its force renew ;
That, when he 's dead, I 'll raise to realms above ;
Let all the powers the righteous act approve."

It is indeed a god speaking of his union with an
earthly Woman, but it expresses the common Roman
thought as to marriage,—the same which permitted a
man to lend his wife to a friend, as if she were a chattel.

" She dwelt but in the suburbs of his good pleasure."

Yet the same city, as I have said, leaned on the worship
of Vesta, the Preserver, and in later times was devoted
to that of Isis.   In Sparta, thought, in this respect as in
all others, was expressed in the characters of real life,
and the women of Sparta were as much Spartans as the
men.   The " citoyen, citoyenne " of France was here
actualized.   Was not the calm equality they enjoyed as
honorable as the devotion of chivalry ?   They intelligently shared the ideal life of their nation.

Like the men they felt

" Honor gone, all 's gone :
Better never have been born."

They were the true friends of men.   The Spartan,
surely, would not think that he received only his body
from his mother.   The sage, had he lived in that community, could not have thought the souls of " vain and

foppish men will be degraded after death to the forms of women; and, if they do not then make great efforts to retrieve themselves, will become birds."

(By the way, it is very expressive of the hard intellectuality of the merely *mannish* mind, to speak thus of birds, chosen always by the *feminine* poet as the symbols of his fairest thoughts.)

We are told of the Greek nations in general, that Woman occupied there an infinitely lower place than Man. It is difficult to believe this, when we see such range and dignity of thought on the subject in the mythologies, and find the poets producing such ideals as Cassandra, Iphigenia, Antigone, Macaria; where Sibylline priestesses told the oracle of the highest god, and he could not be content to reign with a court of fewer than nine muses. Even Victory wore a female form.

But, whatever were the facts of daily life, I cannot complain of the age and nation which represents its thought by such a symbol as I see before me at this moment. It is a zodiac of the busts of gods and goddesses, arranged in pairs. The circle breathes the music of a heavenly order. Male and female heads are distinct in expression, but equal in beauty, strength and calmness. Each male head is that of a brother and a king, — each female of a sister and a queen. Could the thought thus expressed be lived out, there would be nothing more to be desired. There would be unison in variety, congeniality in difference.

Coming nearer our own time, we find religion and poetry no less true in their revelations. The rude man,

just disengaged from the sod, the Adam, accuses Woman
to his God, and records her disgrace to their posterity
He is not ashamed to write that he could be drawn from
heaven by one beneath him,— one made, he says, from
but a small part of himself. But in the same nation,
educated by time, instructed by a succession of prophets,
we find Woman in as high a position as she has ever occupied. No figure that has ever arisen to greet our eyes
has been received with more fervent reverence than that
of the Madonna. Heine calls her the *Dame du Comp-
toir* of the Catholic church, and this jeer well expresses
a serious truth.

And not only this holy and significant image was worshipped by the pilgrim, and the favorite subject of the
artist, but it exercised an immediate influence on the
destiny of the sex. The empresses who embraced the
cross converted sons and husbands. Whole calendars
of female saints, heroic dames of chivalry, binding the
emblem of faith on the heart of the best-beloved, and
wasting the bloom of youth in separation and loneliness,
for the sake of duties they thought it religion to assume,
with innumerable forms of poesy, trace their lineage to
this one. Nor, however imperfect may be the action,
in our day, of the faith thus expressed, and though we
can scarcely think it nearer this ideal than that of India
or Greece was near their ideal, is it in vain that the truth
has been recognized, that Woman is not only a part of
Man, bone of his bone, and flesh of his flesh, born that
men might not be lonely — but that women are in themselves possessors of and possessed by immortal souls.

This truth undoubtedly received a greater outward stability from the belief of the church that the earthly parent of the Saviour of souls was a woman.

The Assumption of the Virgin, as painted by sublime artists, as also Petrarch's Hymn to the Madonna,* cannot have spoken to the world wholly without result, yet oftentimes those who had ears heard not.

See upon the nations the influence of this powerful example. In Spain look only at the ballads. Woman in these is "very Woman;" she is the betrothed, the bride, the spouse of Man; there is on her no hue of the philosopher, the heroine, the savante, but she looks great and noble. Why? Because she is also, through her deep devotion, the betrothed of Heaven. Her upturned eyes have drawn down the light that casts a radiance round her. See only such a ballad as that of "Lady Teresa's Bridal," where the Infanta, given to the Moorish bridegroom, calls down the vengeance of Heaven on his unhallowed passion, and thinks it not too much to expiate by a life in the cloister the involuntary stain upon her princely youth.† It was this constant sense of claims above those of earthly love or happiness that made the Spanish lady who shared this spirit a guerdon to be won by toils and blood and constant purity, rather than a chattel to be bought for pleasure and service.

Germany did not need to *learn* a high view of Woman; it was inborn in that race. Woman was to the Teuton warrior his priestess, his friend, his sister,— in truth, a wife. And the Christian statues of noble pairs, as they

* Appendix B   † Appendix C.

lie above their graves in stone, expressing the meaning
of all the by-gone pilgrimage by hands folded in mutual
prayer, yield not a nobler sense of the place and powers
of Woman than belonged to the *altvater* day. The holy
love of Christ which summoned them, also, to choose
" the better part — that which could not be taken from
them," refined and hallowed in this nation a native faith ;
thus showing that it was not the warlike spirit alone that
left the Latins so barbarous in this respect.

But the Germans, taking so kindly to this thought,
did it the more justice. The idea of Woman in their
literature is expressed both to a greater height and depth
than elsewhere.

I will give as instances the themes of three ballads :

One is upon a knight who had always the name of the
Virgin on his lips. This protected him all his life
through, in various and beautiful modes, both from sin
and other dangers ; and, when he died, a plant sprang
from his grave, which so gently whispered the Ave
Maria that none could pass it by with an unpurified heart.

Another is one of the legends of the famous Dra-
chenfels. A maiden, one of the earliest converts to
Christianity, was carried by the enraged populace to this
dread haunt of " the dragon's fabled brood," to be
their prey. She was left alone, but undismayed, for she
knew in whom she trusted. So, when the dragons
came rushing towards her, she showed them a crucifix
and they crouched reverently at her feet. Next day the
people came, and, seeing these wonders, were all turned to
the faith which exalts the lowly.

The third I have in mind is another of the Rhine
legends. A youth is sitting with the maid he loves on
the shore of an isle, her fairy kingdom, then perfumed
by the blossoming grape-vines which draped its bowers.
They are happy; all blossoms with them, and life promises its richest wine. A boat approaches on the tide;
it pauses at their feet. It brings, perhaps, some joyous
message, fresh dew for their flowers, fresh light on the
wave. No! it is the usual check on such great happiness. The father of the count departs for the crusade;
will his son join him, or remain to rule their domain,
and wed her he loves? Neither of the affianced pair
hesitates a moment. "I must go with my father," —
"Thou must go with thy father." It was one thought,
one word. "I will be here again," he said, "when
these blossoms have turned to purple grapes." "I hope
so," she sighed, while the prophetic sense said "no."

And there she waited, and the grapes ripened, and
were gathered into the vintage, and he came not. Year
after year passed thus, and no tidings; yet still she
waited.

He, meanwhile, was in a Moslem prison. Long he
languished there without hope, till, at last, his patron
saint appeared in vision and announced his release, but
only on condition of his joining the monastic order for
the service of the saint.

And so his release was effected, and a safe voyage
home given. And once more he sets sail upon the
Rhine. The maiden, still watching beneath the vines,
sees at last the object of all this patient love approach--

approach, but not to touch the strand to which she, with
outstretched arms, has rushed. He dares not trust himself to land, but in low, heart-broken tones, tells her of
Heaven's will ; and that he, in obedience to his vow, is
now on his way to a convent on the river-bank, there to
pass the rest of his earthly life in the service of the
shrine. And then he turns his boat, and floats away from
her and hope of any happiness in this world, but urged,
as he believes, by the breath of Heaven.

The maiden stands appalled, but she dares not murmur, and cannot hesitate long. She also bids them prepare her boat. She follows her lost love to the convent
gate, requests an interview with the abbot, and devotes
her Elysian isle, where vines had ripened their ruby
fruit in vain for her, to the service of the monastery
where her love was to serve. Then, passing over to the
nunnery opposite, she takes the veil, and meets her
betrothed at the altar ; and for a life-long union, if not
the one they had hoped in earlier years.

Is not this sorrowful story of a lofty beauty ? Does
it not show a sufficiently high view of Woman, of Marriage? This is commonly the chivalric, still more the
German view.

Yet, wherever there was a balance in the mind of Man,
of sentiment with intellect, such a result was sure. The
Greek Xenophon has not only painted us a sweet picture
of the domestic Woman, in his Economics, but in the
Cyropedia has given, in the picture of Panthea, a view
of Woman which no German picture can surpass, whether
lonely and quiet with veiled lids, the temple of a vestal

loveliness, or with eyes flashing, and hair flowing to the free wind, cheering on the hero to fight for his God, his country, or whatever name his duty might bear at the time. This picture I shall copy by and by. Yet Xenophon grew up in the same age with him who makes Iphigenia say to Achilles,

" Better a thousand women should perish than one man cease to see the light.'

This was the vulgar Greek sentiment. Xenophon, aiming at the ideal Man, caught glimpses of the ideal Woman also. From the figure of a Cyrus the Pantheas stand not afar. They do not in thought; they would not in life.

I could swell the catalogue of instances far beyond the reader's patience. But enough have been brought forward to show that, though there has been great disparity betwixt the nations as between individuals in their culture on this point, yet the idea of Woman has always cast some rays and often been forcibly represented.

Far less has Woman to complain that she has not had her share of power. This, in all ranks of society, except the lowest, has been hers to the extent that vanity would crave, far beyond what wisdom would accept. In the very lowest, where Man, pressed by poverty, sees in Woman only the partner of toils and cares, and cannot hope, scarcely has an idea of, a comfortable home, he often maltreats her, and is less influenced by her. In all ranks, those who are gentle and uncomplaining, too candid to intrigue, too delicate to encroach, suffer

much. They suffer long, and are kind; verily, they
have their reward. But wherever Man is sufficiently
raised above extreme poverty, or brutal stupidity,
to care for the comforts of the fireside, or the bloom
and ornament of life, Woman has always power enough,
if she choose to exert it, and is usually disposed to do
so, in proportion to her ignorance and childish vanity. Unacquainted with the importance of life and its
purposes, trained to a selfish coquetry and love of
petty power, she does not look beyond the pleasure of
making herself felt at the moment, and governments are
shaken and commerce broken up to gratify the pique of
a female favorite. The English shopkeeper's wife does
not vote, but it is for her interest that the politician can-
vasses by the coarsest flattery. France suffers no woman
on her throne, but her proud nobles kiss the dust at the
feet of Pompadour and Dubarry; for such flare in the
lighted foreground where a Roland would modestly aid in
the closet. Spain (that same Spain which sang of Ximena
and the Lady Teresa) shuts up her women in the care of
duennas, and allows them no book but the breviary; but
the ruin follows only the more surely from the worthless
favorite of a worthless queen. Relying on mean precau-
tions, men indeed cry peace, peace, where there is no peace.

It is not the transient breath of poetic incense that
women want; each can receive that from a lover. It is
not life-long sway; it needs but to become a coquette, a
shrew, or a good cook, to be sure of that. It is not
money, nor notoriety, nor the badges of authority which
men have appropriated to themselves. If demands, made

in their behalf, lay stress on any of these particulars,
those who make them have not searched deeply into the
need.   The want is for that which at once includes these
and precludes them ; which would not be forbidden power,
lest there be temptation to steal and misuse it ; which
would not have the mind perverted by flattery from a
worthiness of esteem ; it is for that which is the birthright
of every being capable of receiving it, — the freedom, the
religious, the intelligent freedom of the universe to use
its means, to learn its secret, as far as Nature has enabled
them, with God alone for their guide and their judge.

Ye cannot believe it, men ; but the only reason why
women ever assume what is more appropriate to you, is
because you prevent them from finding out what is fit for
themselves.   Were they free, were they wise fully to
develop the strength and beauty of Woman ; they would
never wish to be men, or man-like.   The well-instructed
moon, flies not from her orbit to seize on the glories of
her partner.   No; for she knows that one law rules, one
heaven contains, one universe replies to them alike.   It
is with women as with the slave :

> " Vor dem Sklaven, wenn er die Kette bricht,
> Vor dem freien Menschen erzittert nicht."

Tremble not before the free man, but before the slave
who has chains to break.

In slavery, acknowledged slavery, women are on a par
with men.   Each is a work-tool, an article of property,
no more !   In perfect freedom, such as is painted in
Olympus, in Swedenborg's angelic state, in the heaven

where there is no marrying nor giving in marriage, each
is a. purified intelligence, an enfranchised soul,— no less.

> " Jene himmlische Gestalten
> Sie fragen nicht nach Mann und Weib,
> Und keine kleider, keine Falten
> Umgeben den verklarten Leib."

The child who sang this was a prophetic form, expressive of the longing for a state of perfect freedom, pure
love. She could not remain here, but was translated
to another air. And it may be that the air of this earth
will never be so tempered that such can bear it long.
But, while they stay, they must bear testimony to the
truth they are constituted to demand.

That an era approaches which shall approximate
nearer to such a temper than any has yet done, there are
many tokens; indeed, so many that only a few of the
most prominent can here be enumerated.

The reigns of Elizabeth of England and Isabella of
Castile foreboded this era. They expressed the beginning
of the new state, while they forwarded its progress.
These were strong characters, and in harmony with the
wants of their time. One showed that this strength did
not unfit a woman for the duties of a wife and a mother;
the other, that it could enable her to live and die alone,
a wide energetic life, a courageous death. Elizabeth is
certainly no pleasing example. In rising above the
weakness, she did not lay aside the foibles ascribed to
her sex; but her strength must be respected now, as it
was in her own time.

Mary Stuart and Elizabeth seem types, moulded by

the spirit of the time, and placed upon an elevated platform, to show to the coming ages Woman such as the
conduct and wishes of Man in general is likely to make,
her. The first shows Woman lovely even to allure-
ment; quick in apprehension and weak in judgment;
with grace and dignity of sentiment, but no principle;
credulous and indiscreet, yet artful; capable of sudden
greatness or of crime, but not of a steadfast wisdom, nor self-restraining virtue. The second reveals
Woman half-emancipated and jealous of her freedom,
such as she has figured before or since in many a combative attitude, mannish, not equally manly; strong and
prudent more than great or wise; able to control vanity,
and the wish to rule through coquetry and passion, but
not to resign these dear deceits from the very foundation, as unworthy a being capable of truth and nobleness. Elizabeth, taught by adversity, put on her virtues as armor, more than produced them in a natural
order from her soul. The time and her position called
on her to act the wise sovereign, and she was proud that
she could do so, but her tastes and inclinations would
have led her to act the weak woman. She was without
magnanimity of any kind.

We may accept as an omen for ourselves that it was
Isabella who furnished Columbus with the means of
coming hither. This land must pay back its debt to
Woman, without whose aid it would not have been
brought into alliance with the civilized world.

A graceful and meaning figure is that introduced to us
by Mr. Prescott, in the Conquest of Mexico, in the

Indian girl Marina, who accompanied Cortez, and was his interpreter in all the various difficulties of his career. She stood at his side, on the walls of the besieged palace, to plead with her enraged countrymen. By her name he was known in New Spain, and, after the conquest, her gentle intercession was often of avail to the conquered. The poem of the Future may be read in some features of the story of " Malinche."

The influence of Elizabeth on literature was real, though, by sympathy with its finer productions, she was no more entitled to give name to an era than Queen Anne. It was simply that the fact of having a female sovereign on the throne affected the course of a writer's thoughts. In this sense, the presence of a woman on the throne always makes its mark. Life is lived before the eyes of men, by which their imaginations are stimulated as to the possibilities of Woman. " We will die for our king, Maria Theresa," cry the wild warriors, clashing their swords ; and the sounds vibrate through the poems of that generation. The range of female character in Spenser alone might content us for one period. Britomart and Belphœbe have as much room on the canvas as Florimel ; and, where this is the case, the haughtiest Amazon will not murmur that Una should be felt to be the fairest type.

Unlike as was the English queen to a fairy queen, we may yet conceive that it was the image of *a* queen before the poet's mind that called up this splendid court of women. Shakspeare's range is also great ; but he has left out the heroic characters, such as the Macaria of

Greece, the Britomart of Spenser. Ford and Massinger have, in this respect, soared to a higher flight of feeling than he. It was the holy and heroic Woman they most loved, and if they could not paint an Imogen, a Desdemona, a Rosalind, yet, in those of a stronger mould, they showed a higher ideal, though with so much less poetic power to embody it, than we see in Portia or Isabella. The simple truth of Cordelia, indeed, is of this sort. The beauty of Cordelia is neither male nor female; it is the beauty of virtue.

The ideal of love and marriage rose high in the mind of all the Christian nations who were capable of grave and deep feeling. We may take as examples of its English aspect the lines,

> " I could not love thee, dear, so much,
> Loved I not honor more."

Or the address of the Commonwealth's man to his wife, as she looked out from the Tower window to see him, for the last time, on his way to the scaffold. He stood up in the cart, waved his hat, and cried, " To Heaven, my love, to Heaven, and leave you in the storm ! "

Such was the love of faith and honor, — a love which stopped, like Colonel Hutchinson's, " on this side idolatry," because it was religious. The meeting of two such souls Donne describes as giving birth to an " abler soul."

Lord Herbert wrote to his love,

> " Were not our souls immortal made,
> Our equal loves can make them such."

In the "Broken Heart," of Ford, Penthea, a character which engages my admiration even more deeply than the famous one of Calanthe, is made to present to the mind the most beautiful picture of what these relations should be in their purity. Her life cannot sustain the violation of what she so clearly feels.

Shakspeare, too, saw that, in true love, as in fire, the utmost ardor is coïncident with the utmost purity. It is a true lover that exclaims in the agony of Othello,

> "If thou art false, O then Heaven mocks itself!"

The son, framed, like Hamlet, to appreciate truth in all the beauty of relations, sinks into deep melancholy when he finds his natural expectations disappointed. He has no other. She to whom he gave the name, disgraces from his heart's shrine all the sex.

> "Frailty, thy name is Woman."

It is because a Hamlet could find cause to say so, that I have put the line, whose stigma has never been removed, at the head of my work. But, as a lover, surely Hamlet would not have so far mistaken, as to have finished with such a conviction. He would have felt the faith of Othello, and that faith could not, in his more dispassionate mind, have been disturbed by calumny.

In Spain, this thought is arrayed in a sublimity which belongs to the sombre and passionate genius of the nation. Calderon's Justina resists all the temptation of the Demon, and raises her lover, with her, above the sweet lures of mere temporal happiness. Their mar-

riage is vowed at the stake; their souls are liberated
together by the martyr flame into "a purer state of sensation and existence."

In Italy, the great poets wove into their lives an ideal
love which answered to the highest wants. It included
those of the intellect and the affections, for it was a love
of spirit for spirit. It was not ascetic, or superhuman,
but, interpreting all things, gave their proper beauty to
details of the common life, the common day. The poet
spoke of his love, not as a flower to place in his bosom,
or hold carelessly in his hand, but as a light toward
which he must find wings to fly, or "a stair to heaven."
He delighted to speak of her, not only as the bride of
his heart, but the mother of his soul; for he saw that, in
cases where the right direction had been taken, the
greater delicacy of her frame and stillness of her life
left her more open than is Man to spiritual influx. So
he did not look upon her as betwixt him and earth, to
serve his temporal needs, but, rather, betwixt him and
heaven, to purify his affections and lead him to wisdom
through love. He sought, in her, not so much the Eve
as the Madonna.

In these minds the thought, which gleams through all
the legends of chivalry, shines in broad intellectual efful-
gence, not to be misinterpreted; and their thought is reverenced by the world, though it lies far from the practice
of the world as yet, — so far that it seems as though a
gulf of death yawned between.

Even with such men the practice was, often, widely
different from the mental faith. I say mental; for if the

heart were thoroughly alive with it, the practice could
not be dissonant.   Lord Herbert's was a marriage of convention, made for him at fifteen; he was not discontented
with it, but looked only to the advantages it brought of
perpetuating his family on the basis of a great fortune.
He paid, in act, what he considered a dutiful attention to
the bond; his thoughts travelled elsewhere; and while
forming a high ideal of the companionship of minds in
marriage, he seems never to have doubted that its realiz-
ation must be postponed to some other state of being.
Dante, almost immediately after the death of Beatrice,
married a lady chosen for him by his friends, and Boc-
caccio, in describing the miseries that attended, in this
case,

"The form of an union where union is none,"

speaks as if these were inevitable to the connection, and
as if the scholar and poet, especially, could expect nothing but misery and obstruction in a domestic partnership
with Woman.

Centuries have passed since, but civilized Europe is
still in a transition state about marriage; not only in
practice but in thought.   It is idle to speak with contempt of the nations where polygamy is an institution, or
seraglios a custom, while practices far more debasing
haunt, well-nigh fill, every city and every town, and so
far as union of one with one is believed to be the only
pure form of marriage, a great majority of societies and
individuals are still doubtful whether the earthly bond
must be a meeting of souls, or only supposes a contract
of convenience and utility.   Were Woman established in

the rights of an immortal being, this could not be. She would not, in some countries, be given away by her father, with scarcely more respect for her feelings than is shown by the Indian chief, who sells his daughter for a horse, and beats her if she runs away from her new home. Nor, in societies where her choice is left free, would she be perverted, by the current of opinion that seizes her, into the belief that she must marry, if it be only to find a protector, and a home of her own. Neither would Man, if he thought the connection of permanent importance, form it so lightly. He would not deem it a trifle, that he was to enter into the closest relations with another soul, which, if not eternal in themselves, must eternally affect his growth. Neither, did he believe Woman capable of friendship,* would he, by rash haste, lose the chance of finding a friend in the person who might, probably, live half a century by his side. Did love, to his mind, stretch forth into infinity, he would not miss his chance of its revelations, that he might the sooner rest from his weariness by a bright fireside, and secure a sweet and graceful attendant " devoted to him alone." Were he a step higher, he would not carelessly enter into a relation where he might not be able to do the duty of a friend, as well as a protector from external ill, to the other party, and have a being in his power pining for sympathy, intelligence and aid, that he could not give.

What deep communion, what real intercourse is im-

---

* See Appendix D, Spinoza's view.

plied in sharing the joys and cares of parentage, when
any degree of equality is admitted between the parties! It is true that, in a majority of instances, the man
looks upon his wife as an adopted child, and places her
to the other children in the relation of nurse or govern-
ess, rather than that of parent. Her influence with them
is sure; but she misses the education which should
enlighten that influence, by being thus treated. It is
the order of nature that children should complete the
education, moral and mental, of parents, by making them
think what is needed for the best culture of human
beings, and conquer all faults and impulses that interfere with their giving this to these dear objects, who represent the world to them. Father and mother should
assist one another to learn what is required for this sublime priesthood of Nature. But, for this, a religious
recognition of equality is required.

Where this thought of equality begins to diffuse itself,
it is shown in four ways.

First;—The household partnership. In our country, the woman looks for a "smart but kind" husband;
the man for a "capable, sweet-tempered" wife. The
man furnishes the house; the woman regulates it.
Their relation is one of mutual esteem, mutual dependence. Their talk is of business; their affection shows
itself by practical kindness. They know that life goes
more smoothly and cheerfully to each for the other's aid;
they are grateful and content. The wife praises her husband as a "good provider;" the husband, in return, com-

pliments her as a "capital housekeeper." This relation
is good so far as it goes.

Next comes a closer tie, which takes the form either of
mutual idolatry or of intellectual companionship. The
first, we suppose, is to no one a pleasing subject of contemplation. The parties weaken and narrow one another;
they lock the gate against all the glories of the universe,
that they may live in a cell together. To themselves
they seem the only wise; to all others, steeped in infatu-
ation; the gods smile as they look forward to the crisis
of cure; to men, the woman seems an unlovely syren; to
women, the man an effeminate boy.

The other form, of intellectual companionship, has
become more and more frequent. Men engaged in public life, literary men, and artists, have often found in
their wives companions and confidants in thought no less
than in feeling. And, as the intellectual development of
Woman has spread wider and risen higher, they have,
not unfrequently, shared the same employment; as in
the case of Roland and his wife, who were friends in the
household and in the nation's councils, read, regulated
home affairs, or prepared public documents together,
indifferently. It is very pleasant, in letters begun by
Roland and finished by his wife, to see the harmony of
mind, and the difference of nature; one thought, but
various ways of treating it.

This is one of the best instances of a marriage of
friendship. It was only friendship, whose basis was
esteem; probably neither party knew love, except by
name. Roland was a good man, worthy to esteem, and be

esteemed; his wife as deserving of admiration as able to do without it.

Madame Roland is the fairest specimen we yet have of her class; as clear to discern her aim, as valiant to pursue it, as Spenser's Britomart; austerely set apart from all that did not belong to her, whether as Woman or as mind. She is an antetype of a class to which the coming time will afford a field — the Spartan matron, brought by the culture of the age of books to intellectual consciousness and expansion. Self-sufficingness, strength, and clearsightedness were, in her, combined with a power of deep and calm affection. She, too, would have given a son or husband the device for his shield, " Return with it or upon it ; " and this, not because she loved little, but much. The page of her life is one of unsullied dignity. Her appeal to posterity is one against the injustice of those who committed such crimes in the name of Liberty. She makes it in behalf of herself and her husband. I would put beside it, on the shelf, a little volume, containing a similar appeal from the verdict of contemporaries to that of mankind, made by Godwin in behalf of his wife, the celebrated, the by most men detested, Mary Wolstonecraft. In his view, it was an appeal from the injustice of those who did such wrong in the name of virtue. Were this little book interesting for no other cause, it would be so for the generous affection evinced under the peculiar circumstances. This man had courage to love and honor this woman in the face of the world's sentence, and of all that was repulsive in her own past history. He believed he saw of what soul she was, and that the impulses she had struggled to act out were noble, though the opinions to which they had led might not be thoroughly weighed. He loved her, and he defended her for the meaning and tendency of her inner life. It was a good fact.

Mary Wolstonecraft, like Madame Dudevant (commonly known as George Sand) in our day, was a woman whose existence better proved the need of some new interpretation of Woman's Rights than anything she wrote. Such beings as these, rich in genius, of most tender sympathies, capable of high virtue and a chastened harmony, ought not to find themselves, by birth, in a place so narrow, that, in breaking bonds, they become outlaws. Were there as much room in the world for such, as in Spenser's poem for Britomart, they would not run their heads so wildly against the walls, but prize their shelter rather. They find their way, at last, to light and air, but the world will not take off the brand it has set upon them. The champion of the Rights of Woman found, in Godwin, one who would plead that cause like a brother. He who delineated with such purity of traits the form of Woman in the Marguerite, of whom the weak St. Leon could never learn to be worthy, — a pearl indeed whose price was above rubies, — was not false in life to the faith by which he had hallowed his romance. He acted, as he wrote, like a brother. This form of appeal rarely fails to touch the basest man : — " Are you acting toward other women in the way you would have men act towards your sister?" George Sand smokes, wears male attire, wishes to be addressed as " Mon frère ; " —

perhaps, if she found those who were as brothers indeed, she would not care whether she were brother or sister.* We rejoice to see that she, who expresses such a painful contempt for men in most of her works, as shows she must have known great wrong from them, depicts, in "La Roche Mauprat," a man raised by the workings of love from the depths of savage sensualism to a moral and intellectual life. It was love for a pure object, for a stead·· fast woman, one of those who, the Italian said, could make the "stair to heaven."

This author, beginning like the many in assault upon bad institutions, and external ills, yet deepening the experience through comparative freedom, sees at last that the only efficient remedy must come from individual character. These bad institutions, indeed, it may always be replied, prevent individuals from forming good character, therefore we must remove them. Agreed; yet keep steadily the higher aim in view. Could you clear away all the bad forms of society, it is vain, unless the individual begin to be ready for better. There must be a parallel movement in these two branches of life.. And all the rules left by Moses availed less to further the best life than the living example of one Messiah.

Still the mind of the age struggles confusedly with these problems, better discerning as yet the ill it can no longer bear, than the good by which it may super-

---

* A note appended by my sister in this place, in the first edition, is here omitted, because it is incorporated in another article in this volume, treating of George Sand more at length. — [ED.]

sede it. But women like Sand will speak now and cannot be silenced; their characters and their eloquence alike foretell an era when such as they shall easier learn to lead true lives. But though such forebode, not such shall be parents of it.* Those who would reform the world must show that they do not speak in the heat of wild impulse; their lives must be unstained by passionate error; they must be severe lawgivers to themselves. They must be religious students of the divine purpose with regard to man, if they would not confound the fancies of a day with the requisitions of eternal good. Their liberty must be the liberty of law and knowledge. But as to the transgressions against custom which have caused such outcry against those of noble intention, it may be observed that the resolve of Eloisa to be only the mistress of Abelard, was that of one who saw in practice around her the contract of marriage made the seal of degradation. Shelley feared not to be fettered, unless so to be was to be false. Wherever abuses are seen, the timid will suffer; the bold will protest. But society has a right to outlaw them till she has revised her law; and this she must be taught to do, by one who speaks with authority, not in anger or haste.

If Godwin's choice of the calumniated authoress of the "Rights of Woman," for his honored wife, be a sign of a new era, no less so is an article to which I have alluded some pages back, published five or six years ago in one of the English Reviews, where the writer, in doing full justice to Eloisa, shows his bitter regret that she lives not

*Appendix E.

now to love him, who might have known better how to prize her love than did the egotistical Abelard.

These marriages, these characters, with all their imperfections, express an onward tendency. They speak of aspiration of soul, of energy of mind, seeking clearness and freedom. Of a like promise are the tracts lately published by Goodwyn Barmby (the European Pariah, as he calls himself) and his wife Catharine. Whatever we may think of their measures, we see in them wedlock; the two minds are wed by the only contract that can permanently avail, that of a common faith and a common purpose.

We might mention instances, nearer home, of minds, partners in work and in life, sharing together, on equal terms, public and private interests, and which wear not, on any side, the aspect of offence shown by those last-named: persons who steer straight onward, yet, in our comparatively free life, have not been obliged to run their heads against any wall. But the principles which guide them might, under petrified and oppressive institutions, have made them warlike, paradoxical, and, in some sense, Pariahs. The phenomena are different, the law is the same, in all these cases. Men and women have been obliged to build up their house anew from the very foundation. If they found stone ready in the quarry, they took it peaceably; otherwise they alarmed the country by pulling down old towers to get materials.

These are all instances of marriage as intellectual companionship. The parties meet mind to mind, and a mutual trust is produced, which can buckler them against

a million. They work together for a common purpose,
and, in all these instances, with the same implement, —
the pen. The pen and the writing-desk furnish forth as
naturally the retirement of Woman as of Man.

A pleasing expression, in this kind, is afforded by the
union in the names of the Howitts. William and Mary
Howitt we heard named together for years, supposing
them to be brother and sister; the equality of labors and
reputation, even so, was auspicious ; more so, now we find
them man and wife. In his late work on Germany,
Howitt mentions his wife, with pride, as one among the
constellation of distinguished English-women, and in a
graceful, simple manner. And still we contemplate with
pleasure the partnership in literature and affection between the Howitts, — the congenial pursuits and productions — the pedestrian tours wherein the married pair
showed that marriage, on a wide enough basis, does not
destroy the "inexhaustible" entertainment which lovers
find in one another's company.

In naming these instances, I do not mean to imply
that community of employment is essential to the union
of husband and wife, more than to the union of friends.
Harmony exists in difference, no less than in likeness, if
only the same key-note govern both parts. Woman the
poem, Man the poet ! Woman the heart, Man the head !
Such divisions are only important when they are never
to be transcended. If nature is never bound down, nor
the voice of inspiration stifled, that is enough. We are
pleased that women should write and speak, if they feel
need of it, from having something to tell; but silence for

ages would be no misfortune, if that silence be from divine command, and not from Man's tradition.

While Goetz Von Berlichingen rides to battle, his wife is busy in the kitchen; but difference of occupation does not prevent that community of inward life, that perfect esteem, with which he says,

"Whom God loves, to him gives he such a wife."

Manzoni thus dedicates his "Adelchi."

"To his beloved and venerated wife, Enrichetta Luigia Blondel, who, with conjugal affection and maternal wisdom, has preserved a virgin mind, the author dedicates this 'Adelchi,' grieving that he could not, by a more splendid and more durable monument, honor the dear name, and the memory of so many virtues."

The relation could not be fairer, nor more equal, if she, too, had written poems. Yet the position of the parties might have been the reverse as well; the Woman might have sung the deeds, given voice to the life of the Man, and beauty would have been the result; as we see, in pictures of Arcadia, the nymph singing to the shepherds, or the shepherd, with his pipe, alluring the nymphs; either makes a good picture. The sounding lyre requires not muscular strength, but energy of soul to animate the hand which would control it. Nature seems to delight in varying the arrangements, as if to show that she will be fettered by no rule; and we must admit the same varieties that she admits.

The fourth and highest grade of marriage union is the religious, which may be expressed as pilgrimage toward a common shrine. This includes the others: home sympathies and household wisdom, for these pilgrims must know how to assist each other along the dusty way; intellectual communion, for how sad it would be on such a journey to have a companion to whom you could not communicate your thoughts and aspirations as they sprang to life; who would have no feeling for the prospects that open, more and more glorious as we advance; who would never see the flowers that may be gathered by the most industrious traveller! It must include all these.

Such a fellow-pilgrim Count Zinzendorf seems to have found in his countess, of whom he thus writes:

"Twenty-five years' experience has shown me that just the help-meet whom I have is the only one that could suit my vocation. Who else could have so carried through my family affairs? Who lived so spotlessly before the world? Who so wisely aided me in my rejection of a dry morality? Who so clearly set aside the Pharisaism which, as years passed, threatened to creep in among us? Who so deeply discerned as to the spirits of delusion which sought to bewilder us? Who would have governed my whole economy so wisely, richly and hospitably, when circumstances commanded? Who have taken indifferently the part of servant or mistress, without, on the one side, affecting an especial spirituality; on the other, being sullied by any worldly pride? Who, in a community where all ranks are eager to be on a level, would, from wise and real causes, have known how to maintain inward and outward distinctions? Who, without a murmur, have seen her husband encounter

such dangers by land and sea? Who undertaken with
him, and *sustained*, such astonishing pilgrimages?
Who, amid such difficulties, would have always held up
her head and supported me? Who found such vast
sums of money, and acquitted them on her own credit?
And, finally, who, of all human beings, could so well
understand and interpret to others my inner and outer
being as this one, of such nobleness in her way of thinking, such great intellectual capacity, and so free from the
theological perplexities that enveloped me ! "

Let any one peruse, with all intentness, the lineaments of this portrait, and see if the husband had not
reason, with this air of solemn rapture and conviction, to
challenge comparison? We are reminded of the majestic
cadence of the line whose feet step in the just proportion
of Humanity,

"Daughter of God and Man, accomplished Eve ! "

An observer* adds this testimony :

"We may, in many marriages, regard it as the best
arrangement, if the man has so much advantage over his
wife, that she can, without much thought of her own, be
led and directed by him as by a father. But it was not
so with the count and his consort. She was not made to
be a copy; she was an original; and, while she loved and
honored him, she thought for herself, on all subjects,
with so much intelligence, that he could and did look on
her as a sister and friend also."

Compare with this refined specimen of a religiously

---

* Spangenberg.

civilized life the following imperfect sketch of a North American Indian, and we shall see that the same causes will always produce the same results. The Flying Pigeon (Ratchewaine) was the wife of a barbarous chief, who had six others; but she was his only true wife, because the only one of a strong and pure character, and, having this, inspired a veneration, as like as the mind of the man permitted to that inspired by the Countess Zinzendorf. She died when her son was only four years old, yet left on his mind a feeling of reverent love worthy the thought of Christian chivalry. Grown to manhood, he shed tears on seeing her portrait.

THE FLYING PIGEON.

"Ratchewaine was chaste, mild, gentle in her disposition, kind, generous, and devoted to her husband. A harsh word was never known to proceed from her mouth; nor was she ever known to be in a passion. Mahaskah used to say of her, after her death, that her hand was shut when those who did not want came into her presence; but when the really poor came in, it was like a strainer full of holes, letting all she held in it pass through. In the exercise of generous feeling she was uniform. It was not indebted for its exercise to whim, nor caprice, nor partiality. No matter of what nation the applicant for her bounty was, or whether at war or peace with her nation; if he were hungry, she fed him; if naked, she clothed him; and, if houseless, she gave him shelter. The continued exercise of this generous feeling kept her poor. And she has been known to give away her last blanket — all the honey that was in the lodge, the last bladder of bear's oil, and the last piece of dried meat.

" She was scrupulously exact in the observance of all the religious rites which her faith imposed upon her. Her conscience is represented to have been extremely tender. She often feared that her acts were displeasing to the Great Spirit, when she would blacken her face, and retire to some lone place, and fast and pray."

To these traits should be added, but for want of room, anecdotes which show the quick decision and vivacity of her mind. Her face was in harmony with this combination. Her brow is as ideal and the eyes and lids as devout and modest as the Italian picture of the Madonna, while the lower part of the face has the simplicity and childish strength of the Indian race. Her picture presents the finest specimen of Indian beauty we have ever seen. Such a Woman is the sister and friend of all beings, as the worthy Man is their brother and helper.

With like pleasure we survey the pairs wedded on the eve of missionary effort. They, indeed, are fellow-pilgrims on the well-made road, and whether or no they accomplish all they hope for the sad Hindoo, or the nearer savage, we feel that in the burning waste their love is like to be a healing dew, in the forlorn jungle a tent of solace to one another. They meet, as children of one Father, to read together one book of instruction.

We must insert in this connection the most beautiful picture presented by ancient literature of wedded love under this noble form.

It is from the romance in which Xenophon, the chivalrous Greek, presents his ideal of what human nature
should be.

The generals of Cyrus had taken captive a princess, a
woman of unequalled beauty, and hastened to present her
to the prince as that part of the spoil he would think
most worthy of his acceptance. Cyrus visits the lady,
and is filled with immediate admiration by the modesty
and majesty with which she receives him. He finds
her name is Panthea, and that she is the wife of Abradatus, a young king whom she entirely loves. He protects
her as a sister, in his camp, till he can restore her to her
husband.

After the first transports of joy at this reünion, the
heart of Panthea is bent on showing her love and gratitude to her magnanimous and delicate protector. And
as she has nothing so precious to give as the aid of Abradatus, that is what she most wishes to offer. Her husband is of one soul with her in this, as in all things.

The description of her grief and self-destruction, after
the death which ensued upon this devotion, I have seen
quoted, but never that of their parting when she sends
him forth to battle. I shall copy both. If they have
been read by any of my readers, they may be so again
with profit in this connection, for never were the heroism
of a true Woman, and the purity of love in a true marriage, painted in colors more delicate and more lively.

"The chariot of Abradatus, that had four perches and
eight horses, was completely adorned for him; and when
he was going to put on his linen corslet, which was a sort

of armor used by those of his country, Panthea brought
him a golden helmet, and arm-pieces, broad bracelets for
his wrists, a purple habit that reached down to his feet,
and hung in folds at the bottom, and a crest dyed of a
violet color. These things she had made, unknown to
her husband, and by taking the measure of his armor.
He wondered when he saw them, and inquired thus of
Panthea : ' And have you made me these arms, woman,
by destroying your own ornaments ? '   ' No, by Jove ! '
said Panthea, ' not what is the most valuable of them ;
for it is you, if you appear to others to be what I think
you, that will be my greatest ornament.'   And, saying
that, she put on him the armor, and, though she endeav-
ored to conceal it, the tears poured down her cheeks.
When Abradatus, who was before a man of fine appearance, was set out in those arms, he appeared the most
beautiful and noble of all, especially being likewise so by
nature.   Then, taking the reins from the driver, he was
just preparing to mount the chariot, when Panthea, after
she had desired all that were there to retire, thus said :

" ' O Abradatus ! if ever there was a woman who had a
greater regard to her husband than to her own soul, I
believe you know that I am such an one ; what need I
therefore speak of things in particular ? for I reckon that
my actions have convinced you more than any words I
can now use.   And yet, though I stand thus affected
toward you, as you know I do, I swear, by this friendship
of mine and yours, that I certainly would rather choose
to be put under ground jointly with you, approving yourself a brave man, than to live with you in disgrace and

shame; so much do I think you and myself worthy of
the noblest things. Then I think that we both lie under
great obligations to Cyrus, that, when I was a captive,
and chosen out for himself, he thought fit to treat me
neither as a slave, nor, indeed, as a woman of mean
account, but he took and kept me for you, as if I were
his brother's wife. Besides, when Araspes, who was my
guard, went away from him, I promised him, that, if he
would allow me to send for you, you would come to him,
and approve yourself a much better and more faithful
friend than Araspes.'

"Thus she spoke; and Abradatus, being struck with
admiration at her discourse, laying his hand gently on
her head, and lifting up his eyes to heaven, made this
prayer : ' Do thou, O greatest Jove! grant me to appear
a husband worthy of Panthea, and a friend worthy of
Cyrus, who has done us so much honor ! '

"Having said this, he mounted the chariot by the door
of the driver's seat; and, after he had got up, when the
driver shut the door, Panthea, who had now no other
way to salute him, kissed the seat of the chariot. The
chariot then moved, and she, unknown to him, followed,
till Abradatus turning about, and seeing her, said : ' Take
courage, Panthea ! Fare you happily and well, and now
go your ways.' On this her women and servants carried
her to her conveyance, and, laying her down, concealed
her by throwing the covering of a tent over her. The
people, though Abradatus and his chariot made a noble
spectacle, were not able to look at him till Panthea was
gone."

After the battle —

" Cyrus calling to some of his servants, ' Tell me, said he, ' has any one seen Abradatus? for I admire that he now does not appear.' One replied, ' My sovereign, it is because he is not living, but died in the battle as he broke in with his chariot on the Egyptians. All the rest, except his particular companions, they say, turned off when they saw the Egyptians' compact body. His wife is now said to have taken up his dead body, to have placed it in the carriage that she herself was conveyed in, and to have brought it hither to some place on the river Pactolus, and her servants are digging a grave on a certain elevation. They say that his wife, after setting him out with all the ornaments she has, is sitting on the ground with his head on her knees.' Cyrus, hearing this, gave himself a blow on the thigh, mounted his horse at a leap, and, taking with him a thousand horse, rode away to this scene of affliction ; but gave orders to Gadatas and Gobryas to take with them all the rich ornaments proper for a friend and an excellent man deceased, and to follow after him ; and whoever had herds of cattle with him, he ordered them to take both oxen, and horses, and sheep in good number, and to bring them away to the place where, by inquiry, they should find him to be, that he might sacrifice these to Abradatus.

" As soon as he saw the woman sitting on the ground, and the dead body there lying, he shed tears at the afflicting sight, and said : ' Alas ! thou brave and faithful soul, hast thou left us, and art thou gone ? ' At the same time he took him by the right hand, and the hand of the deceased came away, for it had been cut off with a sword by the Egyptians. He, at the sight of this, became yet much more concerned than before. The woman shrieked out in a lamentable manner, and, taking the hand from Cyrus, kissed it, fitted it to its proper place again, as well as she could, and said : 'The rest, Cyrus, is in the same condition, but what need you see it? And I know that I was not one of the least concerned in these his sufferings, and, perhaps, you were not less so; for I, fool that I was! frequently exhorted him to behave in such a manner as to appear a friend to you, worthy of notice ; and I know he never thought of what he himself should suffer, but of what he should do to please you. He is dead, therefore,' said she, ' without reproach, and I, who urged him on, sit here alive.' Cyrus, shedding tears for some time in silence, then spoke : —' He has died, woman, the noblest death ; for he has died victorious ! Do you adorn him with these things that I furnish you with.' (Gobryas and Gadatas were then come up, and had brought rich ornaments in great abundance with them.) 'Then,' said he, ' be assured that he shall not want respect and honor in all other things ; but, over and above, multitudes shall concur in raising him a monument that shall be worthy of us, and all the sacrifices shall be made him that are proper to be made in honor of a brave man. You shall not be left destitute, but, for the sake of your modesty and every other virtue, I will pay you all other honors, as well as place those about you who will conduct you wherever you please. Do you but make it known to me where it is that you

desire to be conveyed to.' And Panthea replied : ' Be
confident, Cyrus, I will not conceal from you to whom
it is that I desire to go.'

" He, having said this, went away with great pity for
her that she should have lost such a husband, and for
the man that he should have left such a wife behind him,
never to see her more.   Panthea then gave orders for her
servants to retire, ' till such time,' said she, ' as I shall
have lamented my husband as I please.'   Her nurse she
bid to stay, and gave orders that, when she was dead,
she would wrap her and her husband up in one mantle
together.   The nurse, after having repeatedly begged her
not to do this, and meeting with no success, but observing
her to grow angry, sat herself down, breaking out into
tears.   She, being beforehand provided with a sword,
killed herself, and, laying her head down on her husband's breast, she died.   The nurse set up a lamentable
cry, and covered them both, as Panthea had directed.

" Cyrus, as soon as he was informed of what the woman
had done, being struck with it, went to help her if he
could.   The servants, three in number, seeing what had
been done, drew their swords and killed themselves, as
they stood at the place where she had ordered them.
And the monument is now said to have been raised by
continuing the mound on to the servants ; and on a pillar
above, they say, the names of the man and woman were
written in Syriac letters.

" Below were three pillars, and they were inscribed
thus, ' Of the servants.'   Cyrus, when he came to this
melancholy scene, was struck with admiration of the

woman, and, having lamented over her, went away. He took care, as was proper, that all the funeral rites should be paid them in the noblest manner, and the monument, they say, was raised up to a very great size."

These be the ancients, who, so many assert, had no idea of the dignity of Woman, or of marriage. Such love Xenophon could paint as subsisting between those who after death "would see one another never more." Thousands of years have passed since, and with the reception of the Cross, the nations assume the belief that those who part thus may meet again and forever, if spiritually fitted to one another, as Abradatus and Panthea were, and yet do we see such marriages among them? If at all, how often?

I must quote two more short passages from Xenophon, for he is a writer who pleases me well.

Cyrus, receiving the Armenians whom he had conquered —

" 'Tigranes,' said he, 'at what rate would you purchase the regaining of your wife?' Now Tigranes happened to be *but lately married,* and had a very great love for his wife." (That clause perhaps sounds *modern.*)

" 'Cyrus,' said he, 'I would ransom her at the expense of my life.'

" 'Take then your own to yourself,' said he. * * *

" When they came home, one talked of Cyrus' wisdom, another of his patience and resolution, another of his mildness. One spoke of his beauty and smallness of his person, and, on that Tigranes asked his wife, 'And

do you, Armenian dame, think Cyrus handsome?
'Truly,' said she, 'I did not look at him.' 'At
whom, then, *did* you look?' said Tigranes. 'At him
who said that, to save me from servitude, he would ransom me at the expense of his own life.' "

From the Banquet. —

"Socrates, who observed her with pleasure, said, 'This
young girl has confirmed me in the opinion I have had,
for a long time, that the female sex are nothing inferior
to ours, excepting only in strength of body, or, perhaps,
in steadiness of judgment.' "

In the Economics, the manner in which the husband
gives counsel to his young wife presents the model of
politeness and refinement. Xenophon is thoroughly the
gentleman; gentle in breeding and in soul. All the men
he describes are so, while the shades of manner are distinctly marked. There is the serene dignity of Socrates,
with gleams of playfulness thrown across its cool, religious
shades, the princely mildness of Cyrus, and the more
domestic elegance of the husband in the Economics.

There is no way that men sin more against refinement,
as well as discretion, than in their conduct toward their
wives. Let them look at the men of Xenophon. Such
would know how to give counsel, for they would know how
to receive it. They would feel that the most intimate
relations claimed most, not least, of refined courtesy.
They would not suppose that confidence justified carelessness, nor the reality of affection want of delicacy in the
expression of it.

Such men would be too wise to hide their affairs from the wife, and then expect her to act as if she knew them. They would know that, if she is expected to face calamity with courage, she must be instructed and trusted in prosperity, or, if they had failed in wise confidence, such as the husband shows in the Economics, they would be ashamed of anger or querulous surprise at the results that naturally follow.

Such men would not be exposed to the bad influence of bad wives; for all wives, bad or good, loved or unloved, inevitably influence their husbands, from the power their position not merely gives, but necessitates, of coloring evidence and infusing feelings in hours when the — patient, shall I call him? — is off his guard. Those who understand the wife's mind, and think it worth while to respect her springs of action, know better where they are. But to the bad or thoughtless man, who lives carelessly and irreverently so near another mind, the wrong he does daily back upon himself recoils. A Cyrus, an Abradatus, knows where he stands.

But to return to the thread of my subject.

Another sign of the times is furnished by the triumphs of Female Authorship. These have been great, and are constantly increasing. Women have taken possession of so many provinces for which men had pronounced them unfit, that, though these still declare there are some inaccessible to them, it is difficult to say just *where* they must stop.

The shining names of famous women have cast light upon the path of the sex, and many obstructions have been removed. When a Montague could learn better than her brother, and use her lore afterwards to such purpose as an observer, it seemed amiss to hinder women from preparing themselves to see, or from seeing all they could, when prepared. Since Somerville has achieved so much, will any young girl be prevented from seeking a knowledge of the physical sciences, if she wishes it? De Stael's name was not so clear of offence; she could not forget the Woman in the thought; while she was instructing you as a mind, she wished to be admired as a Woman; sentimental tears often dimmed the eagle glance. Her intellect, too, with all its splendor, trained in a drawing-room, fed on flattery, was tainted and flawed; yet its beams make the obscurest school-house in New England warmer and lighter to the little rugged girls who are gathered together on its wooden bench. They may never through life hear her name, but she is not the less their benefactress.

The influence has been such, that the aim certainly is, now, in arranging school instruction for girls, to give them as fair a field as boys. As yet, indeed, these arrangements are made with little judgment or reflection; just as the tutors of Lady Jane Grey, and other distinguished women of her time, taught them Latin and Greek, because they knew nothing else themselves, so now the improvement in the education of girls is to be made by giving them young men as teachers, who only teach what has been taught themselves at college, while methods and topics need revision for these new subjects, which could better be made by those who had experienced the same wants. Women are, often, at the head of these institutions; but they have, as yet, seldom been thinking women, capable of organizing a new whole for the wants of the time, and choosing persons to officiate in the departments. And when some portion of instruction of a good sort is got from the school, the far greater proportion which is infused from the general atmosphere of society contradicts its purport. Yet books and a little elementary instruction are not furnished in vain. Women are better aware how great and rich the universe is, not so easily blinded by narrowness or partial views of a home circle. "Her mother did so before her" is no longer a sufficient excuse. Indeed, it was never received as an excuse to mitigate the severity of censure, but was adduced as a reason, rather, why there should be no effort made for reformation.

Whether much or little has been done, or will be done, — whether women will add to the talent of narration the power of systematizing, — whether they will carve marble, as well as draw and paint, — is not important. But that it should be acknowledged that they have intellect which needs developing — that they should not be considered complete, if beings of affection and habit alone — is important.

Yet even this acknowledgment, rather conquered by Woman than proffered by Man, has been sullied by the usual selfishness. Too much is said of women being better educated, that they may become better companions and mothers *for men*. They should be fit for such companionship, and we have mentioned, with satisfaction, in-

stances where it has been established.   Earth knows nc
fairer, holier relation than that of a mother.   It is one
which, rightly understood, must both promote and
require the highest attainments.   But a being of infinite
scope must not be treated with an exclusive view to any
one relation.   Give the soul free course, let the organization, both of body and mind, be freely developed, and
the being will be fit for any and every relation to which
it may be called.   The intellect, no more than the sense
of hearing, is to be cultivated merely that Woman may be
a more valuable companion to Man, but because the Power
who gave a power, by its mere existence signifies that it
must be brought out toward perfection.

In this regard of self-dependence, and a greater simplicity and fulness of being, we must hail as a prelimi-
nary the increase of the class contemptuously designated
as " old maids."

We cannot wonder at the aversion with which old
bachelors and old maids have been regarded.   Marriage
is the natural means of forming a sphere, of taking root
in the earth; it requires more strength to do this without
such an opening; very many have failed, and their imperfections have been in every one's way.   They have
been more partial, more harsh, more officious and imper-
tinent, than those compelled by severer friction to render
themselves endurable.   Those who have a more full experience of the instincts have a distrust as to whether the
unmarried can be thoroughly human and humane, such as
is hinted in the saying, " Old maids' and bachelors' chil-

dren are well cared for," which derides at once their
ignorance and their presumption.

Yet the business of society has become so complex,
that it could now scarcely be carried on without the presence of these despised auxiliaries ; and detachments from
the army of aunts and uncles are wanted to stop gaps in
every hedge. They rove about, mental and moral Ishmaelites, pitching their tents amid the fixed and orna-
mented homes of men.

In a striking variety of forms, genius of late, both at
home and abroad, has paid its tribute to the character of
the Aunt and the Uncle, recognizing in these personages
the spiritual parents, who have supplied defects in the
treatment of the busy or careless actual parents.

They also gain a wider, if not so deep experience.
Those who are not intimately and permanently linked
with others, are thrown upon themselves ; and, if they
do not there find peace and incessant life, there is none
to flatter them that they are not very poor, and very
mean.

A position which so constantly admonishes, may be of
inestimable benefit. The person may gain, undistracted
by other relationships, a closer communion with the one.
Such a use is made of it by saints and sibyls. Or she
may be one of the lay sisters of charity, a canoness,
bound by an inward vow, — or the useful drudge of all
men, the Martha, much sought, little prized, — or the
intellectual interpreter of the varied life she sees; the
Urania of a half-formed world's twilight.

Or she may combine all these. Not " needing to

care that she may please a husband," a frail and .imite1 being, her thoughts may turn to the centre, and she may, by steadfast contemplation entering into the secret of truth and love, use it for the good of all men, instead of a chosen few, and interpret through it all the forms of life. It is possible, perhaps, to be at once a priestly servant and a loving muse.

Saints and geniuses have often chosen a lonely position, in the faith that if, undisturbed by the pressure of near ties, they would give themselves up to the inspiring spirit, it would enable them to understand and reproduce life better than actual experience could.

How many "old maids" take this high stand we cannot say : it is an unhappy fact that too many who have come before the eye are gossips rather, and not always good-natured gossips. But if these abuse, and none make the best of their vocation, yet it has not failed to produce some good results. It has been seen by others, if not by themselves, that beings, likely to be left alone, need to be fortified and furnished within themselves; and education and thought have tended more and more to regard these beings as related to absolute Being, as well as to others. It has been seen that, as the breaking of no bond ought to destroy a man, so ought the missing of none to hinder him from growing. And thus a circumstance of the time, which springs rather from its luxury than its purity, has helped to place women on the true platform.

Perhaps the next generation, looking deeper into this matter, will find that contempt is put upon old maids, or

old women, at all, merely because they do not use the
elixir which would keep them always young.   Under its
influence, a gem brightens yearly which is only seen to
more advantage through the fissures Time makes in the
casket.*   No one thinks of Michael Angelo's Persican
Sibyl, or St. Theresa, or Tasso's Leonora, or the Greek
Electra, as an old maid, more than of Michael Angelo or
Canova as old bachelors, though all had reached the
period in life's course appointed to take that degree.

See a common woman at forty; scarcely has she the
remains of beauty, of any soft poetic grace which gave
her attraction as Woman, which kindled the hearts of
those who looked on her to sparkling thoughts, or diffused
round her a roseate air of gentle love.   See her, who was,
indeed, a lovely girl, in the coarse, full-blown dahlia
flower of what is commonly matron-beauty, "fat, fair,
and forty," showily dressed, and with manners as broad
and full as her frill or satin cloak.   People observe,
"How well she is preserved!" "She is a fine woman
still," they say.   This woman, whether as a duchess in
diamonds, or one of our city dames in mosaics, charms
the poet's heart no more, and would look much out
of place kneeling before the Madonna.   She "does
well the honors of her house," — "leads society," — is,
in short, always spoken and thought of upholstery-wise.

Or see that care-worn face, from which every soft line
is blotted,— those faded eyes, from which lonely tears
have driven the flashes of fancy, the mild white beam of

* Appendix F.

a tender enthusiasm.   This woman is not so ornamental to a tea-party ; yet she would please better, in picture. Yet surely she, no more than the other, looks as a human being should at the end of forty years.   Forty years ! have they bound those brows with no garland ? shed in the lamp no drop of ambrosial oil ?

Not so looked the Iphigenia in Aulis.   Her forty years had seen her in anguish, in sacrifice, in utter loneliness.   But those pains were borne for her father and her country; the sacrifice she had made pure for herself and those around her.   Wandering alone at night in the vestal solitude of her imprisoning grove, she has looked up through its " living summits " to the stars, which shed down into her aspect their own lofty melody.   At forty she would not misbecome the marble.

Not so looks the Persica.   She is withered; she is faded; the drapery that enfolds her has in its dignity an angularity, too, that tells of age, of sorrow, of a stern resignation to the *must*.   But her eye, that torch of the soul, is untamed, and, in the intensity of her reading, we see a soul invincibly young in faith and hope.   Her age is her charm, for it is the night of the past that gives this beacon-fire leave to shine.   Wither more and more, black Chrysalid ! thou dost but give the winged beauty time to mature its splendors !

Not so looked Victoria Colonna, after her life of a great hope, and of true conjugal fidelity.   She had been, not merely a bride, but a wife, and each hour had helped tc plume the noble bird.   A coronet of pearls will not shame her brow ; it is white and ample, a worthy altar for love and thought.

Even among the North American Indians, a race of men as completely engaged in mere instinctive life as almost any in the world, and where each chief, keeping many wives as useful servants, of course looks with no kind eye. on celibacy in Woman, it was excused in the following instance mentioned by Mrs. Jameson. A woman dreamt in youth that she was betrothed to the Sun. She built her a wigwam apart, filled it with emblems of her alliance, and means of an independent life. There she passed her days, sustained by her own exertions, and true to her supposed engagement.

In any tribe, we believe, a woman, who lived as if she was betrothed to the Sun, would be tolerated, and the rays which made her youth blossom sweetly, would crown her with a halo in age.

There is, on this subject, a nobler view than heretofore, if not the noblest, and improvement here must coincide with that in the view taken of marriage. "We must have units before we can have union," says one of the ripe thinkers of the times.

If larger intellectual resources begin to be deemed needful to Woman, still more is a spiritual dignity in her, or even the mere assumption of it, looked upon with respect. Joanna Southcote and Mother Anne Lee are sure of a band of disciples; Ecstatica, Dolorosa, of enraptured believers who will visit them in their lowly huts, and wait for days to revere them in their trances. The foreign noble traverses land and sea to hear a few words

from the lips of the lowly peasant girl, whom he believes
especially visited by the Most High.   Very beautiful, in
this way, was the influence of the invalid of St. Peters-
burg, as described by De Maistre.

Mysticism, which may be defined as the brooding soul
of the world, cannot fail of its oracular promise as to
Woman.   "The mothers,"   "The mother of all
things," are expressions of thought which lead the mind
towards this side of universal growth.   Whenever a mystical whisper was heard, from Behmen down to St.
Simon, sprang up the thought, that, if it be true, as the
legend says, that Humanity withers through a fault committed by and a curse laid upon Woman, through her
pure child, or influence, shall the new Adam, the redemption, arise.   Innocence is to be replaced by virtue, dependence by a willing submission, in the heart of the Virgin-
Mother of the new race.

The spiritual tendency is toward the elevation of Woman, but the intellectual by itself is not so.   Plato
sometimes seems penetrated by that high idea of love,
which considers Man and Woman as the two-fold expression of one thought.   This the angel of Swedenborg, the
angel of the coming age, cannot surpass, but only explain
more fully.   But then again Plato, the man of intellect,
treats Woman in the Republic as property, and, in the
Timæus, says that Man, if he misuse the privileges of
one life, shall be degraded into the form of Woman ; and
then, if he do not redeem himself, into that of a bird.
This, as I said above, expresses most happily how anti-
poetical is this state of mind.   For the poet, contemplat-

ing the world of things, selects various birds as the symbols of his most gracious and ethereal thoughts, just as he calls upon his genius as muse rather than as God. But the intellect, cold, is ever more masculine than feminine; warmed by emotion, it rushes toward mother-earth, and puts on the forms of beauty.

The electrical, the magnetic element in Woman has not been fairly brought out at any period. Everything might be expected from it; she has far more of it than Man. This is commonly expressed by saying that her intuitions are more rapid and more correct. You will often see men of high intellect absolutely stupid in regard to the atmospheric changes, the fine invisible links which connect the forms of life around them, while common women, if pure and modest, so that a vulgar self do not overshadow the mental eye, will seize and delineate these with unerring discrimination.

Women who combine this organization with creative genius are very commonly unhappy at present. They see too much to act in conformity with those around them, and their quick impulses seem folly to those who do not discern the motives. This is an usual effect of the apparition of genius, whether in Man or Woman, but is more frequent with regard to the latter, because a harmony, an obvious order and self-restraining decorum, is most expected from her.

Then women of genius, even more than men. are likely to be enslaved by an impassioned sensibility. The world repels them more rudely, and they are of weaker bodily frame

Those who seem overladen with electricity frighten
those around them.   "When she merely enters the room,
I am what the French call *herissé*," said a man of
petty feelings and worldly character of such a woman,
whose depth of eye and powerful motion announced the
conductor of the mysterious fluid.

Woe to such a woman who finds herself linked to such
a man in bonds too close !   It is the cruelest of errors.
He will detest her with all the bitterness of wounded
self-love.   He will take the whole prejudice of manhood
upon himself, and, to the utmost of his power, imprison
and torture her by its imperious rigors.

Yet, allow room enough, and the electric fluid will be
found to invigorate and embellish, not destroy life.   Such
women are the great actresses, the songsters.   Such traits
we read in a late searching, though too French, analysis
of the character of Mademoiselle Rachel, by a modern
La Rochefoucault.   The Greeks thus represent the
muses; they have not the golden serenity of Apollo;
they are *over*flowed with thought; there is something
tragic in their air.   Such are the Sibyls of Guercino;
the eye is overfull of expression, dilated and lustrous;
it seems to have drawn the whole being into it.

Sickness is the frequent result of this overcharged
existence.   To this region, however misunderstood, or
interpreted with presumptuous carelessness, belong the
phenomena of magnetism, or mesmerism, as it is now
often called, where the trance of the Ecstatica purports
to be produced by the agency of one human being or
another, instead of, as in her case, direct from the spirit.

The worldling has his sneer at this as at the services of religion. "The churches can always be filled with women"—"Show me a man in one of your magnetic states, and I will believe."

Women are, indeed, the easy victims both of priest-craft and self-delusion; but this would not be, if the intellect was developed in proportion to the other powers. They would then have a regulator, and be more in equi-poise, yet must retain the same nervous susceptibility while their physical structure is such as it is.

It is with just that hope that we welcome everything that tends to strengthen the fibre and develop the nature on more sides. When the intellect and affections are in harmony; when intellectual consciousness is calm and deep; inspiration will not be confounded with fancy.

> Then, " she who advances
> With rapturous, lyrical glances,
> Singing the song of the earth, singing
> Its hymn to the Gods,"

will not be pitied as a mad-woman, nor shrunk from as unnatural.

The Greeks, who saw everything in forms, which we are trying to ascertain as law, and classify as cause, em-bodied all this in the form of Cassandra. Cassandra was only unfortunate in receiving her gift too soon. The remarks, however, that the world still makes in such cases, are well expressed by the Greek dramatist.

In the Trojan dames there are fine touches of nature with regard to Cassandra. Hecuba shows that mixture of shame and reverence that prosaic kindred always do

toward the inspired child, the poet, the elected sufferer for
the race.

When the herald announces that Cassandra is chosen
to be the mistress of Agamemnon, Hecuba answers, with
indignation, betraying the pride and faith she involun-
tarily felt in this daughter.

> "*Hec.* The maiden of Phoebus, to whom the golden-haired
>   Gave as a privilege a virgin life !
> *Tal.* Love of the inspired maiden hath pierced him.
> *Hec.* Then cast away, my child, the sacred keys, and from thy person
>   The consecrated garlands which thou wearest."

Yet, when, a moment after, Cassandra appears, singing, wildly, her inspired song, Hecuba calls her, "My
frantic child."

Yet how graceful she is in her tragic *raptus*, the
chorus shows.

> "*Chorus.* How sweetly at thy house's ills thou smil'st,
>   Chanting what, haply, thou wilt not show true.'

If Hecuba dares not trust her highest instinct about
her daughter, still less can the vulgar mind of the herald
Talthybius, a man not without feeling, but with no
princely, no poetic blood, abide the wild, prophetic mood
which insults all his prejudices.

> "*Tal.* The venerable, and that accounted wise,
>   Is nothing better than that of no repute ;
>   For the greatest king of all the Greeks,
>   The dear son of Atreus, is possessed with the love
>   Of this mad-woman.   I, indeed, am poor ;
>   Yet I would not receive her to my bed."

The royal Agamemnon could see the beauty of Cassandra ; *he* was not afraid of her prophetic gifts.

The best topic for a chapter on this subject, in the present day, would be the history of the Seeress of Prevorst, the best observed subject of magnetism in our present times, and who, like her ancestresses of Delphos, was roused to ecstasy or phrensy by the touch of the laurel.

I observe in her case, and in one known to me here, that what might have been a gradual and gentle disclosure of remarkable powers was broken and jarred into disease by an unsuitable marriage. Both these persons were unfortunate in not understanding what was involved in this relation, but acted ignorantly, as their friends desired. They thought that this was the inevitable destiny of Woman. But when engaged in the false position, it was impossible for them to endure its dissonances, as those of less delicate perceptions can; and the fine flow of life was checked and sullied. They grew sick; but, even so, learned and disclosed more than those in health are wont to do.

In such cases, worldlings sneer; but reverent men learn wondrous news, either from the person observed, or by thoughts caused in themselves by the observation. Fenelon learns from Guyon, Kerner from his Seeress, what we fain would know. But to appreciate such disclosures one must be a child; and here the phrase, "women and children," may, perhaps, be interpreted aright, that only little children shall enter into the kingdom of heaven.

All these motions of the time, tides that betoken a waxing moon, overflow upon our land. The world at large is readier to let Woman learn and manifest the capacities of her nature than it ever was before, and here is a less encumbered field and freer air than anywhere else. And it ought to be so ; we ought to pay for Isabella's jewels.

The names of nations are feminine — Religion, Virtue and Victory are feminine. To those who have a superstition, as to outward reigns, it is not without significance that the name of the queen of our mother-land should at this crisis be Victoria, — Victoria the First. Perhaps to us it may be given to disclose the era thus outwardly presaged.

Another Isabella too at this time ascends the throne. Might she open a new world to her sex ! But, probably, these poor little women are, least of any, educated to serve as examples or inspirers for the rest. The Spanish queen is younger ; we know of her that she sprained her foot the other day, dancing in her private apartments ; of Victoria, that she reads aloud, in a distinct voice and agreeable manner, her addresses to Parliament on certain solemn days, and, yearly, that she presents to the nation some new prop of royalty. These ladies have, very likely, been trained more completely to the puppet life than any other. The queens, who have been queens indeed, were trained by adverse circumstances to know the world around them and their own powers.

It is moving, while amusing, to read of the Scottish peasant measuring the print left by the queen's foot as she walks, and priding himself on its beauty. It is so natural to wish to find what is fair and precious in high places, — so astonishing to find the Bourbon a glutton, or the Guelph a dullard or gossip.

In our own country, women are, in many respects, better situated than men. Good books are allowed, with more time to read them. They are not so early forced into the bustle of life, nor so weighed down by demands for outward success. The perpetual changes, incident to our society, make the blood circulate freely through the body politic, and, if not favorable at present to the grace and bloom of life, they are so to activity, resource, and would be to reflection, but for a low materialist tendency, from which the women are generally exempt in themselves, though its existence, among the men, has a tendency to repress their impulses and make them doubt their instincts, thus often paralyzing their action during the best years.

But they have time to think, and no traditions chain them, and few conventionalities, compared with what must be met in other nations. There is no reason why they should not discover that the secrets of nature are open, the revelations of the spirit waiting, for whoever will seek them. When the mind is once awakened to this consciousness, it will not be restrained by the habits of the past, but fly to seek the seeds of a heavenly future.

Their employments are more favorable to meditation than those of men.

Woman is not addressed religiously here more than elsewhere. She is told that she should be worthy to be the mother of a Washington, or the companion of some

10

good man. But in many, many instances, she has already learned that all bribes have the same flaw; that truth and good are to be sought solely for their own sakes. And, already, an ideal sweetness floats over many forms, shines in many eyes.

Already deep questions are put by young girls on the great theme : What shall I do to enter upon the eternal life?

Men are very courteous to them. They praise them often, check them seldom. There is chivalry in the feeling toward " the ladies," which gives them the best seats in the stage-coach, frequent admission, not only to lectures of all sorts, but to courts of justice, halls of legislature, reform conventions. The newspaper editor " would be better pleased that the Lady's Book should be filled up exclusively by ladies. It would then, indeed, be a true gem, worthy to be presented by young men to the mistress of their affections." Can gallantry go further?

In this country is venerated, wherever seen, the character which Goethe spoke of as an Ideal, which he saw actualized in his friend and patroness, the Grand Duchess Amelia : " The excellent woman is she, who, if the husband dies, can be a father to the children." And this, if read aright, tells a great deal.

Women who speak in public, if they have a moral power, such as has been felt from Angelina Grimke and Abby Kelly, — that is, if they speak for conscience' sake, to serve a cause which they hold sacred, — invariably subdue the prejudices of their hearers, and excite an interest proportionate to the aversion with which it had been the purpose to regard them.

A passage in a private letter so happily illustrates this, that it must be inserted here.

Abby Kelly in the Town-House of ———.

"The scene was not unheroic — to see that woman, true to humanity and her own nature, a centre of rude eyes and tongues, even gentlemen feeling licensed to make part of a species of mob around a female out of her sphere. As she took her seat in the desk amid the great noise, and in the throng, full, like a wave, of something to ensue, I saw her humanity in a gentleness and unpretension, tenderly open to the sphere around her, and, had she not been supported by the power of the will of genuineness and principle, she would have failed. It led her to prayer, which, in Woman especially, is childlike; sensibility and will going to the side of God and looking up to him; and humanity was poured out in aspiration.

"She acted like a gentle hero, with her mild decision and womanly calmness. All heroism is mild, and quiet, and gentle, for it is life and possession; and combativeness and firmness show a want of actualness. She is as earnest, fresh and simple, as when she first entered the crusade. I think she did much good, more than the men in her place could do, for Woman feels more as being and reproducing — this brings the subject more into home relations. Men speak through, and mostly from intellect, and this addresses itself to that in others which is combative."

Not easily shall we find elsewhere, or before this time,

any written observations on the same subject, so delicate
and profound.

The late Dr. Channing, whose enlarged and tender and
religious nature shared every onward impulse of his time,
though his thoughts followed his wishes with a delibera-
tive caution which belonged to his habits and tempera-
ment, was greatly interested in these expectations for
women. His own treatment of them was absolutely and
thoroughly religious. He regarded them as souls, each
of which had a destiny of its own, incalculable to other
minds, and whose leading it must follow, guided by the
light of a private conscience. He had sentiment, delicacy,
kindness, taste; but they were all pervaded and ruled by
this one thought, that all beings had souls, and must
vindicate their own inheritance. Thus all beings were
treated by him with an equal, and sweet, though solemn,
courtesy. The young and unknown, the woman and the
child, all felt themselves regarded with an infinite expectation, from which there was no reaction to vulgar
prejudice. He demanded of all he met, to use his favorite phrase, "great truths."

His memory, every way dear and reverend, is, by
many, especially cherished for this intercourse of unbroken
respect.

At one time, when the progress of Harriet Martineau
through this country, Angelina Grimke's appearance in
public, and the visit of Mrs. Jameson, had turned his
thoughts to this subject, he expressed high hopes as to
what the coming era would bring to Woman. He had
been much pleased with the dignified courage of Mrs.

Jameson in taking up the defence of her sex in a way from which women usually shrink, because, if they express themselves on such subjects with sufficient force and clearness to do any good, they are exposed to assaults whose vulgarity makes them painful. In intercourse with such a woman, he had shared her indignation at the base injustice, in many respects, and in many regions, done to the sex; and been led to think of it far more than ever before. He seemed to think that he might some time write upon the subject. That his aid is withdrawn from the cause is a subject of great regret; for, on this question as on others, he would have known how to sum up the evidence, and take, in the noblest spirit, middle ground. He always furnished a platform on which opposing parties could stand and look at one another under the influence of his mildness and enlightened candor.

Two younger thinkers, men both, have uttered noble prophecies, auspicious for Woman. Kinmont, all whose thoughts tended towards the establishment of the reign of love and peace, thought that the inevitable means of this would be an increased predominance given to the idea of Woman. Had he lived longer, to see the growth of the Peace Party, the reforms in life and medical practice which seek to substitute water for wine and drugs, pulse for animal food, he would have been confirmed in his view of the way in which the desired changes are to be effected.

In this connection I must mention Shelley, who, like all men of genius, shared the feminine development, and, unlike many, knew it. His life was one of the first pulse-beats in the present reform-growth. He, too, abhorred blood and heat, and, by his system and his song, tended to reinstate a plant-like gentleness in the development of energy. In harmony with this, his ideas of marriage were lofty, and, of course, no less so of Woman, her nature, and destiny.

For Woman, if, by a sympathy as to outward condition, she is led to aid the enfranchisement of the slave, must be no less so, by inward tendency, to favor measures which promise to bring the world more thoroughly and deeply into harmony with her nature. When the lamb takes place of the lion as the emblem of nations, both women and men will be as children of one spirit, perpetual learners of the word and doers thereof, not hearers only.

A writer in the New York Pathfinder, in two articles headed "Femality," has uttered a still more pregnant word than any we have named. He views Woman truly from the soul, and not from society, and the depth and leading of his thoughts are proportionably remarkable. He views the feminine nature as a harmonizer of the vehement elements, and this has often been hinted elsewhere; but what he expresses most forcibly is the lyrical, the inspiring and inspired apprehensiveness of her being.

This view being identical with what I have before attempted to indicate, as to her superior susceptibility to magnetic or electric influence, I will now try to express myself more fully.

There are two aspects of Woman's nature, represented by the ancients as Muse and Minerva. It is the former to which the writer in the Pathfinder looks. It is the latter which Wordsworth has in mind, when he says,

> " With a placid brow,
> Which woman ne'er should forfeit, keep thy vow."

The especial genius of Woman I believe to be electrical in movement, intuitive in function, spiritual in tendency. She excels not so easily in classification, or recreation, as in an instinctive seizure of causes, and a simple breathing out of what she receives, that has the singleness of life, rather than the selecting and energizing of art.

More native is it to her to be the living model of the artist than to set apart from herself any one form in objective reality; more native to inspire and receive the poem, than to create it. In so far as soul is in her completely developed, all soul is the same; but in so far as it is modified in her as Woman, it flows, it breathes, it sings, rather than deposits soil, or finishes work; and that which is especially feminine flushes, in blossom, the face of earth, and pervades, like air and water, all this seeming solid globe, daily renewing and purifying its life. Such may be the especially feminine element spoken of as Femality. But it is no more the order of nature that it should be incarnated pure in any form, than that the masculine energy should exist unmingled with it in any form.

Male and female represent the two sides of the great

radical dualism. But, in fact, they are perpetually passing into one another. Fluid hardens to solid, solid rushes to fluid. There is no wholly masculine man, no purely feminine woman.

History jeers at the attempts of physiologists to bind great original laws by the forms which flow from them. They make a rule; they say from observation what can and cannot be. In vain! Nature provides exceptions to every rule. She sends women to battle, and sets Hercules spinning; she enables women to bear immense burdens, cold, and frost; she enables the man, who feels maternal love, to nourish his infant like a mother. Of late she plays still gayer pranks. Not only she deprives organizations, but organs, of a necessary end. She enables people to read with the top of the head, and see with the pit of the stomach. Presently she will make a female Newton, and a male Syren.

Man partakes of the feminine in the Apollo, Woman of the masculine as Minerva.

What I mean by the Muse is that unimpeded clearness of the intuitive powers, which a perfectly truthful adherence to every admonition of the higher instincts would bring to a finely organized human being. It may appear as prophecy or as poesy. It enabled Cassandra to foresee the results of actions passing round her; the Seeress to behold the true character of the person through the mask of his customary life. (Sometimes she saw a feminine form behind the man, sometimes the reverse.) It enabled the daughter of Linnæus to see the soul of the flowei exhaling from the flower.* It gave a man, but a poet-man, the power of which he thus speaks : " Often in my contemplation of nature, radiant intimations, and as it were sheaves of light, appear before me as to the facts of cosmogony, in which my mind has, perhaps, taken especial part." He wisely adds, " but it is necessary with earnestness to verify the knowledge we gain by these flashes of light." And none should forget this. Sight must be verified by light before it can deserve the honors of piety and genius. Yet sight comes first, and of this sight of the world of causes, this approximation to the region of primitive motions, women I hold to be especially capable. Even without equal freedom with the other sex, they have already shown themselves so ; and should these faculties have free play, I believe they will open new, deeper and purer sources of joyous inspiration than have as yet refreshed the earth.

Let us be wise, and not impede the soul. Let her work as she will. Let us have one creative energy, one incessant revelation. Let it take what form it will, and let us not bind it by the past to man or woman, black or white. Jove sprang from Rhea, Pallas from Jove. So let it be.

If it has been the tendency of these remarks to call Woman rather to the Minerva side,—if I, unlike the

* The daughter of Linnaeus states, that, while looking steadfastly at the red lily, she saw its spirit hovering above it, as a red flame. It is true, this, like many fair spirit-stories, may be explained away as an optical illusion, but its poetic beauty and meaning would, even then, make it valuable, as an illustration of the spiritual fact.

more generous writer, have spoken from society no less than the soul,—let it be pardoned ! It is love that has caused this,—love for many incarcerated souls, that might be freed, could the idea of religious self-dependence be established in them, could the weakening habit of dependence on others be broken up.

Proclus teaches that every life has, in its sphere, a totality or wholeness of the animating powers of the other spheres ; having only, as its own characteristic, a predominance of some one power. Thus Jupiter comprises, within himself, the other twelve powers, which stand thus : The first triad is *demiurgic or fabricative*, that is, Jupiter, Neptune, Vulcan ; the second, *defensive*, Vesta, Minerva, Mars ; the third, *vivific*, Ceres, Juno, Diana ; and the fourth, Mercury, Venus, Apollo, *elevating and harmonic*. In the sphere of Jupiter, energy is predominant — with Venus, beauty ; but each comprehends and apprehends all the others.

When the same community of life and consciousness of mind begin among men, humanity will have, positively and finally, subjugated its brute elements and Titanic childhood ; criticism will have perished ; arbitrary limits and ignorant censure be impossible ; all will have entered upon the liberty of law, and the harmony of common growth.

Then Apollo will sing to his lyre what Vulcan forges on the anvil, and the Muse weave anew the tapestries of Minerva.

It is, therefore, only in the present crisis that the preference is given to Minerva. The power of continence must establish the legitimacy of freedom, the power of self-poise the perfection of motion.

Every relation, every gradation of nature is incalculably precious, but only to the soul which is poised upon itself, and to whom no loss, no change, can bring dull discord, for it is in harmony with the central soul.

If any individual live too much in relations, so that he becomes a stranger to the resources of his own nature, he falls, after a while, into a distraction, or imbecility, from which he can only be cured by a time of isolation, which gives the renovating fountains time to rise up. With a society it is the same. Many minds, deprived of the traditionary or instinctive means of passing a cheerful existence, must find help in self-impulse, or perish. It is therefore that, while any elevation, in the view of union, is to be hailed with joy, we shall not decline celibacy as the great fact of the time. It is one from which no vow, no arrangement, can at present save a thinking mind. For now the rowers are pausing on their oars ; they wait a change before they can pull together. All tends to illustrate the thought of a wise cotemporary. Union is only possible to those who are units. To be fit for relations in time, souls, whether of Man or Woman, must be able to do without them in the spirit.

It is therefore that I would have Woman lay aside all thought, such as she habitually cherishes, of being taught and led by men. I would have her, like the Indian girl, dedicate herself to the Sun, the Sun of Truth, and go nowhere if his beams did not make clear the path. I would have her free from compromise, from complaisance, from helplessness, because I would have her good enough and strong enough to love one and all beings, from the fulness, not the poverty of being.

Men, as at present instructed, will not help this work, because they also are under the slavery of habit. I have seen with delight their poetic impulses. A sister is the fairest ideal, and how nobly Wordsworth, and even Byron, have written of a sister!

There is no sweeter sight than to see a father with his little daughter. Very vulgar men become refined to the eye when leading a little girl by the hand. At that moment, the right relation between the sexes seems established, and you feel as if the man would aid in the noblest purpose, if you ask him in behalf of his little daughter. Once, two fine figures stood before me, thus. The father of very intellectual aspect, his falcon eye softened by affection as he looked down on his fair child; she the image of himself, only more graceful and brilliant in expression. I was reminded of Southey's Kehama; when, lo, the dream was rudely broken! They were talking of education, and he said,

"I shall not have Maria brought too forward. If she knows too much, she will never find a husband; superior women hardly ever can."

"Surely," said his wife, with a blush, "you wish Maria to be as good and wise as she can, whether it will help her to marriage or not."

"No," he persisted, "I want her to have a sphere and a home, and some one to protect her when I am gone."

It was a trifling incident, but made a deep impression. I felt that the holiest relations fail to instruct the unprepared and perverted mind. If this man, indeed, could have looked at it on the other side, he was the last that would have been willing to have been taken himself for the home and protection he could give, but would have been much more likely to repeat the tale of Alcibiades with his phials.

But men do *not* look at both sides, and women must leave off asking them and being influenced by them, but retire within themselves, and explore the ground-work of life till they find their peculiar secret. Then, when they come forth again, renovated and baptized, they will know how to turn all dross to gold, and will be rich and free though they live in a hut, tranquil if in a crowd. Then their sweet singing shall not be from passionate impulse, but the lyrical overflow of a divine rapture, and a new music shall be evolved from this many-chorded world.

Grant her, then, for a while, the armor and the javelin. Let her put from her the press of other minds, and meditate in virgin loneliness. The same idea shall reäppear in due time as Muse, or Ceres, the all-kindly, patient Earth-Spirit.

Among the throng of symptoms which denote the present tendency to a crisis in the life of Woman, — which resembles the change from girlhood, with its beautiful instincts, but unharmonized thoughts, its blind pupilage and restless seeking, to self-possessed, wise and graceful womanhood, — I have attempted to select a few.

One of prominent interest is the unison upon the subject of three male minds, which, for width of culture,
power of self-concentration and dignity of aim, take rank
as the prophets of the coming age, while their histories
and labors are rooted in the past.

Swedenborg came, he tells us, to interpret the past revelation and unfold a new. He announces the New Church
that is to prepare the way for the New Jerusalem, a city
built of precious stones, hardened and purified by secret
processes in the veins of earth through the ages.

Swedenborg approximated to that harmony between
the scientific and poetic lives of mind, which we hope
from the perfected man. The links that bind together
the realms of nature, the mysteries that accompany her
births and growths, were unusually plain to him. He
seems a man to whom insight was given at a period when
the mental frame was sufficiently matured to retain and
express its gifts.

His views of Woman are, in the main, satisfactory.
In some details we may object to them, as, in all his
system, there are still remains of what is arbitrary and
seemingly groundless — fancies that show the marks of
old habits, and a nature as yet not thoroughly leavened
with the spiritual leaven. At least, so it seems to me
now. I speak reverently, for I find such reason to ven-
erate Swedenborg, from an imperfect knowledge of his
mind, that I feel one more perfect might explain to me
much that does not now secure my sympathy.

His idea of Woman is sufficiently large and noble to
interpose no obstacle to her progress. His idea of mar-

riage is consequently sufficient. Man and Woman share
an angelic ministry; the union is of one with one, permanent and pure.

As the New Church extends its ranks, the needs of
Woman must be more considered.

Quakerism also establishes Woman on a sufficient
equality with Man. But, though the original thought
of Quakerism is pure, its scope is too narrow, and its influence, having established a certain amount of good and
made clear some truth, must, by degrees, be merged in
one of wider range.* The mind of Swedenborg appeals
to the various nature of Man, and allows room for æsthetic
culture and the free expression of energy.

As apostle of the new order, of the social fabric that
is to rise from love, and supersede the old that was based
on strife, Charles Fourier comes next, expressing, in an
outward order, many facts of which Swedenborg saw the
secret springs. The mind of Fourier, though grand and
clear, was, in some respects, superficial. He was a
stranger to the highest experiences. His eye was fixed
on the outward more than the inward needs of Man. Yet
he, too, was a seer of the divine order, in its musical
expression, if not in its poetic soul. He has filled one
department of instruction for the new era, and the harmony in action, and freedom for individual growth, he
hopes shall exist; and, if the methods he proposes should
not prove the true ones, yet his fair propositions shall

---

* In worship at stated periods, in daily expression, whether by
word or deed, the Quakers have placed Woman on the same platform
with Man. Can any one assert that they have reason to repent this?

give many hints, and make room for the inspiration needed for such.

He, too, places Woman on an entire equality with Man, and wishes to give to one as to the other that independence which must result from intellectual and practical development.

Those who will consult him for no other reason, might do so to see how the energies of Woman may be made available in the pecuniary way. The object of Fourier was to give her the needed means of self-help, that she might dignify and unfold her life for her own happiness, and that of society. The many, now, who see their daughters liable to destitution, or vice to escape from it, may be interested to examine the means, if they have not yet soul enough to appreciate the ends he proposes.

On the opposite side of the advancing army leads the great apostle of individual culture, Goethe. Swedenborg makes organization and union the necessary results of solitary thought. Fourier, whose nature was, above all, constructive, looked to them too exclusively. Better institutions, he thought, will make better men. Goethe expressed, in every way, the other side. If one man could present better forms, the rest could not use them till ripe for them.

Fourier says, As the institutions, so the men! All follies are excusable and natural under bad institutions.

Goethe thinks, As the man, so the institutions! There is no excuse for ignorance and folly. A man can grow in any place, if he will.

Ay! but, Goethe, bad institutions are prison-walls and

impure air, that make him stupid, so that he does not will.

And thou, Fourier, do not expect to change mankind at once, or even "in three generations," by arrangement of groups and series, or flourish of trumpets for attractive industry. If these attempts are made by unready men, they will fail.

Yet we prize the theory of Fourier no less than the profound suggestion of Goethe. Both are educating the age to a clearer consciousness of what Man needs, what Man can be; and better life must ensue.

Goethe, proceeding on his own track, elevating the human being, in the most imperfect states of society, by continual efforts at self-culture, takes as good care of women as of men. His mother, the bold, gay Frau Aja, with such playful freedom of nature; the wise and gentle maiden, known in his youth, over whose sickly solitude "the Holy Ghost brooded as a dove;" his sister, the intellectual woman *par excellence;* the Duchess Amelia; Lili, who combined the character of the woman of the world with the lyrical sweetness of the shepherdess, on whose chaste and noble breast flowers and gems were equally at home; all these had supplied abundant suggestions to his mind, as to the wants and the possible excellences of Woman. And from his poetic soul grew up forms new and more admirable than life has yet produced, for whom his clear eye marked out paths in the future.

In Faust Margaret represents the redeeming power, which, at present, upholds Woman, while waiting for a

better day. The lovely little girl, pure in instinct, ignorant in mind, is misled and profaned by man abusing her confidence.* To the Mater *Dolorosa* she appeals for aid. It is given to the soul, if not against outward sorrow; and the maiden, enlightened by her sufferings, refusing to receive temporal salvation by the aid of an evil power, obtains the eternal in its stead.

In the second part, the intellectual man, after all his manifold strivings, owes to the interposition of her whom he had betrayed *his* salvation. She intercedes, this time, herself a glorified spirit, with the Mater *Gloriosa*.

Leonora, too, is Woman, as we see her now, pure, thoughtful, refined by much acquaintance with grief.

Iphigenia he speaks of in his journals as his " daughter," and she is the daughter † whom a man will wish, even if he has chosen his wife from very mean motives. She is the virgin, steadfast soul, to whom falsehood is more dreadful than any other death.

But it is to Wilhelm Meister's Apprenticeship and

---

* As Faust says, her only fault was a " kindly delusion," — " ein guter wahn."

† Goethe was as false to his ideas, in practice, as Lord Herbert. And his punishment was the just and usual one of connections formed beneath the standard of right, from the impulses of the baser self. Iphigenia was the worthy daughter of his mind ; but the son, child of his degrading connection in actual life, corresponded with that connection. This son, on whom Goethe vainly lavished so much thought and care, was like his mother, and like Goethe's attachment for his mother. " This young man," says a late well-informed writer (M. Henri Blaze), " Wieland, with good reason, called the son of the servant, *der Sohn der Magd.* He inherited from his father only his name and his *physique.*"

Wandering Years that I would especially refer, as these volumes contain the sum of the Sage's observations during a long life, as to what Man should do, under present circumstances, to obtain mastery over outward, through an initiation into inward life, and severe discipline of faculty.

As Wilhelm advances into the upward path, he becomes acquainted with better forms of Woman, by knowing how to seek, and how to prize them when found. For the weak and immature man will, often, admire a superior woman, but he will not be able to abide by a feeling which is too severe a tax on his habitual existence. But, with Wilhelm, the gradation is natural, and expresses ascent in the scale of being. At first, he finds charm in Mariana and Philina, very common forms of feminine character, not without redeeming traits, no less than charms, but without wisdom or purity. Soon he is attended by Mignon, the finest expression ever yet given to what I have called the lyrical element in Woman. She is a child, but too full-grown for this man; he loves, but cannot follow her; yet is the association not without an enduring influence. Poesy has been domesticated in his life; and, though he strives to bind down her heavenward impulse, as art or apothegm, these are only the tents, beneath which he may sojourn for a while, but which may be easily struck, and carried on limitless wanderings.

Advancing into the region of thought, he encounters a wise philanthropy in Natalia (instructed, let us observe, by an *uncle*); practical judgment and the outward economy of life in Theresa; pure devotion in the Fair Saint.

Further, and last, he comes to the house of Macaria, the soul of a star; that is, a pure and perfected intelligence embodied in feminine form, and the centre of a world whose members revolve harmoniously around her. She instructs him in the archives of a rich human history, and introduces him to the contemplation of the heavens.

From the hours passed by the side of Mariana to these with Macaria, is a wide distance for human feet to traverse. Nor has Wilhelm travelled so far, seen and suffered so much, in vain. He now begins to study how he may aid the next generation; he sees objects in harmonious arrangement, and from his observations deduces precepts by which to guide his course as a teacher and a master, "help-full, comfort-full."

In all these expressions of Woman, the aim of Goethe is satisfactory to me. He aims at a pure self-subsistence, and a free development of any powers with which they may be gifted by nature as much for them as for men. They are units, addressed as souls. Accordingly, the meeting between Man and Woman, as represented by him, is equal and noble; and, if he does not depict marriage, he makes it possible.

In the Macaria, bound with the heavenly bodies in fixed revolutions, the centre of all relations, herself unrelated, he expresses the Minerva side of feminine nature. It was not by chance that Goethe gave her this name. Macaria, the daughter-of Hercules, who offered herself as a victim for the good of her country, was canon-

ized by the Greeks, and worshipped as the Goddess of true
Felicity. Goethe has embodied this Felicity as the
Serenity that arises from Wisdom, a Wisdom such as the
Jewish wise man venerated, alike instructed in the designs
of heaven, and the methods necessary to carry them into
effect upon earth.

Mignon is the electrical, inspired, lyrical nature. And
wherever it appears we echo in our aspirations that of the
child,

> "So let me seem until I be : —
> Take not the *white robe* away."

> *   *   *   *   *

> "Though I lived without care and toil,
> Yet felt I sharp pain enough :
> Make me again forever young."

All these women, though we see them in relations, we
can think of as unrelated. They all are very individual,
yet seem nowhere restrained. They satisfy for the present,
yet arouse an infinite expectation.

The economist Theresa, the benevolent Natalia, the
fair Saint, have chosen a path, but their thoughts are not
narrowed to it. The functions of life to them are not
ends, but suggestions.

Thus, to them, all things are important, because none
is necessary. Their different characters have fair play,
and each is beautiful in its minute indications, for nothing
is enforced or conventional; but everything, however
slight, grows from the essential life of the being.

Mignon and Theresa wear male attire when they like,
and it is graceful for them to do so, while Macaria is

confined to her arm-chair behind the green curtain, and the Fair Saint could not bear a speck of dust on her robe.

All things are in their places in this little world, because all is natural and free, just as " there is room for everything out of doors." Yet all is rounded in by natural harmony, which will always arise where Truth and Love are sought in the light of Freedom.

Goethe's book bodes an era of freedom like its own of " extraordinary, generous seeking," and new revelations. New individualities shall be developed in the actual world, which shall advance upon it as gently as the figures come out upon his canvas.

I have indicated on this point the coincidence between his hopes and those of Fourier, though his are directed by an infinitely higher and deeper knowledge of human nature. But, for our present purpose, it is sufficient to show how surely these different paths have conducted to the same end two earnest thinkers. In some other place I wish to point out similar coincidences between Goethe's model school and the plans of Fourier, which may cast light upon the page of prophecy.

Many women have observed that the time drew nigh for a better care of the sex, and have thrown out hints that may be useful. Among these may be mentioned —

Miss Edgeworth, who, although restrained by the habits of her age and country, and belonging more to the eighteenth than the nineteenth century, has done excellently as far as she goes. She had a horror of sentimentalism, and of the love of notoriety, and saw how likely women, in the early stages of culture, were to aim at these. Therefore she bent her efforts to recommending domestic life. But the methods she recommends are such as will fit a character for any position to which it may be called. She taught a contempt of falsehood, no less in its most graceful, than in its meanest apparitions; the cultivation of a clear, independent judgment, and adherence to its dictates; habits of various and liberal study and employment, and a capacity for friendship. Her standard of character is the same for both sexes,— Truth, honor, enlightened benevolence, and aspiration after knowledge. Of poetry, she knows nothing, and her religion consists in honor and loyalty to obligations once assumed — in short, in "the great idea of duty which holds us upright." Her whole tendency is practical.

Mrs. Jameson is a sentimentalist, and, therefore, suits us ill in some respects, but she is full of talent, has a just and refined perception of the beautiful, and a genuine courage when she finds it necessary. She does not appear to have thought out, thoroughly, the subject on which we are engaged, and her opinions, expressed as opinions, are sometimes inconsistent with one another. But from the refined perception of character, admirable suggestions are given in her "Women of Shakspeare," and "Loves of the Poets."

But that for which I most respect her is the decision with which she speaks on a subject which refined women are usually afraid to approach, for fear of the insult and scurrile jest they may encounter; but on which she neither can nor will restrain the indignation of a full heart. I refer to the degradation of a large portion of women into the sold and polluted slaves of men, and the daring with which the legislator and man of the world lifts his head beneath the heavens, and says, "This must be; it cannot be helped; it is a necessary accompaniment of *civilization.*"

So speaks the *citizen*. Man born of Woman, the father of daughters, declares that he will and must buy the comforts and commercial advantages of his London, Vienna, Paris, New York, by conniving at the moral death, the damnation, so far as the action of society can insure it, of thousands of women for each splendid metropolis.

O men! I speak not to you. It is true that your wickedness (for you must not deny that at least nine thousand out of the ten fall through the vanity you have systematically flattered, or the promises you have treacherously broken); yes, it is true that your wickedness is its own punishment. Your forms degraded and your eyes clouded by secret sin; natural harmony broken and fineness of perception destroyed in your mental and bodily organization; God and love shut out from your hearts by the foul visitants you have permitted there; incapable of pure marriage; incapable of pure parentage; incapable of worship; O wretched men, your sin is its own punishment! You have lost the world in losing yourselves. Who ruins another has admitted the worm to the root of his own tree, and the fuller ye fill the cup of evil, the deeper must be your own bitter draught. But I speak not to you — you need to teach and warn one

another.   And more than one voice rises in earnestness.
And all that *women* say to the heart that has once chosen the evil path is considered prudery, or ignorance, or
perhaps a feebleness of nature which exempts from similar temptations.

But to you, women, American women, a few words
may not be addressed in vain.   One here and there may
listen.

You know how it was in the Oriental clime.   One
man, if wealth permitted, had several wives and many
handmaidens.   The chastity and equality of genuine
marriage, with "the thousand decencies that flow" from
its communion, the precious virtues that gradually may
be matured within its enclosure, were unknown.

But this man did not wrong according to his light.
What he did, he might publish to God and Man ; it was
not a wicked secret that hid in vile lurking-places and
dens, like the banquets of beasts of prey.   Those women
were not lost, not polluted in their own eyes, nor those
of others.   If they were not in a state of knowledge and
virtue, they were at least in one of comparative innocence.

You know how it was with the natives of this con-
tinent.   A chief had many wives, whom he maintained
and who did his household work ; those women were but
servants, still they enjoyed the respect of others and
their own.   They lived together in peace.   They knew
that a sin against what was in their nation esteemed
virtue, would be as strictly punished in Man as in Woman.

Now pass to the countries where marriage is between
one and one.   I will not speak of the Pagan nations,

but come to those which own the Christian rule. We all know what that enjoins ; there is a standard to appeal to.

See, now, not the mass of the people, for we all know that it is a proverb and a bitter jest to speak of the " down-trodden million." We know that, down to our own time, a principle never had so fair a chance to pervade the mass of the people, but that we must solicit its illustration from select examples.

Take the Paladin, take the Poet. Did *they* believe purity more impossible to Man than to Woman? Did they wish Woman to believe that Man was less amenable to higher motives,— that pure aspirations would not guard him against bad passions,— that honorable employments and temperate habits would not keep him free from slavery to the body? O no! Love was to them a part of heaven, and they could not even wish to receive its happiness, unless assured of being worthy of it. Its highest happiness to them was that it made them wish to be worthy. They courted probation. They wished not the title of knight till the banner had been upheld in the heats of battle, amid the rout of cowards.

I ask of you, young girls — I do not mean *you* whose heart is that of an old coxcomb, though your locks have not yet lost their sunny tinge. Not of you whose whole character is tainted with vanity, inherited or taught, who have early learned the love of coquettish excitement, and whose eyes rove restlessly in search of a " conquest " or a " beau ;" you who are ashamed *not* to be seen by others the mark of the most contemptuous flattery or injurious desire. To such I do not speak. But to thee, maiden,

who, if not so fair, art yet of that unpolluted nature
which Milton saw when he dreamed of Comus and the
Paradise. Thou, child of an unprofaned wedlock, brought
up amid the teachings of the woods and fields, kept
fancy-free by useful employment and a free flight into
the heaven of thought, loving to please only those whom
thou wouldst not be ashamed to love; I ask of thee,
whose cheek has not forgotten its blush nor thy heart its
lark-like hopes, if he whom thou mayest hope the Father
will send thee, as the companion of life's toils and joys,
is not to thy thought pure? Is not manliness to thy
thought purity, *not* lawlessness? Can his lips speak
falsely? Can he do, in secret, what he could not avow
to the mother that bore him? O say, dost thou not look
for a heart free, open as thine own, all whose thoughts
may be avowed, incapable of wronging the innocent, or
still further degrading the fallen — a man, in short, in
whom brute nature is entirely subject to the impulses of
his better self?

Yes! it was thus that thou didst hope; for I have
many, many times seen the image of a future life, of a
destined spouse, painted on the tablets of a virgin heart.

It might be that she was not true to these hopes. She
was taken into what is called "the world," froth and
scum as it mostly is on the social caldron. There, she
saw fair Woman carried in the waltz close to the heart of
a being who appeared to her a Satyr. Being warned by
a male friend that he was in fact of that class, and not fit
for such familiar nearness to a chaste being, the advised
replied that "women should know nothing about such

things." She saw one fairer given in wedlock to a man
of the same class. " Papa and mamma said that ' all
men were faulty at some time in their lives ; they had
a great many temptations.' Frederick would be so happy
at home ; he would not want to do wrong." She turned
to the married women ; they, O tenfold horror ! laughed
at her supposing " men were like women." Sometimes,
I say, she was not true, and either sadly accommodated
herself to " Woman's lot," or acquired a taste for satyr-
society, like some of the Nymphs, and all the Bacchanals
of old. But to those who could not and would not
accept a mess of pottage, or a Circe cup, in lieu of their
birthright, and to these others who have yet their choice
to make, I say, Courage ! I have some words of cheer
for you. A man, himself of unbroken purity, reported
to me the words of a foreign artist, that " the world
would never be better till men subjected themselves to
the same laws they had imposed on women ; " that artist,
he added, was true to the thought. The same was true
of Canova, the same of Beethoven. " Like each other
demi-god, they kept themselves free from stain ; " and
Michael Angelo, looking over here from the loneliness
of his century, might meet some eyes that need not shun
his glance.

In private life, I am assured by men who are not so
sustained and occupied by the worship of pure beauty,
that a similar consecration is possible, is practised ; that
many men feel that no temptation can be too strong for
the will of man, if he invokes the aid of the Spirit
instead of seeking extenuation from the brute alliances

of his nature.   In short, what the child fancies is really
true, though almost the whole world declares it a lie.
Man is a child of God; and if he seeks His guidance to
keep the heart with diligence, it will be so given that all
the issues of life may be pure.   Life will then be a
temple.

> The temple round
> Spread green the pleasant ground ;
> The fair colonnade
> Be of pure marble pillars made ;
> Strong to sustain the roof,
> Time and tempest proof ;
> Yet, amidst which, the lightest breeze
> Can play as it please ;
> The audience hall
> Be free to all
> Who revere
> The power worshipped here,
> Sole guide of youth,
> Unswerving Truth.
> In the inmost shrine
> Stands the image divine,
> Only seen
> By those whose deeds have worthy been —
> Priestlike clean.
> Those, who initiated are,
> Declare,
> As the hours
> Usher in varying hopes and powers ;
> It changes its face,
> It changes its age,
> Now a young, beaming grace,
> Now Nestorian sage :
> But, to the pure in heart,
> This shape of primal art

In age is fair,
In youth seems wise,
Beyond compare,
Above surprise ;
What it teaches native seems,
Its new lore our ancient dreams ;
Incense rises from the ground ;
Music flows around ;
Firm rest the feet below, clear gaze the eyes above,
When Truth, to point the way through life, assumes the wand of Love;
But, if she cast aside the robe of green,
Winter's silver sheen,
White, pure as light,
Makes gentle shroud as worthy weed as bridal robe had been.*

We are now in a transition state, and but few steps
have yet been taken. From polygamy, Europe passed
to the marriage *de convenance*. This was scarcely an
improvement. An attempt was then made to substitute
genuine marriage (the mutual choice of souls inducing
a permanent union), as yet baffled on every side by the
haste, the ignorance, or the impurity of Man.

Where Man assumes a high principle to which he is
not yet ripened, it will happen, for a long time, that the
few will be nobler than before; the many, worse. Thus
now. In the country of Sidney and Milton, the metrop-

---

* As described by the historian : —
" The temple of Juno is like what the character of Woman should be.
Columns ! graceful decorums, attractive yet sheltering.
Porch ! noble, inviting aspect of the life.
Kaos ! receives the worshippers. See here the statue of the
Divinity.
Ophistodomos ! Sanctuary where the most precious possessions
were kept safe from the hand of the spoiler and the eye of the world."

olis is a den of wickedness, and a sty of sensuality; in the country of Lady Russell, the custom of English peeresses, of selling their daughters to the highest bidder, is made the theme and jest of fashionable novels by unthinking children who would stare at the idea of sending them to a Turkish slave-dealer, though the circumstances of the bargain are there less degrading, as the will and thoughts of the person sold are not so degraded by it, and it is not done in defiance of an acknowledged law of right in the land and the age.

I must here add that I do not believe there ever was put upon record more depravation of Man, and more despicable frivolity of thought and aim in Woman, than in the novels which purport to give the picture of English fashionable life, which are read with such favor in our drawing-rooms, and give the tone to the manners of some circles.   Compared with the cold, hard-hearted folly there described, crime is hopeful; for it, at least, shows some power remaining in the mental constitution.

To return:— Attention has been awakened among men to the stains of celibacy, and the profanations of marriage.   They begin to write about it and lecture about it. It is the tendency now to endeavor to help the erring by showing them the physical law.   This is wise and excellent; but forget not the better half.   Cold bathing and exercise will not suffice to keep a life pure, without an inward baptism, and noble, exhilarating employment for the thoughts and the passions.   Early marriages are desirable, but if (and the world is now so out of joint that there are a hundred thousand chances to one against it) a man does not early, or at all, find the person to whom he can be united in the marriage of souls, will you give him in the marriage *de convenance?* or, if not married, can you find no way for him to lead a virtuous and happy life? Think of it well, ye who think yourselves better than pagans, for many of *them* knew this sure way.*

To you, women of America, it is more especially my business to address myself on this subject, and my advice may be classed under three heads :

Clear your souls from the taint of vanity.

Do not rejoice in conquests, either that your power to allure may be seen by other women, or for the pleasure of rousing passionate feelings that gratify your love of excitement.

It must happen, no doubt, that frank and generous women will excite love they do not reciprocate, but, in nine cases out of ten, the woman has, half consciously, done much to excite. In this case, she shall not be held guiltless, either as to the unhappiness or injury of the lover. Pure love, inspired by a worthy object, must ennoble

* The Persian sacred books, the Desatir, describe the great and holy prince Ky Khosrou, as being " an angel, and the son of an angel," one to whom the Supreme says, " Thou art not absent from before me for one twinkling of an eye. I am never out of thy heart. And I am contained in nothing but in thy heart, and in a heart like thy heart. And I am nearer unto thee than thou art to thyself." This prince had in his Golden Seraglio three ladies of surpassing beauty, and all four, in this royal monastery, passed their lives, and left the world as virgins.

The Persian people had no scepticism when the history of such a mind was narrated.

and bless, whether mutual or not; but that which is
excited by coquettish attraction of any grade of refinement, must cause bitterness and doubt, as to the reality
of human goodness, so soon as the flush of passion is
over   And, that you may avoid all taste for these false
pleasures,

> " Steep the soul
> In one pure love, and it will last thee long."

The love of truth, the love of excellence, whether
you clothe them in the person of a special object or not
will have power to save you from following Duessa,
and lead you in the green glades where Una's feet have
trod.

It was on this one subject that a venerable champion
of good, the last representative of the spirit which sanctified the Revolution, and gave our country such a sunlight
of hope in the eyes of the nations, the same who lately,
in Boston, offered anew to the young men the pledge
taken by the young men of his day, offered, also, his
counsel, on being addressed by the principal of a girl's
school, thus : —

REPLY OF MR. ADAMS.

Mr. Adams was so deeply affected by the address of
Miss Foster, as to be for some time inaudible. When
heard, he spoke as follows :

" This is the first instance in which a lady has thus
addressed me personally; and I trust that all the ladies
present will be able sufficiently to enter into my feelings

to know that I am more affected by this honor than by any other I could have received.

"You have been pleased, madam, to allude to the character of my father, and the history of my family, and their services to the country. It is indeed true that, from the existence of the republic as an independent nation, my father and myself have been in the public service of the country, almost without interruption. I came into the world, as a person having personal responsibilities, with the Declaration of Independence, which constituted us a nation. I was a child at that time, and had then perhaps the greatest of blessings that can be bestowed on man — a mother who was anxious and capable to form her children to be what they ought to be. From that mother I derived whatever instruction — religious especially and moral — has pervaded a long life; I will not say perfectly, and as it ought to be; but I will say, because it is justice only to the memory of her whom I revere, that if, in the course of my life, there has been any imperfection, or deviation from what she taught me, the fault is mine, and not hers.

"With such a mother, and such other relations with the sex, of sister, wife, and daughter, it has been the perpetual instruction of my life to love and revere the female sex. And in order to carry that sentiment of love and reverence to its highest degree of perfection, I know of nothing that exists in human society better adapted to produce that result, than institutions of the character that I have now the honor to address.

"I have been taught, as I have said, through the

course of my life, to love and to revere the female sex; but I have been taught, also — and that lesson has perhaps impressed itself on my mind even more strongly, it may be, than the other — I have been taught not to flatter them. It is not unusual, in the intercourse of Man with the other sex — and especially for young men — to think that the way to win the hearts of ladies is by flattery. To love and to revere the sex, is what I think the duty of Man; but *not to flatter them;* and this I would say to the young ladies here — and if they, and others present, will allow me, with all the authority which nearly four score years may have with those who have not yet attained one score — I would say to them what I have no doubt they say to themselves, and are taught here, not to take the flattery of men as proof of perfection.

"I am now, however, I fear, assuming too much of a character that does not exactly belong to me. I therefore conclude, by assuring you, madam, that your reception of me has affected me, as you perceive, more than I can express in words; and that I shall offer my best prayers, till my latest hour, to the Creator of us all, that this institution especially, and all others of a similar kind, designed to form the female mind to wisdom and virtue, may prosper to the end of time."

It will be interesting to add here the character of Mr. Adams' mother, as drawn by her husband, the first John Adams, in a family letter * written just before his death.

"I have reserved for the last the life of Lady Russell

* Journal and Correspondence of Miss Adams, vol. i., p. 246.

This I have not yet read, because I read it more than forty years ago. On this hangs a tale which you ought to know and communicate it to your children. I bought the Life and Letters of Lady Russell in the year 1775, and sent it to your grandmother, with an express intent and desire that she should consider it a mirror in which to contemplate herself; for, at that time, I thought it extremely probable, from the daring and dangerous career I was determined to run, that she would one day find herself in the situation of Lady Russell, her husband without a head. This lady was more beautiful than Lady Russell, had a brighter genius, more information, a more refined taste, and, at least, her equal in the virtues of the heart; equal fortitude and firmness of character, equal resignation to the will of Heaven, equal in all the virtues and graces of the Christian life. Like Lady Russell, she never, by word or look, discouraged me from running all hazards for the salvation of my country's liberties; she was willing to share with me, and that her children should share with us both, in all the dangerous consequences we had to hazard."

Will a woman who loves flattery or an aimless excitement, who wastes the flower of her mind on transitory sentiments, ever be loved with a love like that, when fifty years' trial have entitled to the privileges of " the golden marriage ? "

Such was the love of the iron-handed warrior for her, not his hand-maid, but his help-meet :

" Whom God loves, to him gives he such a wife."

I find the whole of what I want in this relation, in the

two epithets by which Milton makes Adam address *his* wife.

In the intercourse of every day he begins :

" Daughter of God and man, *accomplished* Eve." *

In a moment of stronger feeling,

" Daughter of God and man, IMMORTAL Eve."

What majesty in the cadence of the line; what dignity, what reverence in the attitude both of giver and receiver !

The woman who permits, in her life, the alloy of vanity ; the woman who lives upon flattery, coarse or fine, shall never be thus addressed. She is *not* immortal so far as her will is concerned, and every woman who does so creates miasma, whose spread is indefinite. The hand which casts into the waters of life a stone of offence knows not how far the circles thus caused may spread their agitations.

A little while since I was at one of the most fashionable places of public resort. I saw there many women, dressed without regard to the season or the demands of the place, in apery, or, as it looked, in mockery, of European fashions. I saw their eyes restlessly courting attention. I saw the way in which it was paid : the style of devotion, almost an open sneer, which it pleased those ladies to receive from men whose expression marked their own low position in the moral and intellectual world. Those women went to their pillows with their

* See Appendix H.

heads full of folly, their hearts of jealousy, or gratified
vanity; those men, with the low opinion they already
entertained of Woman confirmed. These were American
ladies; that is, they were of that class who have wealth
and leisure to make full use of the day, and confer benefits on others. They were of that class whom the possession of external advantages makes of pernicious example
to many, if these advantages be misused.

Soon after, I met a circle of women, stamped by society
as among the most degraded of their sex. "How," it
was asked of them, "did you come here?" for by the
society that I saw in the former place they were shut up
in a prison. The causes were not difficult to trace : love
of dress, love of flattery, love of excitement. They had
not dresses like the other ladies, so they stole them; they
could not pay for flattery by distinctions, and the dower
of a worldly marriage, so they paid by the profanation
of their persons. In excitement, more and more madly
sought from day to day, they drowned the voice of conscience.

Now I ask you, my sisters, if the women at the fashionable house be not answerable for those women being in
the prison?

As to position in the world of souls, we may suppose the women of the prison stood fairest, both because
they had misused less light, and because loneliness and
sorrow had brought some of them to feel the need of better life, nearer truth and good. This was no merit in
them, being an effect of circumstance, but it was hopeful.
But you, my friends (and some of you I have already

met), consecrate yourselves without waiting for reproof, in free love and unbroken energy, to win and to
diffuse a better life. Offer beauty, talents, riches, on the
altar; thus shall ye keep spotless your own hearts, and
be visibly or invisibly the angels to others.

I would urge upon those women who have not yet considered this subject, to do so. Do not forget the unfor-
tunates who dare not cross your guarded way. If it do
not suit you to act with those who have organized
measures of reform, then hold not yourself excused from
acting in private. Seek out these degraded women, give
them tender sympathy, counsel, employment. Take the
place of mothers, such as might have saved them
originally.

If you can do little for those already under the ban of
the world, — and the best-considered efforts have often
failed, from a want of strength in those unhappy ones to
bear up against the sting of shame and the prejudices of
the world, which makes them seek oblivion again in their
old excitements, — you will at least leave a sense of love
and justice in their hearts, that will prevent their becoming utterly embittered and corrupt. And you may learn
the means of prevention for those yet uninjured. These
will be found in a diffusion of mental culture, simple
tastes, best taught by your example, a genuine self-
respect, and, above all, what the influence of Man tends
to hide from Woman, the love and fear of a divine, in
preference to a human tribunal.

But suppose you save many who would have lost their
bodily innocence (for as to mental, the loss of that is

incalculably more general), through mere vanity and folly; there still remain many, the prey and spoil of the brute passions of Man; for the stories frequent in our newspapers outshame antiquity, and vie with the horrors of war.

As to this, it must be considered that, as the vanity and proneness to seduction of the imprisoned women represented a general degradation in their sex; so do these acts a still more general and worse in the male. Where so many are weak, it is natural there should be many lost; where legislators admit that ten thousand prostitutes are a fair proportion to one city, and husbands tell their wives that it is folly to expect chastity from men, it is inevitable that there should be many monsters of vice.

I must in this place mention, with respect and gratitude, the conduct of Mrs. Child in the case of Amelia Norman. The action and speech of this lady was of straightforward nobleness, undeterred by custom or cavil from duty toward an injured sister. She showed the case and the arguments the counsel against the prisoner had the assurance to use in their true light to the public. She put the case on the only ground of religion and equity. She was successful in arresting the attention of many who had before shrugged their shoulders, and let sin pass as necessarily a part of the company of men. They begin to ask whether virtue is not possible, perhaps necessary, to Man as well as to Woman. They begin to fear that the perdition of a woman must involve that of

a man. This is a crisis. The results of this case will
be important.

In this connection I must mention Eugene Sue, the
French novelist, several of whose works have been lately
translated among us, as having the true spirit of reform
as to women. Like every other French writer, he is still
tainted with the transmissions of the old *regime.* Still,
falsehood may be permitted for the sake of advancing
truth, evil as the way to good. Even George Sand, who
would trample on every graceful decorum, and every
human law, for the sake of a sincere life, does not see that
she violates it by making her heroines able to tell falsehoods in a good cause. These French writers need ever
to be confronted by the clear perception of the English
and German mind, that the only good man, consequently
the only good reformer, is he

" Who bases good on good alone, and owes
To virtue every triumph that he knows."

Still, Sue has the heart of a reformer, and especially
towards women; he sees what they need, and what causes
are injuring them. From the histories of Fleur de
Marie and La Louve, from the lovely and independent
character of Rigolette, from the distortion given to Ma-
tilda's mind, by the present views of marriage, and from
the truly noble and immortal character of the "hump-
backed Sempstress" in the "Wandering Jew," may be
gathered much that shall elucidate doubt and direct
inquiry on this subject. In reform, as in philosophy,
the French are the interpreters to the civilized world.

Their own attainments are not great, but they make clear the past, and break down barriers to the future.

Observe that the good man of Sue is as pure as Sir Charles Grandison.

Apropos to Sir Charles. Women are accustomed to be told by men that the reform is to come *from them*. "You," say the men, "must frown upon vice; you must decline the attentions of the corrupt; you must not submit to the will of your husband when it seems to you unworthy, but give the laws in marriage, and redeem it from its present sensual and mental pollutions."

This seems to us hard. Men have, indeed, been, for more than a hundred years, rating women for countenancing vice. But, at the same time, they have carefully hid from them its nature, so that the preference often shown by women for bad men arises rather from a confused idea that they are bold and adventurous, acquainted with regions which women are forbidden to explore, and the curiosity that ensues, than a corrupt heart in the woman. As to marriage, it has been inculcated on women, for centuries, that men have not only stronger passions than they, but of a sort that it would be shameful for them to share or even understand; that, therefore, they must "confide in their husbands," that is, submit implicitly to their will; that the least appearance of coldness or withdrawal, from whatever cause, in the wife is wicked, because liable to turn her husband's thoughts to illicit indulgence; for a man is so constituted that he must indulge his passions or die !

Accordingly, a great part of women look upon men as

a kind of wild beasts, but "suppose they are all alike;" the unmarried are assured by the married that, "if they knew men as they do," that is, by being married to them, "they would not expect continence or self-government from them."

I might accumulate illustrations on this theme, drawn from acquaintance with the histories of women, which would startle and grieve all thinking men, but I forbear. Let Sir Charles Grandison preach to his own sex; or if none there be who feels himself able to speak with authority from a life unspotted in will or deed, let those who are convinced of the practicability and need of a pure life, as the foreign artist was, advise the others, and warn them by their own example, if need be.

The following passage, from a female writer, on female affairs, expresses a prevalent way of thinking on this subject:

"It may be that a young woman, exempt from all motives of vanity, determines to take for a husband a man who does not inspire her with a very decided inclination. Imperious circumstances, the evident interest of her family, or the danger of suffering celibacy, may explain such a resolution. If, however, she were to endeavor to surmount a personal repugnance, we should look upon this as *injudicious*. Such a rebellion of nature marks the limit that the influence of parents, or the self-sacrifice of the young girl, should never pass. *We shall be told that this repugnance is an affair of the imagination.* It may be so; but imagination is a power which it is temerity to brave ; and its antipathy is more difficult to conquer than its preference." *

Among ourselves, the exhibition of such a repugnance from a woman who had been given in marriage "by advice of friends," was treated by an eminent physician as sufficient proof of insanity. If he had said sufficient cause for it, he would have been nearer right.

It has been suggested by men who were pained by seeing bad men admitted, freely, to the society of modest women, — thereby encouraged to vice by impunity, and corrupting the atmosphere of homes,— that there should be a senate of the matrons in each city and town, who should decide what candidates were fit for admission to their houses and the society of their daughters. †

Such a plan might have excellent results ; but it argues a moral dignity and decision which does not yet exist, and needs to be induced by knowledge and reflection. It has been the tone to keep women ignorant on these subjects, or, when they were not, to command that they should seem so. "It is indelicate," says the father or husband, "to inquire into the private character of such an one. It is sufficient that I do not think him unfit to visit you." And so, this man, who would not tolerate these pages in his house, "unfit for family reading," because they speak plainly, introduces there a man whose shame is written on his brow, as well as the open secret of the whole town, and, presently, if *respectable* still,

* Madame Necker de Saussure.

† See Goethe's Tasso. "A synod of good women should decide,' — if the golden age is to be restored.

and rich enough, gives him his daughter to wife. The mother affects ignorance, "supposing he is no worse than most men." The daughter *is* ignorant; something in the mind of the new spouse seems strange to her, but she supposes it is "woman's lot" not to be perfectly happy in her affections; she has always heard, "men could not understand women," so she weeps alone, or takes to dress and the duties of the house. The husband, of course, makes no avowal, and dreams of no redemption.

"In the heart of every young woman," says the female writer above quoted, addressing herself to the husband, "depend upon it, there is a fund of exalted ideas; she conceals, represses, without succeeding in smothering them. *So long as these ideas in your wife are directed to* YOU, *they are, no doubt, innocent,* but take care that they be not accompanied with *too much* pain. In other respects, also, spare her delicacy. Let all the antecedent parts of your life, if there are such, which would give her pain, be concealed from her; *her happiness and her respect for you would suffer from this misplaced confidence.* Allow her to retain that flower of purity, *which should distinguish her, in your eyes, from every other woman.*" We should think so truly, under this canon. Such a man must esteem purity an exotic that could only be preserved by the greatest care. Of the degree of mental intimacy possible, in such a marriage, let every one judge for himself!

On this subject, let every woman, who has once begun to think, examine herself; see whether she does not suppose virtue possible and necessary to Man, and whether she would not desire for her son a virtue which aimed at a fitness for a divine life, and involved, if not asceticism, that degree of power over the lower self, which shall "not exterminate the passions, but keep them chained at the feet of reason." The passions, like fire, are a bad master; but confine them to the hearth and the altar, and they give life to the social economy, and make each sacrifice meet for heaven.

When many women have thought upon this subject, some will be fit for the senate, and one such senate in operation would affect the morals of the civilized world.

At present I look to the young. As preparatory to the senate, I should like to see a society of novices, such as the world has never yet seen, bound by no oath, wearing no badge. In place of an oath, they should have a religious faith in the capacity of Man for virtue; instead of a badge, should wear in the heart a firm resolve not to stop short of the destiny promised him as a son of God. Their service should be action and conservatism, not of old habits, but of a better nature, enlightened by hopes that daily grow brighter.

If sin was to remain in the world, it should not be by their connivance at its stay, or one moment's concession to its claims.

They should succor the oppressed, and pay to the upright the reverence due in hero-worship by seeking to emulate them. They would not denounce the willingly bad, but they could not be with them, for the two classes could not breathe the same atmosphere.

They would heed no detention from the time-serving, the worldly and the timid.

They could love no pleasures that were not innocent and capable of good fruit.

I saw, in a foreign paper, the title now given to a party abroad, "Los Exaltados." Such would be the title now given these children by the world: Los Exaltados, Las Exaltadas; but the world would not sneer always, for from them would issue a virtue by which it would, at last, be exalted too.

I have in my eye a youth and a maiden whom I look to as the nucleus of such a class. They are both in early youth; both as yet uncontaminated; both aspiring, without rashness; both thoughtful; both capable of deep affection; both of strong nature and sweet feelings ; both capable of large mental development. They reside in different regions of earth, but their place in the soul is the same. To them I look, as, perhaps, the harbingers and leaders of a new era, for never yet have I known minds so truly virgin, without narrowness or ignorance.

When men call upon women to redeem them, they mean such maidens. But such are not easily formed under the present influences of society. As there are more such young men to help give a different tone, there will be more such maidens.

The English, novelist, D'Israeli, has, in his novel of " The Young Duke," made a man of the most depraved stock be redeemed by a woman who despises him when he has only the brilliant mask of fortune and beauty to cover the poverty of his heart and brain, but knows how to encourage him when he enters on a better course. But this woman was educated by a father who valued character in women.

Still, there will come now and then one who will, as I hope of my young Exaltada, be example and instruction for the rest. It was not the opinion of Woman current among Jewish men that formed the character of the mother of Jesus.

Since the sliding and backsliding men of the world, no less than the mystics, declare that, as through Woman Man was lost, so through Woman must Man be redeemed, the time must be at hand. When she knows herself indeed as "accomplished," still more as "immortal Eve," this may be.

As an immortal, she may also know and inspire immortal love, a happiness not to be dreamed of under the circumstances advised in the last quotation. Where love is based on concealment, it must, of course, disappear when the soul enters the scene of clear vision!

And, without this hope, how worthless every plan, every bond, every power!

"The giants," said the Scandinavian Saga, "had induced Loke (the spirit that hovers between good and ill) to steal for them Iduna (Goddess of Immortality) and her apples of pure gold. He lured her out, by promising to show, on a marvellous tree he had discovered, apples beautiful as her own, if she would only take them with her for a comparison. Thus having lured her beyond the heavenly domain, she was seized and carried away captive by the powers of misrule.

"As now the gods could not find their friend Iduna, they were confused with grief; indeed, they began visibly to grow old and gray. Discords arose, and love grew cold. Indeed, Odur, spouse of the goddess of love and beauty, wandered away, and returned no more. At last, however, the gods, discovering the treachery of Loke, obliged him to win back Iduna from the prison in which she sat mourning. He changed himself into a falcon, and brought her back as a swallow, fiercely pursued by the Giant King, in the form of an eagle. So she strives to return among us, light and small as a swallow. We must welcome her form as the speck on the sky that assures the glad blue of Summer. Yet one swallow does not make a summer. Let us solicit them in flights and flocks!"

Returning from the future to the present, let us see what forms Iduna takes, as she moves along the declivity of centuries to the valley where the lily flower may concentrate all its fragrance.

It would seem as if this time were not very near to one fresh from books, such as I have of late been — no: *not* reading, but sighing over. A crowd of books having been sent me since my friends knew me to be engaged in this way, on Woman's "Sphere," Woman's "Mission," and Woman's "Destiny," I believe that almost all that is extant of formal precept has come under my eye. Among these I read with refreshment a little one called "The Whole Duty of Woman," "indited by a noble lady at the request of a noble lord," and which has this much of nobleness, that the view it takes is a religious one. It aims to fit Woman for heaven; the main bent of most of the others is to fit her to please, or, at least, not to disturb, a husband.

Among these I select, as a favorable specimen, the book I have already quoted, " The Study* of the Life of Woman, by Madame Necker de Saussure, of Geneva, translated from the French." This book was published at Philadelphia, and has been read with much favor here. Madame Necker is the cousin of Madame de Stael, and has taken from her works the motto prefixed to this.

" Cette vie n'a quelque prix que si elle sert a' l'education morale de notre cœur."

Mde. Necker is, by nature, capable of entire consistency in the application of this motto, and, therefore, the qualifications she makes, in the instructions given to her own sex, show forcibly the weight which still paralyzes and distorts the energies of that sex.

The book is rich in passages marked by feeling and good suggestions; but, taken in the whole, the impression it leaves is this:

Woman is, and *shall remain*, inferior to Man and subject to his will, and, in endeavoring to aid her, we must anxiously avoid anything that can be misconstrued into expression of the contrary opinion, else the men will be alarmed, and combine to defeat our efforts.

The present is a good time for these efforts, for men are less occupied about women than formerly. Let us,

* This title seems to be incorrectly translated from the French. I have not seen the original.

then, seize upon the occasion, and do what we can to make our lot tolerable. But we must sedulously avoid encroaching on the territory of Man. If we study natural history, our observations may be made useful, by some male naturalist; if we draw well, we may make our services acceptable to the artists. But our names must not be known; and, to bring these labors to any result, we must take some man for our head, and be his hands.

The lot of Woman is sad. She is constituted to expect and need a happiness that cannot exist on earth. She must stifle such aspirations within her secret heart, and fit herself, as well as she can, for a life of resignations and consolations.

She will be very lonely while living with her husband. She must not expect to open her heart to him fully, or that, after marriage, he will be capable of the refined service of love. The man is not born for the woman, only the woman for the man. " Men cannot understand the hearts of women." The life of Woman must be outwardly a well-intentioned, cheerful dissimulation of her real life.

Naturally, the feelings of the mother, at the birth of a female child, resemble those of the Paraguay woman, described by Southey as lamenting in such heart-breaking tones that her mother did not kill her the hour she was born, — "her mother, who knew what the life of a woman must be; " — or of those women seen at the north by Sir A. Mackenzie, who performed this pious duty towards female infants whenever they had an opportunity.

" After the first delight, the young mother experiences

feelings a little different, according as the birth of a son
or a daughter has been announced.

" Is it a son ?   A sort of glory swells at this thought
the heart of the mother ; she seems to feel that she is
entitled to gratitude.   She has given a citizen, a defender,
to her country ; to her husband an heir of his name ; to
herself a protector.   And yet the contrast of all these
fine titles with this being, so humble, soon strikes her.
At the aspect of this frail treasure, opposite feelings
agitate her heart ; she seems to recognize in him *a nature
superior to her own*, but subjected to a low condition,
and she honors a future greatness in the object of extreme
compassion.   Somewhat of that respect and adoration
for a feeble child, of which some fine pictures offer the
expression in the features of the happy Mary, seem re-
produced with the young mother who has given birth to
a son.

" Is it a daughter ?   There is usually a slight degree
of regret ; so deeply rooted is the idea of the superiority
of Man in happiness and dignity ; and yet, as she looks
upon this child, she is more and more *softened* towards
it.   A deep sympathy — a sentiment of identity with this
delicate being — takes possession of her ; an extreme pity
for so much weakness, a more pressing need of prayer,
stirs her heart.   Whatever sorrows she may have felt,
she dreads for her daughter ; but she will guide her to
become much wiser, much better than herself.   And then
the gayety, the frivolity of the young woman have their
turn.   This little creature is a flower to cultivate, a doll
to decorate.'

Similar sadness at the birth of a daughter I have heard mothers express not unfrequently.

As to this living so entirely for men, I should think when it was proposed to women they would feel, at least, some spark of the old spirit of races allied to our own. "If he is to be my bridegroom *and lord*," cries Brunhilda,* "he must first be able to pass through fire and water." "I will serve at the banquet," says the Walkyrie, "but only him who, in the trial of deadly combat, has shown himself a hero."

If women are to be bond-maids, let it be to men superior to women in fortitude, in aspiration, in moral power, in refined sense of beauty! You who give yourselves "to be supported," or because "one must love something," are they who make the lot of the sex such that mothers are sad when daughters are born.

It marks the state of feeling on this subject that it was mentioned, as a bitter censure on a woman who had influence over those younger than herself, — "She makes those girls want to see heroes?"

"And will that hurt them?"

"Certainly; how *can* you ask? They will find none, and so they will never be married."

"*Get* married" is the usual phrase, and the one that correctly indicates the thought; but the speakers, on this occasion, were persons too outwardly refined to use it. They were ashamed of the word, but not of the thing. Madame Necker, however, sees good possible in celibacy.

Indeed, I know not how the subject could be better

* See the Nibelungen Lays.

14*

illustrated, than by separating the wheat from the chaff in Madame Necker's book; place them in two heaps, and then summon the reader to choose; giving him first a near-sighted glass to examine the two;—it might be a Christian, an astronomical, or an artistic glass,—any kind of good glass to obviate acquired defects in the eye. I would lay any wager on the result.

But time permits not here a prolonged analysis. I have given the clues for fault-finding.

As a specimen of the good take the following passage, on the phenomena of what I have spoken of, as the lyrical or electric element in Woman.

" Women have been seen to show themselves poets in the most pathetic pantomimic scenes, where all the passions were depicted full of beauty ; and these poets used a language unknown to themselves, and, the performance once over, their inspiration was a forgotten dream. Without doubt there is an interior development to beings so gifted; but their sole mode of communication with us is their talent.   They are, in all besides, the inhabitants of another planet."

Similar observations have been made by those who have seen the women at Irish wakes, or the funeral ceremonies of modern Greece or Brittany, at times when excitement gave the impulse to genius; but, apparently, without a thought that these rare powers belonged to no other planet, but were a high development of the growth of this, and might, by wise and reverent treatment, be made to inform and embellish the scenes of every day. But, when Woman has her fair chance, she will do so, and the poem of the hour will vie with that of the ages.

I come now with satisfaction to my own country, and to a writer, a female writer, whom I have selected as the clearest, wisest, and kindliest, who has, as yet, used pen here on these subjects. This is Miss Sedgwick.

Miss Sedgwick, though she inclines to the private path, and wishes that, by the cultivation of character, might should vindicate right, sets limits nowhere, and her objects and inducements are pure. They are the free and careful cultivation of the powers that have been given, with an aim at moral and intellectual perfection. Her speech is moderate and sane, but never palsied by fear or sceptical caution.

Herself a fine example of the independent and beneficent existence that intellect and character can give to Woman, no less than Man, if she know how to seek and prize it,—also, that the intellect need not absorb or weaken, but rather will refine and invigorate, the affections,—the teachings of her practical good sense come with great force, and cannot fail to avail much. Every way her writings please me both as to the means and the ends. I am pleased at the stress she lays on observance of the physical laws, because the true reason is given. Only in a strong and clean body can the soul do its message fitly.

She shows the meaning of the respect paid to personal neatness, both in the indispensable form of cleanliness, and of that love of order and arrangement, that must issue from a true harmony of feeling.

The praises of cold water seem to me an excellent

sign in the age. They denote a tendency to the true life. We are now to have, as a remedy for ills, not orvietan, or opium, or any quack medicine, but plenty of air and water, with due attention to warmth and freedom in dress, and simplicity of diet.

Every day we observe signs that the natural feelings on these subjects are about to be reinstated, and the body to claim care as the abode and organ of the soul ; not as the tool of servile labor, or the object of voluptuous indulgence.

A poor woman, who had passed through the lowest grades of ignominy, seemed to think she had never been wholly lost, "for," said she, " I would always have good under-clothes ; " and, indeed, who could doubt that this denoted the remains of private self-respect in the mind?

A woman of excellent sense said, " It might seem childish, but to her one of the most favorable signs of the times was that the ladies had been persuaded to give up corsets."

Yes ! let us give up all artificial means of distortion Let life be healthy, pure, all of a piece. Miss Sedgwick, in teaching that domestics must have the means of bathing as much as their mistresses, and time, too, to bathe, has symbolized one of the most important of human rights.

Another interesting sign of the time is the influence exercised by two women, Miss Martineau and Miss Barrett, from their sick-rooms. The lamp of life which, if it had been fed only by the affections, depended on precarious human relations, would scarce have been able to maintain a feeble glare in the lonely prison, now shines far and wide over the nations, cheering fellow-sufferers and hallowing the joy of the healthful.

These persons need not health or youth, or the charms of personal presence, to make their thoughts available. A few more such, and "old woman" * shall not be the synonyme for imbecility, nor "old maid" a term of contempt, nor Woman be spoken of as a reed shaken by the wind.

It is time, indeed, that men and women both should cease to grow old in any other way than as the tree does, full of grace and honor. The hair of the artist turns white, but his eye shines clearer than ever, and we feel that age brings him maturity, not decay. So would it be with all, were the springs of immortal refreshment but unsealed within the soul; then, like these women, they would see, from the lonely chamber window, the glories of the universe; or, shut in darkness, be visited by angels.

I now touch on my own place and day, and, as I write, events are occurring that threaten the fair fabric approached by so long an avenue. Week before last, the Gentile was requested to aid the Jew to return to Palestine; for the Millennium, the reign of the Son of Mary was near. Just now, at high and solemn mass, thanks were returned to the Virgin for having delivered O'Connell from unjust imprisonment, in requital of his having consecrated to her the league formed in behalf of Liberty

* An apposite passage is quoted in Appendix F.

on Tara's Hill. But last week brought news which threatens that a cause identical with the enfranchisement of Jews, Irish, women, ay, and of Americans in general, too, is in danger, for the choice of the people threatens to rivet the chains of slavery and the leprosy of sin permanently on this nation, through the Annexation of Texas!

Ah! if this should take place, who will dare again to feel the throb of heavenly hope, as to the destiny of this country? The noble thought that gave unity to all our knowledge, harmony to all our designs, — the thought that the progress of history had brought on the era, the tissue of prophecies pointed out the spot, where humanity was, at last, to have a fair chance to know itself, and all men be born free and equal for the eagle's flight, — flutters as if about to leave the breast, which, deprived of it, will have no more a nation, no more a home on earth.

Women of my country! — Exaltadas! if such there be, — women of English, old English nobleness, who understand the courage of Boadicea, the sacrifice of Godiva, the power of Queen Emma to tread the red-hot iron unharmed, — women who share the nature of Mrs. Hutchinson, Lady Russell, and the mothers of our own revolution, — have you nothing to do with this? You see the men, how they are willing to sell shamelessly the happiness of countless generations of fellow-creatures, the honor of their country, and their immortal souls, for a money market and political power. Do you not feel within you that which can reprove them, which can check, which can convince them? You would not speak in vain; whether each in her own home, or banded in unison.

Tell these men that you will not accept the glittering baubles, spacious dwellings, and plentiful service, they mean to offer you through these means. Tell them that the heart of Woman demands nobleness and honor in Man, and that, if they have not purity, have not mercy, they are no longer fathers, lovers, husbands, sons of yours.

This cause is your own, for, as I have before said, there is a reason why the foes of African Slavery seek more freedom for women; but put it not upon that ground. but on the ground of right.

If you have a power, it is a moral power. The films of interest are not so close around you as around the men. If you will but think, you cannot fail to wish to save the country from this disgrace. Let not slip the occasion, but do something to lift off the curse incurred by Eve.

You have heard the women engaged in the Abolition movement accused of boldness, because they lifted the voice in public, and lifted the latch of the stranger. But were these acts, whether performed judiciously or no, *so* bold. as to dare before God and Man to partake the fruits of such offence as this?

You hear much of the modesty of your sex. Preserve it by filling the mind with noble desires that shall ward off the corruptions of vanity and idleness. A profligate woman, who left her accustomed haunts and took service in a New York boarding-house, said "she had never heard talk so vile at the Five Points, as from the ladies at the boarding-house." And why? Because they were idle; because, having nothing worthy to engage them, they dwelt, with unnatural curiosity, on the ill they dared not go to see.

It will not so much injure your modesty to have your name, by the unthinking, coupled with idle blame, as to have upon your soul the weight of not trying to save a whole race of women from the scorn that is put upon *their* modesty.

Think of this well! I entreat, I conjure you, before it is too late. It is my belief that something effectual might be done by women, if they would only consider the subject, and enter upon it in the true spirit,— a spirit gentle, but firm, and which feared the offence of none, save One who is of purer eyes than to behold iniquity.

And now I have designated in outline, if not in fulness, the stream which is ever flowing from the heights of my thought.

In the earlier tract I was told I did not make my meaning sufficiently clear. In this I have consequently tried to illustrate it in various ways, and may have been guilty of much repetition. Yet, as I am anxious to leave no room for doubt, I shall venture to retrace, once more, the scope of my design in points, as was done in old-fashioned sermons.

Man is a being of two-fold relations, to nature beneath, and intelligences above him. The earth is his school, if not his birth-place; God his object; life and thought his means of interpreting nature, and aspiring to God.

Only a fraction of this purpose is accomplished in the life of any one man. Its entire accomplishment is to be hoped only from the sum of the lives of men, or Man considered as a whole.

As this whole has one soul and one body, any injury or obstruction to a part, or to the meanest member, affects the whole. Man can never be perfectly happy or virtuous, till all men are so.

To address Man wisely, you must not forget that his life is partly animal, subject to the same laws with Nature.

But you cannot address him wisely unless you consider him still more as soul, and appreciate the conditions and destiny of soul.

The growth of Man is two-fold, masculine and feminine.

So far as these two methods can be distinguished, they are so as

Energy and Harmony;
Power and Beauty;
Intellect and Love;

or by some such rude classification; for we have not language primitive and pure enough to express such ideas with precision.

These two sides are supposed to be expressed in Man and Woman, that is, as the more and the less, for the faculties have not been given pure to either, but only in preponderance. There are also exceptions in great num-

15

ber, such as men of far more beauty than power, and the reverse. But, as a general rule, it seems to have been the intention to give a preponderance on the one side, that is called masculine, and on the other, one that is called feminine.

There cannot be a doubt that, if these two developments were in perfect harmony, they would correspond to and fulfil one another, like hemispheres, or the tenor and bass in music.

But there is no perfect harmony in human nature; and the two parts answer one another only now and then; or, if there be a persistent consonance, it can only be traced at long intervals, instead of discoursing an obvious melody.

What is the cause of this?

Man, in the order of time, was developed first; as energy comes before harmony; power before beauty.

Woman was therefore under his care as an elder. He might have been her guardian and teacher.

But, as human nature goes not straight forward, but by excessive action and then reäction in an undulated course, he misunderstood and abused his advantages, and became her temporal master instead of her spiritual sire.

On himself came the punishment. He educated Woman more as a servant than a daughter, and found himself a king without a queen.

The children of this unequal union showed unequal natures, and, more and more, men seemed sons of the handmaid, rather than princess.

At last, there were so many Ishmaelites that the rest

grew frightened and indignant. They laid the blame on Hagar, and drove her forth into the wilderness.

But there were none the fewer Ishmaelites for that.

At last men became a little wiser, and saw that the infant Moses was, in every case, saved by the pure instincts of Woman's breast. For, as too much adversity is better for the moral nature than too much prosperity, Woman, in this respect, dwindled less than Man, though in other respects still a child in leading-strings.

So Man did her more and more justice, and grew more and more kind.

But yet — his habits and his will corrupted by the past — he did not clearly see that Woman was half himself; that her interests were identical with his; and that, by the law of their common being, he could never reach his true proportions while she remained in any wise shorn of hers.

And so it has gone on to our day ; both ideas developing, but more slowly than they would under a clearer recognition of truth and justice, which would have permitted the sexes their due influence on one another, and mutual improvement from more dignified relations.

Wherever there was pure love, the natural influences were, for the time, restored.

Wherever the poet or artist gave free course to his genius, he saw the truth, and expressed it in worthy forms, for these men especially share and need the feminine principle. The divine birds need to be brooded into life and song by mothers.

Wherever religion (I mean the thirst for truth and

good, not the love of sect and dogma) had its course, the original design was apprehended in its simplicity, and the dove presaged sweetly from Dodona's oak.

I have aimed to show that no age was left entirely without a witness of the equality of the sexes in function, duty and hope.

Also that, when there was unwillingness or ignorance, which prevented this being acted upon, women had not the less power for their want of light and noble freedom. But it was power which hurt alike them and those against whom they made use of the arms of the servile, — cunning, blandishment, and unreasonable emotion.

That now the time has come when a clearer vision and better action are possible — when Man and Woman may regard one another as brother and sister, the pillars of one porch, the priests of one worship.

I have believed and intimated that this hope would receive an ampler fruition, than ever before, in our own land.

And it will do so if this land carry out the principles from which sprang our national life.

I believe that, at present, women are the best helpers of one another.

Let them think; let them act; till they know what they need.

We only ask of men to remove arbitrary barriers. Some would like to do more. But I believe it needs that Woman show herself in her native dignity, to teach them how to aid her; their minds are so encumbered by tradition.

When Lord Edward Fitzgerald travelled with the Indians, his manly heart obliged him at once to take the packs from the squaws and carry them. But we do not read that tle red men followed his example, though they are ready enough to carry the pack of the white woman, because she seems to them a superior being.

Let Woman appear in the mild majesty of Ceres, and rudest churls will be willing to learn from her.

You ask, what use will she make of liberty, when she has so long been sustained and restrained?

I answer; in the first place, this will not be suddenly given. I read yesterday a debate of this year on the subject of enlarging women's rights over property. It was a leaf from the class-book that is preparing for the needed instruction. The men learned visibly as they spoke. The champions of Woman saw the fallacy of arguments on the opposite side, and were startled by their own convictions. With their wives at home, and the readers of the paper, it was the same. And so the stream flows on; thought urging action, and action leading to the evolution of still better thought.

But, were this freedom to come suddenly, I have no fear of the consequences. Individuals might commit excesses, but there is not only in the sex a reverence for decorums and limits inherited and enhanced from generation to generation, which many years of other life could not efface, but a native love, in Woman as Woman, of proportion, of "the simple art of not too much,"—a Greek moderation, which would create immediately a restraining party, the natural legislators and instructors

15*

of the rest, and would gradually establish such rules as are needed to guard, without impeding, life.

The Graces would lead the choral dance, and teach the rest to regulate their steps to the measure of beauty.

But if you ask me what offices they may fill, I reply — any. I do not care what case you put; let them be sea-captains, if you will. I do not doubt there are women well fitted for such an office, and, if so, I should be as glad to see them in it, as to welcome the maid of Saragossa, or the maid of Missolonghi, or the Suliote heroine, or Emily Plater.

I think women need, especially at this juncture, a much greater range of occupation than they have, to rouse their latent powers. A party of travellers lately visited a lonely hut on a mountain. There they found an old woman, who told them she and her husband had lived there forty years. "Why," they said, "did you choose so barren a spot?" She "did not know; *it was the man's notion.*"

And, during forty years, she had been content to act, without knowing why, upon "the man's notion." I would not have it so.

In families that I know, some little girls like to saw wood, others to use carpenters' tools. Where these tastes are indulged, cheerfulness and good-humor are promoted. Where they are forbidden, because "such things are not proper for girls," they grow sullen and mischievous.

Fourier had observed these wants of women, as no one can fail to do who watches the desires of little girls, or knows the ennui that haunts grown women, except where they make to themselves a serene little world by art of some kind. He, therefore, in proposing a great variety of employments, in manufactures or the care of plants and animals, allows for one third of women as likely to have a taste for masculine pursuits, one third of men for feminine.

Who does not observe the immediate glow and serenity that is diffused over the life of women, before restless or fretful, by engaging in gardening, building, or the lowest department of art ? Here is something that is not routine, something that draws forth life towards the infinite.

I have no doubt, however, that a large proportion of women would give themselves to the same employments as now, because there are circumstances that must lead them. Mothers will delight to make the nest soft and warm. Nature would take care of that; no need to clip the wings of any bird that wants to soar and sing, or finds in itself the strength of pinion for a migratory flight unusual to its kind. The difference would be that *all* need not be constrained to employments for which *some* are unfit.

I have urged upon the sex self-subsistence in its two forms of self-reliance and self-impulse, because I believe them to be the needed means of the present juncture.

I have urged on Woman independence of Man, not that I do not think the sexes mutually needed by one another, but because in Woman this fact has led to an excessive devotion, which has cooled love, degraded marriage, and prevented either sex from being what it should be to itself or the other.

I wish Woman to live, *first* for God's sake. Then she will not make an imperfect man her god, and thus sink to idolatry. Then she will not take what is not fit for her from a sense of weakness and poverty. Then, if she finds what she needs in Man embodied, she will know how to love, and be worthy of being loved.

By being more a soul, she will not be less Woman, for nature is perfected through spirit.

Now there is no woman, only an overgrown child.

That her hand may be given with dignity, she must be able to stand alone. I wish to see men and women capable of such relations as are depicted by Landor in his Pericles and Aspasia, where grace is the natural garb of strength, and the affections are calm, because deep. The softness is that of a firm tissue, as when

> " The gods approve
> The depth, but not the tumult of the soul,
> A fervent, not ungovernable love."

A profound thinker has said, " No married woman can represent the female world, for she belongs to her husband. The idea of Woman must be represented by a virgin."

But that is the very fault of marriage, and of the present relation between the sexes, that the woman *does* belong to the man, instead of forming a whole with him. Were it otherwise, there would be no such limitation to the thought.

Woman, self-centred, would never be absorbed by any relation; it would be only an experience to her as to

man. It is a vulgar error that love, *a* love, to Woman
is her whole existence; she also is born for Truth and
Love in their universal energy. Would she but assume
her inheritance, Mary would not be the only virgin
mother. Not Manzoni alone would celebrate in his wife
the virgin mind with the maternal wisdom and conjugal
affections. The soul is ever young, ever virgin.

And will not she soon appear? — the woman who shall
vindicate their birthright for all women; who shall
teach them what to claim, and how to use what they
obtain? Shall not her name be for her era Victoria, for
her country and life Virginia? Yet predictions are
rash; she herself must teach us to give her the fitting
name.

An idea not unknown to ancient times has of late been
revived, that, in the metamorphoses of life, the soul
assumes the form, first of Man, then of Woman, and
takes the chances, and reaps the benefits of either lot.
Why then, say some, lay such emphasis on the rights or
needs of Woman? What she wins not as Woman will
come to her as Man.

That makes no difference. It is not Woman, but the
law of right, the law of growth, that speaks in us, and
demands the perfection of each being in its kind — apple
as apple, Woman as Woman. Without adopting your
theory, I know that I, a daughter, live through the life
of Man; but what concerns me now is, that my life be a
beautiful, powerful, in a word, a complete life in its
kind. Had I but one more moment to live I must wish
the same.

Suppose, at the end of your cycle, your great world-year, all will be completed, whether I exert myself or not (and the supposition is *false*, — but suppose it true), am I to be indifferent about it? Not so! I must beat my own pulse true in the heart of the world; for *that* is virtue, excellence, health.

Thou, Lord of Day! didst leave us to-night so calmly glorious, not dismayed that cold winter is coming, not postponing thy beneficence to the fruitful summer! Thou didst smile on thy day's work when it was done, and adorn thy down-going as thy up-rising, for thou art loyal, and it is thy nature to give life, if thou canst, and shine at all events!

I stand in the sunny noon of life. Objects no longer glitter in the dews of morning, neither are yet softened by the shadows of evening. Every spot is seen, every chasm revealed. Climbing the dusty hill, some fair effigies that once stood for symbols of human destiny have been broken; those I still have with me show defects in this broad light. Yet enough is left, even by experience, to point distinctly to the glories of that destiny; faint, but not to be mistaken streaks of the future day. I can say with the bard,

"Though many have suffered shipwreck, still beat noble hearts."

Always the soul says to us all, Cherish your best hopes as a faith, and abide by them in action. Such shall be the effectual fervent means to their fulfilment;

For the Power to whom we bow
Has given its pledge that, if not now,

They of pure and steadfast mind,
By faith exalted, truth refined,
Shall hear all music loud and clear,
Whose first notes they ventured here.
Then fear not thou to wind the horn,
Though elf and gnome thy courage scorn;
Ask for the castle's King and Queen;
Though rabble rout may rush between,
Beat thee senseless to the ground,
In the dark beset thee round;
Persist to ask, and it will come;
Seek not for rest in humbler home;
So shalt thou see, what few have seen,
The palace home of King and Queen.

15th November, 1844.

PART II.

MISCELLANIES.

MISCELLANIES.

AGLAURON AND LAURIE.

A DRIVE THROUGH THE COUNTRY NEAR BOSTON.

AGLAURON and Laurie are two of the pleasantest men I know. Laurie combines, with the external advantages of a beautiful person and easy address, all the charm which quick perceptions and intelligent sympathy give to the intercourse of daily life. He has an extensive, though not a deep, knowledge of men and books, — his naturally fine taste has been more refined by observation, both at home and abroad, than is usual in this busy country; and, though not himself a thinker, he follows with care and delight the flights of a rapid and inventive mind. He is one of those rare persons who, without being servile or vacillating, present on no side any barrier to the free action of another mind. Yes, he is really an agreeable companion. I do not remember ever to have been wearied or chilled in his company.

Aglauron is a person of far greater depth and force than his friend and cousin, but by no means as agreeable. His mind is ardent and powerful, rather than brilliant and ready, — neither does he with ease adapt himself to the course of another. But, when he is once kindled, the blaze of light casts every object on which it falls into a bold relief, and gives every scene a lustre unknown before. He is not, perhaps, strictly original in his thoughts ; but the severe truth of his character, and the searching force of his attention, give the charm of originality to what he says. Accordingly, another cannot, by repetition, do it justice. I have never any doubt when I write down or tell what Laurie says, but Aglauron must write for himself.

Yet I almost always take notes of what has passed, for the amusement of a distant friend, who is learning, amidst the western prairies, patience, and an appreciation of the poor benefits of our imperfectly civilized state. And those I took this day, seemed not unworthy of a more general circulation. The sparkle of talk, the free breeze that swelled its current, are always fled when you write it down ; but there is a gentle flow, and truth to the moment, rarely attained in more elaborate compositions.

My two friends called to ask if I would drive with them into the country, and I gladly consented. It was a beautiful afternoon of the last week in May. Nature seemed most desirous to make up for the time she had lost in an uncommonly cold and wet spring. The leaves were bursting from their sheaths with such rapidity that the trees seemed actually to greet you as you passed along. The vestal choirs of snow-drops and violets were chanting their gentle hopes from every bank, the orchards were white with blossoms, and the birds singing in almost tumultuous glee.

We drove for some time in silence, perhaps fearful to disturb the universal song by less melodious accents, when Aglauron said :

"How entirely are we new-born to-day ! How are all the past cold skies and hostile breezes vanished before this single breath of sweetness ! How consoling is the truth thus indicated ! "

Laurie. It is indeed the dearest fact of our consciousness, that, in every moment of joy, pain is annihilated. There is no past, and the future is only the sunlight streaming into the far valley.

Aglauron. Yet it was the night that taught us to prize the day.

Laurie. Even so. And I, you know, object to none of the " dark masters."

Aglauron. Nor I, — because I am sure that whatever is, is good ; and to find out the *why* is all our employment here. But one feels so *at home* in such a day as this !

Laurie. As this, indeed ! I never heard so many birds, nor saw so many flowers. Do you not like these yellow flowers ?

Aglauron. They gleam upon the fields as if to express the bridal kiss of the sun. He seems most happy, if not most wealthy, when first he is wed to the earth.

Laurie. I believe I have some such feeling about these golden flowers. When I did not know what was the Asphodel, so celebrated by the poets, I thuoght it was a golden flower; yet this yellow is so ridiculed as vulgar.

16*

Aglauron. It is because our vulgar luxury depreciates objects not fitted to adorn our dwellings. These yellow flowers will not bear being taken out of their places and brought home to the centre-table. But, when enamelling the ground. the cowslip, the king-cup, — nay, the marigold and dandelion even, — are resplendently beautiful.

Laurie. They are the poor man's gold. See that dark, unpainted house, with its lilac shrubbery. As it stands, undivided from the road to which the green bank slopes down from the door, is not the effect of that enamel of gold dandelions beautiful?

Aglauron. It seems as if a stream of peace had flowed from the door-step down to the very dust, in waves of light, to greet the passer-by. That is, indeed, a quiet house. It looks as if somebody's grandfather lived there still.

Laurie. It is most refreshing to see the dark boards amid those houses of staring white. Strange that, in the extreme heat of summer, aching eyes don't teach the people better.

Aglauron. We are still, in fact, uncivilized, for all our knowledge of what is done "in foreign parts" cannot make us otherwise. Civilization must be homogeneous,— must be a natural growth. This glistening white paint was long preferred because the most expensive; just as in the West, I understand, they paint houses red to make them resemble the hideous red brick. And the eye, thus spoiled by excitement, prefers red or white to the stone-color, or the browns, which would harmonize with other hues.

Laurie. I should think the eye could never be spoiled so far as to like these white palings. These bars of glare amid the foliage are unbearable.

Myself. What color should they be?

Laurie. An invisible green, as in all civilized parts of the globe. Then your eye would rest on the shrubbery undisturbed.

Myself. Your vaunted Italy has its palaces of white stucco and buildings of brick.

Laurie. Ay, — but the stucco is by the atmosphere soon mellowed into cream-color, the brick into rich brown.

Myself. I have heard a connoisseur admire our own red brick in the afternoon sun, above all other colors.

Laurie. There are some who delight too much in the stimulus of color to be judges of harmony of coloring. It is so, often, with the Italians. No color is too keen for the eye of the Neapolitan. He thinks, with little Riding-hood, there is no color like red. I have seen one of the most beautiful new palaces paved with tiles of a brilliant red. But this, too, is barbarism.

Myself. You are pleased to call it so, because you make the English your arbiters in point of taste; but I do not think they, on your own principle, are our proper models. With their ever-weeping skies, and seven-piled velvet of verdure, they are no rule for us, whose eyes are accustomed to the keen blue and brilliant clouds of our own realm, and who see the earth wholly green scarce two months in the year. No white is more glistening than our January snows; no house here hurts my eye more than the fields of white-weed will, a fortnight hence.

Laurie. True refinement of taste would bid the eye seek repose the more. But, even admitting what you say, there is no harmony. The architecture is borrowed from England; why not the rest?

Aglauron. But, my friend, surely these piazzas and pipe-stem pillars are all American.

Laurie. But the cottage to which they belong is English. The inhabitants, suffocating in small rooms, and beneath sloping roofs, because the house is too low to admit any circulation of air, are in need, we must admit, of the piazza, for elsewhere they must suffer all the torments of Mons. Chaubert in his first experience of the oven. But I do not assail the piazzas, at any rate; they are most desirable, in these hot summers of ours, were they but in proportion with the house, and their pillars with one another. But I do object to houses which are desirable neither as summer nor winter residences here. The shingle palaces, celebrated by Irving's wit, were far more appropriate, for they, at least, gave free course to the winds of heaven, when the thermometer stood at ninety-five degrees in the shade.

Aglauron. Pity that American wit nipped in the bud those early attempts at an American architecture. Here in the East, alas! the case is become hopeless. But in the West the log-cabin still promises a proper basis.

Laurie. You laugh at me. But so it is. I am not so silly as to insist upon American architecture, American art, in the 4th of July style, merely for the gratification of national vanity. But a building, to be beautiful, should harmonize exactly with the uses to which it is to be put, and be an index to the climate and habits of the people. There is no objection to borrowing good thoughts from other nations, if we adopt the new style because we find it will serve our convenience, and not merely because it looks pretty outside.

Aglauron. I agree with you that here, as well as in manners and in literature, there is too ready access to the old stock, and, though I said it in jest, my hope is, in truth, the log-cabin. This the settler will enlarge, as his riches and his family increase; he will beautify as his character refines, and as his eye becomes accustomed to observe objects around him for their loveliness as well as for their utility. He will borrow from Nature the forms and coloring most in harmony with the scene in which his dwelling is placed. Might growth here be but slow enough! Might not a greediness for gain and show cheat men of all the real advantages of their experience!

(Here a carriage passed.)

Laurie. Who is that beautiful lady to whom you bowed?

Aglauron. Beautiful do you think her? At this distance, and with the freshness which the open air gives to her complexion, she certainly does look so, and was so still, five years ago, when I knew her abroad. It is Mrs. V——.

Laurie. I remember with what interest you mentioned her in your letters. And you promised to tell me her true story.

Aglauron. I was much interested, then, both in her and her story. But, last winter, when I met her at the South, she had altered, and seemed so much less attractive than before, that the bright colors of the picture are well-nigh effaced.

Laurie. The pleasure of telling the story will revive them again. Let us fasten our horses and go into this little wood. There is a seat near the lake which is pretty enough to tell a story upon.

Aylauron. In all the idyls I ever read, they were told in caves, or beside a trickling fountain.

Laurie. That was in the last century. We will innovate. Let us begin that American originality we were talking about, and make the bank of a lake answer our purpose.

We dismounted accordingly, but, on reaching the spot, Aglauron at first insisted on lying on the grass, and gazing up at the clouds in a most uncitizen-like fashion, and it was some time before we could get the promised story. At last, —

I first saw Mrs. V—— at the opera in Vienna. Abroad, I scarcely cared for anything in comparison with music. In many respects the Old World disappointed my hopes; society was, in essentials, no better, nor worse, than at home, and I too easily saw through the varnish of conventional refinement. Lions, seen near, were scarcely more interesting than tamer cattle, and much more annoying in their gambols and caprices. Parks and orna-

mental grounds pleased me less than the native forests and
wide-rolling rivers of my own land. But in the Arts, and
most of all in Music, I found all my wishes more than
realized. I found the soul of man uttering itself with
the swiftness, the freedom and the beauty, for which I had
always pined. I easily conceived how foreigners, once
acquainted with this diverse language, pass their lives
without a wish for pleasure or employment beyond hearing the great works of the masters. It seemed to me
that here was wealth to feed the thoughts for ages.
This lady fixed my attention by the rapturous devotion
with which she listened. I saw that she too had here found
her proper home. Every shade of thought and feeling
expressed in the music was mirrored in her beautiful
countenance. Her rapture of attention, during some passages, was enough of itself to make you hold your breath;
and a sudden stroke of genius lit her face into a very
heaven with its lightning. It seemed to me that in her I
should find one who would truly sympathize with me, one
who looked on the art not as a connoisseur, but a votary.

I took the speediest opportunity of being introduced to
her at her own house by a common friend.

But what a difference! At home I scarcely knew her.
Still she was beautiful; but the sweetness, the elevated
expression, which the satisfaction of an hour had given
her, were entirely fled. Her eye was restless, her
cheek pale and thin, her whole expression perturbed and
sorrowful. Every gesture spoke the sickliness of a spirit
long an outcast from its natural home, bereft of happiness, and hopeless of good.

I perceived, at first sight of her every-day face, that
it was not unknown to me. Three or four years earlier,
staying in the country-house of one of her friends, I had
seen her picture. The house was very dull,— as dull as
placid content with the mere material enjoyments of life,
and an inert gentleness of nature, could make its inhabitants. They were people to be loved, but loved without
a thought. Their wings had never grown, nor their eyes
coveted a wider prospect than could be seen from the
parent nest. The friendly visitant could not discompose
them by a remark indicating any expansion of mind or
life. Much as I enjoyed the beauty of the country around,
when out in the free air, my hours within the house
would have been dull enough but for the contemplation
of this picture. While the round of common-place songs
was going on, and the whist-players were at their work, I
used to sit and wonder how this being, so sovereign in the
fire of her nature, so proud in her untamed loveliness,
could ever have come of their blood. Her eye, from the
canvas, even, seemed to annihilate all things low or little,
and able to command all creation in search of the object
of its desires. She had not found it, though ; I felt this
on seeing her now. She, the queenly woman, the Boadicea of a forlorn hope, as she seemed born to be, the
only woman whose face, to my eye, had ever given promise of a prodigality of nature sufficient for the entertainment of a poet's soul, was — I saw it at a glance —
a captive in her life, and a beggar in her affections.

Laurie. A dangerous object to the traveller's eye,
methinks !

Aglauron. Not to mine! The picture had been so; but, seeing her now, I felt that the glorious promise of her youthful prime had failed. She had missed her course; and the beauty, whose charm to the imagination had been that it seemed invincible, was now subdued and mixed with earth.

Laurie. I can never comprehend the cruelty in your way of viewing human beings, Aglauron. To err, to suffer, is their lot; all who have feeling and energy of character must share it; and I could not endure a woman who at six-and-twenty bore no trace of the past.

Aglauron. Such women and such men are the companions of every-day life. But the angels of our thoughts are those moulds of pure beauty which must break with a fall. The common air must not touch them, for they make their own atmosphere. I admit that such are not for the tenderness of daily life; their influence must be high, distant, starlike, to be pure.

Such was this woman to me before I knew her; one whose splendid beauty drew on my thoughts to their future home. In knowing her, I lost the happiness I had enjoyed in knowing what she should have been. At first the disappointment was severe, but I have learnt to pardon her, as others who get mutilated or worn in life, and show the royal impress only in their virgin courage. But this subject would detain me too long. Let me rather tell you of Mrs. V——'s sad history.

A friend of mine has said that beautiful persons seem rarely born to their proper family, but amidst persons

so rough and uncongenial that *their* presei.ce commands
like that of a reproving angel, or pains like that of some
poor prince changed at nurse, and bound for life to the
society of churls.

So it was with Emily. Her father was sordid, her
mother weak ; persons of great wealth and greater selfishness. She was the youngest by many years, and left
alone in her father's house. Notwithstanding the want
of intelligent sympathy while she was growing up, and
the want of all intelligent culture, she was not an
unhappy child. The unbounded and foolish indulgence
with which she was treated did not have an obviously bad
effect upon her then ; it did not make her selfish, sensual, or vain. Her character was too powerful to dwell
upon such boons as those nearest her could bestow. She
negligently received them all as her due. It was later
that the pernicious effects of the absence of all discipline
showed themselves ; but in early years she was happy in
her lavish feelings, and in beautiful nature, on which she
could pour them, and in her own pursuits. Music was
her passion ; in it she found food, and an answer for feelings destined to become so fatal to her peace, but which
then glowed so sweetly in her youthful form as to enchant
the most ordinary observer.

When she was not more than fifteen, and expanding
like a flower in each sunny day, it was her misfortune
that her first husband saw and loved her. Emily, though
pleased by his handsome person and gay manners, never
bestowed a serious thought on him. If she had, it would
have been the first ever disengaged from her life of pleas-

urable sensation. But when he did plead his cause
with all the ardor of youth, and the flourishes which have
been by usage set apart for such occasions, she listened
with delight; for all his talk of boundless love, undying
faith, etc., seemed her native tongue. It was like the
most glowing sunset sky. It swelled upon the ear like
music. It was the only way she ever wished to be
addressed, and she now saw plainly why all talk of every-
day people had fallen unheeded on her ear. She could
have listened all day. But when, emboldened by the
beaming eye and ready smile with which she heard, he
pressed his suit more seriously, and talked of marriage.
she drew back astonished. Marry yet? — impossible!
She had never thought of it; and as she thought now
of marriages, such as she had seen them, there was nothing in marriage to attract. But L—— was not so easily
repelled; he made her every promise of pleasure, as one
would to a child. He would take her away to journey
through scenes more beautiful than she had ever dreamed
of; he would take her to a city where, in the fairest
home, she should hear the finest music, and he himself,
in every scene, would be her devoted slave, too happy if
for every new pleasure he received one of those smiles
which had become his life.

He saw her yielding, and hastened to secure her. Her
father was delighted, as fathers are strangely wont to be,
that he was likely to be deprived of his child, his pet,
his pride. The mother was threefold delighted that she
would have a daughter married *so young*,— at least three
years younger than any of her elder sisters were

married. Both lent their influence; and Emily, accustomed to rely on them against all peril and annoyance,
till she scarcely knew there was pain or evil in the world,
gave her consent, as she would have given it to a pleasure-
party for a day or a week.

The marriage was hurried on; L—— intent on gaining his object, as men of strong will and no sentiment are
wont to be, the parents thinking of the éclat of the
match. Emily was amused by the preparations for the
festivity, and full of excitement about the new chapter
which was to be opened in her life. Yet so little idea had
she of the true business of life, and the importance of its
ties, that perhaps there was no figure in the future that
occupied her less than that of her bridegroom, a handsome man, with a sweet voice, her captive, her adorer.
She neither thought nor saw further, lulled by the pictures
of bliss and adventure which were floating before her
fancy, the more enchanting because so vague.

It was at this time that the picture that so charmed
me was taken. The exquisite rose had not yet opened
its leaves so as to show its heart; but its fragrance and
blushful pride were there in perfection.

Poor Emily! She had the promised journeys, the
splendid home. Amid the former her mind, opened by
new scenes, already learned that something she seemed to
possess was wanting in the too constant companion of her
days. In the splendid home she received not only
musicians, but other visitants, who taught her strange
things.

Four little months after her leaving home, her parents

were astonished by receiving a letter in which she told them they had parted with her too soon; that she was not happy with Mr L——, as he had promised she should be, and that she wished to have her marriage broken. She urged her father to make haste about it, as she had particular reasons for impatience. You may easily conceive of the astonishment of the good folks at home. Her mother wondered and cried. Her father immediately ordered his horses, and went to her.

He was received with rapturous delight, and almost at the first moment thanked for his speedy compliance with her request. But when she found that he opposed her desire of having her marriage broken, and when she urged him with vehemence and those marks of caressing fondness she had been used to find all-powerful, and he told her at last it could not be done, she gave way to a paroxysm of passion; she declared that she could not and would not live with Mr. L——; that, so soon as she saw anything of the world, she saw many men that she infinitely preferred to him; and that, since her father and mother, instead of guarding her, so mere a child as she was, so entirely inexperienced, against a hasty choice, had persuaded and urged her to it, it was their duty to break the match when they found it did not make her happy.

"My child, you are entirely unreasonable."

"It is not a time to be patient; and I was too yielding before. I am not seventeen. Is the happiness of my whole life to be sacrificed?"

"Emily, you terrify me! Do you love anybody else?"

"Not yet; but I am sure I shall find some one to love. now I know what it is. I have seen already many whom I prefer to Mr. L——."

"Is he not kind to you?"

"Kind! yes; but he is perfectly uninteresting. I hate to be with him. I do not wish his kindness, nor to remain in his house."

In vain her father argued; she insisted that she could never be happy as she was; that it was impossible the law could be so cruel as to bind her to a vow she had taken when so mere a child; that she would go home with her father now, and they would see what could be done. She added that she had already told her husband her resolution.

"And how did he bear it?"

"He was very angry; but it is better for him to be angry once than unhappy always, as I should certainly make him did I remain here."

After long and fruitless attempts to reason her into a different state of mind, the father went in search of the husband. He found him irritated and mortified. He loved his wife, in his way, for her personal beauty. He was very proud of her; he was piqued to the last degree by her frankness. He could not but acknowledge the truth of what she said, that she had been persuaded into the match when but a child; for she seemed a very infant now, in wilfulness and ignorance of the world But I believe neither he nor her father had one compunctious misgiving as to their having profaned the holiness of marriage by such an union. Their minds had never been opened to the true meaning of life, and, though they thought themselves so much wiser, they were in truth much less so than the poor, passionate Emily,— for her heart, at least, spoke clearly, if her mind lay in darkness.

They could do nothing with her, and her father was at length compelled to take her home, hoping that her mother might be able to induce her to see things in a different light. But father, mother, uncles, brothers, all reasoned with her in vain. Totally unused to disappointment, she could not for a long time believe that she was forever bound by a bond that sat uneasily on her untamed spirit. When at last convinced of the truth, her despair was terrible.

" Am I his? his forever? Must I never then love? Never marry one whom I could really love? Mother! it is too cruel. I cannot, will not believe it. You always wished me to belong to him. You do not now wish to aid me, or you are afraid! O, you would not be so, could you but know what I feel ! "

At last convinced, she then declared that if she could not be legally separated from L——, but must consent to bear his name, and never give herself to another, she would at least live with him no more. She would not again leave her father's house. Here she was deaf to all argument, and only force could have driven her away. Her indifference to L—— had become hatred, in the course of these thoughts and conversations. She regarded herself as his victim, and him as her betrayer, since, she said, he was old enough to know the importance of the step to which he led her. Her mind, naturally noble, though now in this wild state, refused to admit his love as an excuse. "Had he loved me," she said, "he would have wished to teach me to love him, before securing me as his property. He is as selfish as he is dull and uninteresting. No! I will drag on my miserable years here alone, but I will not pretend to love him, nor gratify him by the sight of his slave!"

A year and more passed, and found the unhappy Emily inflexible. Her husband at last sought employment abroad, to hide his mortification.

After his departure, Emily relaxed once from the severe coldness she had shown since her return home. She had passed her time there with her music, in reading poetry, in solitary walks. But as the person who had been, however unintentionally, the means of making her so miserable, was further removed from her, she showed willingness to mingle again with the family, and see one or two young friends.

One of these, Almeria, effected what all the armament of praying and threatening friends had been unable to do. She devoted herself to Emily. She shared her employments and her walks ; she sympathized with all her feelings, even the morbid ones which she saw to be sincerity, tenderness and delicacy gone astray,— perverted and soured by the foolish indulgence of her education, and the severity of her destiny made known suddenly to a mind quite unprepared. At last, having won the confidence and esteem of Emily, by the wise and gentle check her justice and clear perceptions gave to all extravagance,

Almeria ventured on representing to Emily her conduct as the world saw it.

To this she found her quite insensible. "What is the world to me?" she said. "I am forbidden to seek there all it can offer of value to Woman — sympathy and a home."

"It is full of beauty still," said Almeria, looking out into the golden and perfumed glories of a June day.

"Not to the prisoner and the slave," said Emily.

"All are such, whom God hath not made free;" and Almeria gently ventured to explain the hopes of larger span which enable the soul that can soar upon their wings to disregard the limitations of seventy years.

Emily listened with profound attention. The words were familiar to her, but the tone was not; it was that which rises from the depths of a purified spirit,— purified by pain, softened into peace.

"Have you made any use of these thoughts in your life, Almeria?"

The lovely preacher hesitated not to reveal a tale before unknown except to her own heart. of woe, renunciation, and repeated blows from a hostile fate.

Emily heard it in silence, but she understood. The great illusions of youth vanished. She did not suffer alone; her lot was not peculiar. Another, perhaps many, were forbidden the bliss of sympathy and a congenial environment. And what had Almeria done? Revenged herself? Tormented all around her? Clung with wild passion to a selfish resolve? Not at all. She had made the best of a wreck of life, and deserved a blessing on a

new voyage. She had sought consolation in disinterestea
tenderness for her fellow-sufferers, and she deserved tc
cease to suffer.

The lesson was taken home, and gradually leavened the
whole being of this spoiled but naturally noble child.

A few weeks afterwards, she asked her father wheu
Mr. L—— was expected to return.

" In about three months," he replied, much surprised.

" I should like to have you write to him for me."

" What new absurdity ? " said the father, who, long
mortified and harassed, had ceased to be a fond father to
his once adored Emily.

" Say that my views are unchanged as to his soliciting
a marriage with me when too childish to know my own
mind on that or any other subject; but I have now seen
enough of the world to know that he meant no ill, if no
good, and was no more heedless in this great matter than
many others are. He is not born to know what one constituted like me must feel, in a home where I found no
rest for my heart. I have now read, seen and thought,
what has made me a woman. I can be what you call
reasonable, though not perhaps in your way. I see that
my misfortune is irreparable. I heed not the world's
opinion, and would, for myself, rather remain here, and
keep up no semblance of a connection which my matured
mind disclaims. But that scandalizes you and my
mother, and makes your house a scene of pain and mortification in your old age. I know you, too, did not
neglect the charge of me, in your own eyes. I owe you
gratitude for your affectionate intentions at least.

"L—— too is as miserable as mortification can make one like him. Write, and ask him if he wishes my presence in his house on my own terms. He must not expect from me the affection, or marks of affection, of a wife. I should never have been his wife had I waited till I understood life or myself. But I will be his attentive and friendly companion, the mistress of his house, if he pleases. To the world it will seem enough,— he will be more comfortable there,— and what he wished of me was, in a great measure, to show me to the world. I saw that, as soon as we were in it, I could not give him happiness if I would, for we have not a thought nor employment in common. But if we can agree on the way, we may live together without any one being very miserable except myself, and I have made up my mind."

The astonishment of the father may be conceived, and his cavils ; L——'s also.

To cut the story short, it was settled in Emily's way, for she was one of the sultana kind, dread and dangerous. L—— hardly wished her to love him now, for he half hated her for all she had done ; yet he was glad to have her back, as she had judged, for the sake of appearances. All was smoothed over by a plausible story. People, indeed, knew the truth as to the fair one's outrageous conduct perfectly, but Mr. L—— was rich, his wife beautiful, and gave good parties ; so society, as such, bowed and smiled, while individuals scandalized the pair.

They had been living on this footing for several years, when I saw Emily at the opera. She was a much altered being. Debarred of happiness in her affections, she had turned for solace to the intellectual life, and her naturally powerful and brilliant mind had matured into a splendor which had never been dreamed of by those who had seen her amid the freaks and day-dreams of her early youth.

Yet, as I said before, she was not captivating to me, as her picture had been. She was, in a different way, as beautiful in feature and coloring as in her spring-time. Her beauty, all moulded and mellowed by feeling, was far more eloquent; but it had none of the virgin magnificence, the untouched tropical luxuriance, which had fired my fancy. The false position in which she lived had shaded her expression with a painful restlessness; and her eye proclaimed that the conflicts of her mind had strengthened, had deepened, but had not yet hallowed, her character.

She was, however, interesting, deeply so; one of those rare beings who fill your eye in every mood. Her passion for music, and the great excellence she had attained as a performer, drew us together. I was her daily visitor; but, if my admiration ever softened into tenderness, it was the tenderness of pity for her unsatisfied heart, and cold, false life.

But there was one who saw with very different eyes. V—— had been intimate with Emily some time before my arrival, and every day saw him more deeply enamored.

Laurie. And pray where was the husband all this time?

Aglauron. L—— had sought consolation in ambition He was a man of much practical dexterity, but of little

thought, and less heart. He had at first been jea.ous of
Emily for his honor's sake,— not for any reality,— for
she treated him with great attention as to the comforts of
daily life ; but otherwise, with polite, steady coldness.
Finding that she received the court, which many were disposed to pay her, with grace and affability, but at heart
with imperial indifference, he ceased to disturb himself ;
for, as she rightly thought, he was incapable of understanding her. A coquette he could have interpreted ;
but a romantic character like hers, born for a grand
passion, or no love at all, he could not. Nor did he see
that V—— was likely to be more to her than any of her
admirers.

Laurie. I am afraid I should have shamed his obtuse-
ness. V—— has nothing to recommend him that I know
of, except his beauty, and that is the beauty of a *petit-
maître* — effeminate, without character, and very unlikely,
I should judge, to attract such a woman as you give me
the idea of.

Aglauron. You speak like a man, Laurie ; but have
you never heard tales of youthful minstrels and pages
being preferred by princesses, in the land of chivalry, to
stalwart knights, who were riding all over the land, doing
their devoirs maugre scars and starvation ? And why ?
One want of a woman's heart is to admire and be protected ; but another is to be understood in all her delicate
feelings, and have an object who shall know how to
receive all the marks of her inventive and bour.teous affection. V—— is such an one ; a being of infinite grace

and tenderness, and an equal capacity for prizing the same in another.

Effeminate, say you? Lovely, rather, and lovable. He was not, indeed, made to grow old; but I never saw a fairer spring-time than shone in his eye when life, and thought, and love, opened on him all together.

He was to Emily like the soft breathing of a flute in some solitary valley; indeed, the delicacy of his nature made a solitude around him in the world. So delicate was he, and Emily for a long time so unconscious, that nobody except myself divined how strong was the attraction which, as it drew them nearer together, invested both with a lustre and a sweetness which charmed all around them.

But I see the sun is declining, and warns me to cut short a tale which would keep us here till dawn if I were to detail it as I should like to do in my own memories. The progress of this affair interested me deeply; for, like all persons whose perceptions are more lively than their hopes, I delight to live from day to day in the more ardent experiments of others. I looked on with curiosity, with sympathy, with fear. How could it end? What would become of them, unhappy lovers? One too noble, the other too delicate, ever to find happiness in an unsanctioned tie.

I had, however, no right to interfere, and did not, even by a look, until one evening, when the occasion was forced upon me.

There was a summer fête given at L——'s. I had mingled for a while with the guests in the brilliant apartments; but the heat oppressed, the conversation failed to interest me. An open window tempted me to the garden, whose flowers and tufted lawns lay bathed in moonlight. I went out alone; but the music of a superb band followed my steps, and gave impulse to my thoughts. A dreaming state, pensive though not absolutely sorrowful, came upon me,— one of those gentle moods when thoughts flow through the mind amber-clear and soft, noiseless, because unimpeded. I sat down in an arbor to enjoy it, and probably stayed much longer than I could have imagined; for when I reëntered the large saloon it was deserted. The lights, however, were not extinguished, and, hearing voices in the inner room, I supposed some guests still remained; and, as I had not spoken with Emily that evening, I ventured in to bid her good-night. I started, repentant, on finding her alone with V——, and in a situation that announced their feelings to be no longer concealed from each other. She, leaning back on the sofa, was weeping bitterly, while V——, seated at her feet, holding her hands within his own, was pouring forth his passionate words with a fervency which prevented him from perceiving my entrance. But Emily perceived me at once, and starting up, motioned me not to go, as I had intended. I obeyed, and sat down. A pause ensued, awkward for me and for V——, who sat with his eyes cast down and blushing like a young girl detected in a burst of feeling long kept secret. Emily sat buried in thought, the tears yet undried upon her cheeks. She was pale, but nobly beautiful, as I had never yet seen her.

After a few moments I broke the silence, and attempted

to tell why I had returned so late. She interrupted me: "No matter, Aglauron, how it happened; whatever the chance, it promises to give both V—— and myself, what we greatly need, a calm friend and adviser. You are the only person among these crowds of men whom I could consult; for I have read friendship in your eye, and I know you have truth and honor. V—— thinks of you as I do, and he too is, or should be, glad to have some counsellor beside his own wishes."

V—— did not raise his eyes; neither did he contradict her. After a moment he said, "I believe Aglauron to be as free from prejudice as any man, and most true and honorable; yet who can judge in this matter but ourselves?"

"No one shall judge," said Emily; "but I want counsel. God help me! I feel there is a right and wrong; but how can my mind, which has never been trained to discern between them, be confident of its power at this important moment? Aglauron, what remains to me of happiness,— if anything do remain; perhaps the hope of heaven, if, indeed, there be a heaven,— is at stake! Father and brother have failed their trust. I have no friend able to understand, wise enough to counsel me. The only one whose words ever came true to my thoughts, and of whom you have often reminded me, is distant. Will you, this hour, take her place?"

"To the best of my ability," I replied without hesitation, struck by the dignity of her manner.

"You know," she said, "all my past history; all do so here, though they do not talk loudly of it. You and all others have probably blamed me. You know not, you cannot guess, the anguish, the struggles of my childish mind when it first opened to the meaning of those words, Love, Marriage, Life. When I was bound to Mr. L——, by a vow which from my heedless lips was mockery of all thought, all holiness, I had never known a duty, I had never felt the pressure of a tie. Life had been, so far, a sweet, voluptuous dream, and I thought of this seemingly so kind and amiable person as a new and devoted ministrant to me of its pleasures. But I was scarcely in his power when I awoke. I perceived the unfitness of the tie; its closeness revolted me.

"I had no timidity; I had always been accustomed to indulge my feelings, and I displayed them now. L——, irritated, asserted his mastery; this drove me wild; I soon hated him, and despised too his insensibility to all which I thought most beautiful. From all his faults, and the imperfection of our relation, grew up in my mind the knowledge of what the true might be to me. It is astonishing how the thought grew upon me day by day. I had not been married more than three months before I knew what it would be to love, and I longed to be free to do so. I had never known what it was to be resisted, and the thought never came to me that I could now, and for all my life, be bound by so early a mistake. I thought only of expressing my resolve to be free.

"How I was repulsed, how disappointed, you know, or could divine if you did not know; for all but me have been trained to bear the burden from their youth up, and accustomed to have the individual will fettered for the advantage of society. For the same reason, you cannot guess the silent fury that filled my mind when I at last found that I had struggled in vain, and that I must remain in the bondage that I had ignorantly put on.

" My affections were totally alienated from my family, for I felt they had known what I had not, and had neither put me on my guard, nor warned me against precipitation whose consequences must be fatal. I saw, indeed, that they did not look on life as I did, and could be content without being happy; but this observation was far from making me love them more. I felt alone, bitterly, contemptuously alone. I hated men who had made the laws that bound me. I did not believe in God; for why had He permitted the dart to enter so unprepared a breast? I determined never to submit, though I disdained to struggle, since struggle was in vain. In passive, lonely wretchedness I would pass my days. I would not feign what I did not feel, nor take the hand which had poisoned for me the cup of life before I had sipped the first drops.

" A friend — the only one I have ever known — taught me other thoughts. She taught me that others, perhaps all others, were victims, as much as myself. She taught me that if all the wrecked submitted to be drowned, the world would be a desert. She taught me to pity others, even those I myself was paining; for she showed me that they had sinned in ignorance, and that I had no right to make them suffer so long as I myself di1, merely because they were the authors of my suffering.

"She showed me, by her own pure example, what were Duty and Benevolence and Employment to the soul, even when baffled and sickened in its dearest wishes. That example was not wholly lost: I freed my parents, at least, from their pain, and, without falsehood, became less cruel and more calm.

"Yet the kindness, the calmness, have never gone deep. I have been forced to live out of myself; and life, busy or idle, is still most bitter to the homeless heart. I cannot be like Almeria; I am more ardent; and, Aglauron, you see now I might be happy."

She looked towards V——. I followed her eye, and was well-nigh melted too by the beauty of his gaze.

"The question in my mind is," she resumed, "have I not a right to fly? To leave this vacant life, and a tie which, but for worldly circumstances, presses as heavily on L—— as on myself. I shall mortify him; but that is a trifle compared with actual misery. I shall grieve my parents; but, were they truly such, would they not grieve still more that I must reject the life of mutual love? I have already sacrificed enough; shall I sacrifice the happiness of one I could really bless for those who do not know one native heart-beat of my life?"

V—— kissed her hand.

"And yet," said she, sighing, "it does not always look so. We must, in that case, leave the world; it will not tolerate us. Can I make V—— happy in solitude?

And what would Almeria think? Often it seems that she would feel that now I do love, and could make a green spot in the desert of life over which she mourned, she would rejoice to have me do so. Then, again, something whispers she might have objections to make; and I wish — O, I long to know them! For I feel that this is the great crisis of my life, and that if I do not act wisely, now that I have thought and felt, it will be unpardonable. In my first error I was ignorant what I wished, but now I know, and ought not to be weak or deluded."

I said, "Have you no religious scruples? Do you never think of your vow as sacred?"

"Never!" she replied, with flashing eyes. "Shall the woman be bound by the folly of the child? No! — I have never once considered myself as L——'s wife. If I have lived in his house, it was to make the best of what was left, as Almeria advised. But what I feel he knows perfectly. I have never deceived him. But O! I hazard all! all! and should I be again ignorant, again deceived" ——

V—— here poured forth all that can be imagined.

I rose: "Emily, this case seems to me so extraordinary that I must have time to think. You shall hear from me. I shall certainly give you my best advice, and I trust you will not over-value it."

"I am sure," she said, "it will be of use to me, and will enable me to decide what I shall do. V——, now go away with Aglauron it is too late for you to stay here."

I do not know if I have made obvious, in this account, what struck me most in the interview, — a certain savage force in the character of this beautiful woman, quite independent of the reasoning power. I saw that, as she could give no account of the past, except that she saw it was fit, or saw it was not, so she must be dealt with now by a strong instalment made by another from his own point of view, which she would accept or not, as suited her.

There are some such characters, which, like plants, stretch upwards to the light; they accept what nourishes, they reject what injures them. They die if wounded,—blossom if fortunate ; but never learn to analyze all this, or find its reasons ; but, if they tell their story, it is in Emily's way ; — " it was so ; " " I found it so."

I talked with V——, and found him, as I expected, not the peer of her he loved, except in love. His passion was at its height. Better acquainted with the world than Emily, — not because he had seen it more, but because he had the elements of the citizen in him, — he had been at first equally emboldened and surprised by the ease with which he won her to listen to his suit. But he was soon still more surprised to find that she would only listen. She had no regard for her position in society as a married woman, — none for her vow. She frankly confessed her love, so far as it went, but doubted as to whether it was *her whole love*, and doubted still more her right to leave L——, since she had returned to him, and could not break the bond so entirely as to give them firm foot-hold in the world.

"I may make you unhappy," she said, "and then be unhappy myself; these laws, this society, are so strange, I can make nothing of them. In music I am at home. Why is not all life music? We instantly know when we are going wrong there. Convince me it is for the best, and I will go with you at once. But now it seems wrong, unwise, scarcely better than to stay as we are. We must go secretly, must live obscurely in a corner. That I cannot bear, — all is wrong yet. Why am I not at liberty to declare unblushingly to all men that I will leave the man whom I *do not* love, and go with him I *do* love? That is the only way that would suit me, — I cannot see clearly to take any other course."

I found V—— had no scruples of conscience, any more than herself. He was wholly absorbed in his passion, and his only wish was to persuade her to elope, that a divorce might follow, and she be all his own.

I took my part. I wrote next day to Emily. I told her that my view must differ from hers in this: that I had, from early impressions, a feeling of the sanctity of the marriage vow. It was not to me a measure intended merely to insure the happiness of two individuals, but a solemn obligation, which, whether it led to happiness or not, was a means of bringing home to the mind the great idea of Duty, the understanding of which, and not happiness, seemed to be the end of life. Life looked not clear to me otherwise. I entreated her to separate herself from V—— for a year, before doing anything decisive; she could then look at the subject from other points of view, and see the bearing on mankind as well as on herself alone. If she still found that happiness and V—— were her chief objects, she might be more sure of herself after such a trial. I was careful not to add one word of persuasion or exhortation, except that I recommended her to the enlightening love of the Father of our spirits.

Laurie. With or without persuasion, your advice had small chance, I fear, of being followed.

Aglauron. You err. Next day V—— departed. Emily, with a calm brow and earnest eyes, devoted herself to thought, and such reading as I suggested.

Laurie. And the result?

Aglauron. I grieve not to be able to point my tale with the expected moral, though perhaps the true denouement may lead to one as valuable. L—— died within the year, and she married V——.

Laurie. And the result?

Aglauron. Is for the present utter disappointment in him. She was infinitely blest, for a time, in his devotion, but presently her strong nature found him too much hers, and too little his own. He satisfied her as little as L—— had done, though always lovely and dear. She saw with keen anguish, though this time without bitterness, that we are never wise enough to be sure any measure will fulfil our expectations.

But — I know not how it is — Emily does not yet command the changes of destiny which she feels so keenly and faces so boldly. Born to be happy only in the clear light of religious thought, she still seeks happiness elsewhere. She is now a mother, and all other thoughts are merged in that. But she will not long be permitted to abide there. One more pang, and I look to see her find her central point, from which all the paths she has taken lead. She loves truth so ardently, though as yet only in detail, that she will yet know truth as a whole. She will see that she does not live for Emily, or for V——, or for her ·child, but as one link in a divine purpose. Her large nature must at last serve knowingly.

Myself. I cannot understand you, Aglauron; I do not guess the scope of your story, nor sympathize with your feeling about this lady. She is a strange, and, I think, very unattractive person. I think her beauty must have fascinated you. Her character seems very inconsistent.

Aglauron. Because I have drawn from life.

Myself. But, surely, there should be a harmony somewhere.

Aglauron. Could we but get the right point of view.

Laurie. And where is that?

He pointed to the sun, just sinking behind the pine-grove. We mounted and rode home without a word more. But I do not understand Aglauron yet, nor what he expects from this Emily. Yet her character, though almost featureless at first, gains distinctness as I think of it more. Perhaps in this life I shall find its key.

THE WRONGS OF AMERICAN WOMEN. THE DUTY OF AMERICAN WOMEN.

THE same day brought us a copy of Mr. Burdett's little book, — in which the sufferings and difficulties that beset the large class of women who must earn their subsistence in a city like New York, are delineated with so much simplicity, feeling, and exact adherence to the facts, — and a printed circular, containing proposals for immediate practical adoption of the plan more fully described in a book published some weeks since, under the title, " The Duty of American Women to their Country," which was ascribed alternately to Mrs. Stowe and Miss Catharine Beecher. The two matters seemed linked to one another by natural parity. Full acquaintance with the wrong must call forth all manner of inventions for its redress.

The circular, in showing the vast want that already exists of good means for instructing the children of this nation, especially in the West, states also the belief that among women, as being less immersed in other cares and toils, from the preparation it gives for their task as mothers, and from the necessity in which a great proportion stand of earning a subsistence somehow, at least during the years which precede marriage, if they *do* marry, must the number of teachers wanted be found, which is estimated already at *sixty thousand*.

We cordially sympathize with these views.

Much has been written about woman's keeping within her sphere, which is defined as the domestic sphere. As a little girl she is to learn the lighter family duties, while she acquires that limited acquaintance with the realm of literature and science that will enable her to superintend the instruction of children in their earliest years. It is not generally proposed that she should be sufficiently instructed and developed to understand the pursuits or aims of her future husband; she is not to be a help-meet to him in the way of companionship and counsel, except in the care of his house and children. Her youth is to be passed partly in learning to keep house and the use of the needle, partly in the social circle, where her manners may be formed, ornamental accomplishments perfected and displayed, and the husband found who shall give her the domestic sphere for which she is exclusively to be prepared.

Were the destiny of Woman thus exactly marked out; did she invariably retain the shelter of a parent's or guardian's roof till she married; did marriage give her a sure home and protector; were she never liable to remain a widow, or, if so, sure of finding immediate protection from a brother or new husband, so that she might never be forced to stand alone one moment; and were her mind given for this world only, with no faculties capable of eternal growth and infinite improvement; we would still demand for her a far wider and more generous culture, than is proposed by those who so anxiously define her sphere. We would demand it that she might not ignorantly or frivolously thwart the designs of her husband; that she might be the respected friend of her sons, not less than of her daughters; that she might give more refinement, elevation and attraction, to the society which is needed to give the characters of *men* polish and plasticity,— no less so than to save them from vicious and sensual habits. But the most fastidious critic on the departure of Woman from her sphere can scarcely fail to see, at present, that a vast proportion of the sex, if not the better half, do not, *cannot* have this domestic sphere. Thousands and scores of thousands in this country, no less than in Europe, are obliged to maintain themselves alone. Far greater numbers divide with their husbands the care of earning a support for the family. In England, now, the progress of society has reached so admirable a pitch, that the position of the sexes is frequently reversed, and the husband is obliged to stay at home and "mind the house and bairns," while the wife goes forth to the employment she alone can secure.

We readily admit that the picture of this is most painful;— that Nature made an entirely opposite distribution of functions between the sexes. We believe the natural order to be the best, and that, if it could be followed in an enlightened spirit, it would bring to Woman all she wants, no less for her immortal than her mortal destiny. We are not surprised that men who do not look deeply and carefully at causes and tendencies, should be led, by disgust at the hardened, hackneyed characters which

the present state of things too often produces in women,
to such conclusions as they are. We, no more than
they, delight in the picture of the poor woman digging
in the mines in her husband's clothes. We, no more
than they, delight to hear their voices shrilly raised in
the market-place, whether of apples, or of celebrity.
But we see that at present they must do as they do for
bread. Hundreds and thousands must step out of that
hallowed domestic sphere, with no choice but to work or
steal, or belong to men, not as wives, but as the wretched
slaves of sensuality.

And this transition state, with all its revolting features,
indicates, we do believe, an approach of a nobler era than
the world has yet known. We trust that by the stress
and emergencies of the present and coming time the minds
of women will be formed to more reflection and higher
purposes than heretofore ; their latent powers developed,
their characters strengthened and eventually beautified
and harmonized. Should the state of society then be
such that each may remain, as Nature seems to have intended, Woman the tutelary genius of home, while Man
manages the out-door business of life, both may be done
with a wisdom, a mutual understanding and respect, unknown at present. Men will be no less gainers by this
than women, finding in pure and more religious marriages
the joys of friendship and love combined, — in their
mothers and daughters better instruction, sweeter and
nobler companionship, and in society at large, an excitement to their finer powers and feelings unknown at
present, except in the region of the fine arts.

Blest be the generous, the wise, who seek to forward hopes like these, instead of struggling, against the fiat of Providence and the march of Fate, to bind down rushing life to the standard of the past! Such efforts are vain, but those who make them are unhappy and unwise.

It is not, however, to such that we address ourselves, but to those who seek to make the best of things as they are, while they also strive to make them better. Such persons will have seen enough of the state of things in London, Paris, New York, and manufacturing regions everywhere, to feel that there is an imperative necessity for opening more avenues of employment to women, and fitting them better to enter them, rather than keeping them back.

Women have invaded many of the trades and some of the professions. Sewing, to the present killing extent, they cannot long bear. Factories seem likely to afford them permanent employment. In the culture of fruit, flowers, and vegetables, even in the sale of them, we rejoice to see them engaged. In domestic service they will be aided, but can never be supplanted, by machinery. As much room as there is here for Woman's mind and Woman's labor, will always be filled. A few have usurped the martial province, but these must always be few; the nature of Woman is opposed to war. It is natural enough to see "female physicians," and we believe that the lace cap and work-bag are as much at home here as the wig and gold-headed cane. In the priesthood, they have, from all time, shared more or less — in many eras more than at the present. We believe there has been no female lawyer, and probably will be none. The pen, many of the fine arts, they have made their own; and in the more refined countries of the world, as writers, as musicians, as painters, as actors, women occupy as advantageous ground as men. Writing and music may be esteemed professions for them more than any other.

But there are two others — where the demand must invariably be immense, and for which they are naturally better fitted than men — for which we should like to see them better prepared and better rewarded than they are. These are the professions of nurse to the sick, and of the teacher. The first of these professions we have warmly desired to see dignified. It is a noble one, now most unjustly regarded in the light of menial service. It is one which no menial, no servile nature can fitly occupy. We were rejoiced when an intelligent lady of Massachusetts made the refined heroine of a little romance select this calling. This lady (Mrs. George Lee) has looked on society with unusual largeness of spirit and healthiness of temper. She is well acquainted with the world of conventions, but sees beneath it the world of nature. She is a generous writer, and unpretending as the generous are wont to be. We do not recall the name of the tale, but the circumstance above mentioned marks its temper. We hope to see the time when the refined and cultivated will choose this profession, and learn it, not only through experience and under the direction of the doctor, but by acquainting themselves with the laws of matter and of mind, so that all they do shall be intelligently done, and afford them the means of developing intelligence, as well as the nobler, tenderer feelings of humanity; for even this last part of the benefit they cannot receive if their work be done in a selfish or mercenary spirit.

The other profession is that of teacher, for which women are peculiarly adapted by their nature, superiority in tact, quickness of sympathy, gentleness, patience, and a clear and animated manner in narration or description. To form a good teacher, should be added to this, sincere modesty combined with firmness, liberal views, with a power and will to liberalize them still further, a good method, and habits of exact and thorough investigation. In the two last requisites women are generally deficient, but there are now many shining examples to prove that if they are immethodical and superficial as teachers, it is because it is the custom so to teach them, and that when aware of these faults, they can and will correct them.

The profession is of itself an excellent one for the improvement of the teacher during that interim between youth and maturity when the mind needs testing, tempering, and to review and rearrange the knowledge it has acquired. The natural method of doing this for one's self, is to attempt teaching others; those years also are the best of the practical teacher. The teacher should be near the pupil, both in years and feelings; no oracle, but the eldest brother or sister of the pupil. More experience and years form the lecturer and director of studies, but injure the powers as to familiar teaching.

These are just the years of leisure in the lives even of those women who are to enter the domestic sphere, and

this calling most of all compatible with a constant progress as to qualifications for that.

Viewing the matter thus, it may well be seen that we
should hail with joy the assurance that sixty thousand
female teachers are wanted, and more likely to be, and
that a plan is projected which looks wise, liberal and
generous, to afford the means, to those whose hearts
answer to this high calling, of obeying their dictates.

The plan is to have Cincinnati as a central point,
where teachers shall be for a short time received, examined, and prepared for their duties. By mutual agreement and coöperation of the various sects, funds are to be
raised, and teachers provided, according to the wants and
tendencies of the various locations now destitute. What
is to be done for them centrally, is for suitable persons to
examine into the various kinds of fitness, communicate
some general views whose value has been tested, and
counsel adapted to the difficulties and advantages of their
new positions. The central committee are to have the
charge of raising funds, and finding teachers, and places
where teachers are wanted.

The passage of thoughts, teachers and funds, will be
from East to West — the course of sunlight upon this
earth.

The plan is offered as the most extensive and pliant
means of doing a good and preventing ill to this nation,
by means of a national education, whose normal school
shall have an invariable object in the search after truth,
and the diffusion of the means of knowledge, while its
form shall be plastic according to the wants of the time

This normal school promises to have good effects, for it proposes worthy aims through simple means, and the motive for its formation and support seems to be disinterested philanthropy.

It promises to eschew the bitter spirit of sectarianism and proselytism, else we, for one party, could have nothing to do with it.   Men, no doubt, have oftentimes been kept from absolute famine by the wheat with which such tares are mingled; but we believe the time is come when a purer and more generous food is to be offered to the people at large.   We believe the aim of all education to be to rouse the mind to action, show it the means of discipline and of information; then leave it free, with God, Conscience, and the love of Truth, for its guardians and teachers.   Woe be to those who sacrifice these aims of universal and eternal value to the propagation of a set of opinions !   We can accept such doctrine as is offered by Rev. Calvin E. Stowe, one of the committee, in the following passage :

"In judicious practice, I am persuaded there will seldom be any very great difficulty, especially if there be excited in the community anything like a whole-hearted and enlightened sincerity in the cause of public instruction.

"It is all right for people to suit their own taste and convictions in respect to sect; and by fair means, and at proper times, to teach their children and those under their influence to prefer the denominations which they prefer; but further than this no one has any right to go. It is all wrong to hazard the well-being of the soul, to jeopardize great public interests for the sake of advancing the interests of a sect. People must learn to practise some self-denial, on Christian principles, in respect to their denominational prejudices as well as in respect to other things, before pure religion can ever gain a com-plete victory over every form of human selfishness."

The persons who propose themselves to the examination and instruction of the teachers at Cincinnati, till the plan shall be sufficiently under way to provide regularly for the office, are Mrs. Stowe and Miss Catharine Beecher, ladies well known to fame, as possessing unusual qualifications for the task.

As to finding abundance of teachers, who that reads this little book of Mr. Burdett's, or the account of the compensation of female labor in New York, and the hopeless, comfortless, useless, pernicious lives of those who have even the advantage of getting work must lead, with the sufferings and almost inevitable degradation to which those who cannot are exposed, but must long to snatch such as are capable of this better profession (and among the multitude there must be many who are or could be made so) from their present toils, and make them free, and the means of freedom and growth in others ?

To many books on such subjects — among others to " Woman in the Nineteenth Century " — the objection has been made, that they exhibit ills without specifying any practical means for their remedy. The writer of the last-named essay does indeed think that it contains one great rule which, if laid to heart, would prove a practical remedy for many ills, and of such daily and hourly

efficacy in the conduct of life, that any extensive observance of it for a single year would perceptibly raise the
tone of thought, feeling and conduct, throughout the civilized world.   But to those who ask not only such a principle, but an external method for immediate use, we say
that here is one proposed which looks noble and promising ; the proposers offer themselves to the work with
heart and hand, with time and purse.   Go ye and do
likewise.

GEORGE SAND.

WHEN I first knew George Sand, I thought to have found tried the experiment I wanted. I did not value Bettine so much. She had not pride enough for me. Only now, when I am sure of myself, can I pour out my soul at the feet of another. In the assured soul it is kingly prodigality; in one which cannot forbear it is mere babyhood. I love "abandon" only when natures are capable of the extreme reverse. I knew Bettine would end in nothing; when I read her book I knew she could not outlive her love.

But in "*Les Sept Cordes de la Lyre,*" which I read first, I saw the knowledge of the passions and of social institutions, with the celestial choice which rose above them. I loved Helène, who could hear so well the terrene voices, yet keep her eye fixed on the stars. That would be my wish also, — to know all, and then choose. I even revered her, for I was not sure that I could have resisted the call of the *now ;* could have left the spirit and gone to God; and at a more ambitious age I could not have refused the philosopher. But I hoped much from her steadfastness, and I thought I heard the last tones of a purified life. Gretchen, in the golden cloud, is raised above all past delusions, worthy to redeem and

upbear the wise man who stumbled into the pit of error
while searching for truth.

Still, in " André " and " Jacques," I trace the same
high morality of one who had tried the liberty of circumstance only to learn to appreciate the liberty of law ; —
to know that license is the foe of freedom ; and, though
the sophistry of Passion in these books disgusted me,
flowers of purest hue seemed to grow upon the dark and
dirty ground. I thought she had cast aside the slough
of her past life, and begun a new existence beneath the
sun of a new ideal.

But here, in the " *Lettres d'un Voyageur*," what do
I see ? An unfortunate, wailing her loneli ss, wailing
her mistakes, *writing for money !* She has genius, and
a manly grasp of mind, but not a manly heart. Will
there never be a being to combine a man's mind and a
woman's heart, and who yet finds life too rich to weep
over ? Never ?

When I read in " *Leon Leoni* " the account of the
jeweller's daughter's life with her mother, passed in
dressing, and learning to be looked at when dressed,
"*avec un front impassible*," it reminded me of —— and
her mother. What a heroine she would be for Sand !
She has the same fearless softness with Juliet, and a
sportive *naïveté*, a mixture of bird and kitten, unknown
to the dupe of Leoni.

If I were a man, and wished a wife, as many do,
merely as an ornament, a silken toy, I would take ——
as soon as any I know. Her fantastic, impassioned and
mutable nature would yield an inexhaustible amusement.

She is capable of the most romantic actions, — wild as the falcon, voluptuous as the tuberose ; yet she has not in her the elements of romance, like a deeper or less susceptible nature.   My cold and reasoning ——, with her one love lying, perhaps never to be unfolded, beneath such sheaths of pride and reserve, would make a far better heroine.

—— and her mother differ from Juliet and *her* mother by the impulse a single strong character gave them.   Even at this distance of time there is a light but perceptible taste of iron in the water.

George Sand disappoints me, as almost all beings do, especially since I have been brought close to her person by the " *Lettres d'un Voyageur.*"   Her remarks on Lavater seem really shallow, *à la mode du genre feminin.*   No self-ruling Aspasia she, but a frail woman, mourning over her lot.   Any peculiarity in her destiny seems accidental ; she is forced to this and to that to earn her bread, forsooth !

Yet her style — with what a deeply smouldering fire it burns ! Not vehement, but intense, like Jean Jacques.

FROM A NOTICE OF GEORGE SAND.

* * * * * * *

It is probably known to a great proportion of readers
that this writer is a woman, who writes under the name,
and frequently assumes the dress and manners, of a
man. It is also known that she has not only broken
the marriage-bond, and, since that, formed other connections, independent of the civil and ecclesiastical sanction.
but that she first rose into notice through works which
systematically assailed the present institution of marriage, and the social bonds which are connected with it.

No facts are more adapted to startle every feeling of
our community; but, since the works of Sand are read
here, notwithstanding, and cannot fail to be so while
they exert so important an influence abroad, it would be
well they should be read intelligently, as to the circumstances of their birth and their tendency.

George Sand we esteem to be a person of strong passions, but of original nobleness and a love of right sufficient to guide them all to the service of worthy aims. But
she fell upon evil times. She was given in marriage, according to the fashion of the old régime; she was taken
from a convent, where she had heard a great deal about the
law of God and the example of Jesus, into a society
where no vice was proscribed, if it would only wear the

cl)ak of hypocrisy. She found herself impatient of deception, and loudly appealed to by passion; she yielded, but she could not do so, as others did, sinning against what she owned to be the rule of right and the will of Heaven. She protested, she examined, she " hacked into the roots of things," and the bold sound of her axe called around her every foe that finds a home amid the growths of civilization. Still she persisted. " If it be real," thought she, " it cannot be destroyed; as to what is false, the sooner it goes the better; and I, for one, would rather perish by its fall, than wither in its shade."

Schiller puts into the mouth of Mary Stuart these words, as her only plea: " The world knows the worst of me, and I may boast that, though I have erred, I am better than my reputation." Sand may say the same. All is open, noble; the free descriptions, the sophistry of passion, are, at least, redeemed by a desire for truth as strong as ever beat in any heart. To the weak or unthinking, the reading of such books may not be desirable, for only those who take exercise as men can digest strong meat. But to any one able to understand the position and circumstances, we believe this reading cannot fail of bringing good impulses, valuable suggestions; and it is quite free from that subtle miasma which taints so large a portion of French literature, not less since the Revolution than before. This we say to the foreign reader. To her own country, Sand is a boon precious and prized, both as a warning and a leader, for which none there can be ungrateful. She has dared to probe its festering wounds; and if they be not past all surgery, she is one who, most of any, helps towards a cure.

Would, indeed, the surgeon had come with quite clean hands! A woman of Sand's genius — as free, as bold, and pure from even the suspicion of error — might have filled an apostolic station among her people. *Then* with what force had come her cry, " If it be false, give it up ; but if it be true, keep to it, — one or the other ! "

But we have read all we wish to say upon this subject lately uttered just from the quarter we could wish. It is such a woman, so unblemished in character, so high in aim, so pure in soul, that should address this other, as noble in nature, but clouded by error, and struggling with circumstances. It is such women that will do such others justice. They are not afraid to look for virtue, and reply to aspiration, among those who have *not* dwelt " in decencies forever." It is a source of pride and happiness to read this address from the heart of Elizabeth Barrett : —

TO GEORGE SAND.

A DESIRE.

Thou large-brained woman and large-hearted man,
  Self-called George Sand ! whose soul amid the lions
  Of thy tumultuous senses moans defiance,
And answers roar for roar, as spirits can, —
I would some wild, miraculous thunder ran
  Above the applauding circus, in appliance
  Of thine own nobler nature's strength and science,
Drawing two pinions, white as wings of swan,
From the strong shoulders, to amaze the place
  With holier light ! That thou, to woman's claim,

And man's, might join, beside, the angel's grace
Of a pure genius, sanctified from blame,
Till child and maiden pressed to thine embrace,
To kiss upon thy lips a stainless fame !

TO THE SAME.

A RECOGNITION.

True genius, but true woman ! dost deny
Thy woman's nature with a manly scorn,
And break away the gauds and armlets worn
By weaker woman in captivity ?
Ah, vain denial ! that revolted cry
Is sobbed in by a woman's voice forlorn : —
Thy woman's hair, my sister ! all unshorn,
Floats back dishevelled strength in agony,
Disproving thy man's name ; and while before
The world thou burnest in a poet-fire,
We see thy woman-heart beat evermore
Through the large flame.   Beat purer, heart ! and higher,
Till God unsex thee on the spirit-shore,
To which, alone unsexing, purely aspire !

This last sonnet seems to have been written after seeing the picture of Sand, which represents her in a man's
dress, but with long, loose hair, and an eye whose mournful fire is impressive, even in the caricatures.

For some years Sand has quitted her post of assail-
ant.   She has seen that it is better to seek some form of
life worthy to supersede the old, than rudely to destroy
it, heedless of the future.   Her force is bending towards
philanthropic measures.   She does not appear to possess
much of the constructive faculty ; and, though her writings command a great pecuniary compensation, and have

a wide sway, it is rather for their tendency than for their thought. She has reached no commanding point of view from which she may give orders to the advanced corps. She is still at work with others in the breach, though she works with more force than almost any.

In power, indeed, Sand bears the palm above all other French novelists. She is vigorous in conception, often great in the apprehension and the contrast of characters. She knows passion, as has been hinted, at a *white* heat, when all the lower particles are remoulded by its power. Her descriptive talent is very great, and her poetic feeling exquisite. She wants but little of being a poet, but that little is indispensable. Yet she keeps us always hovering on the borders of enchanted fields. She has, to a signal degree, that power of exact transcript from her own mind, in which almost all writers fail. There is no veil, no half-plastic integument between us and the thought; we vibrate perfectly with it.

This is her chief charm, and next to it is one in which we know no French writer that resembles her, except Rousseau, though he, indeed, is vastly her superior in it; that is, of concentrated glow. Her nature glows beneath the words, like fire beneath ashes,— deep, deep !

Her best works are unequal; in many parts written hastily, or carelessly, or with flagging spirits. They all promise far more than they can perform; the work is not done masterly; she has not reached that point where a writer sits at the helm of his own genius.

Sometimes she plies·the oar,— sometimes she drifts. But what greatness she has is genuine; there is no tinsel of any kind, no drapery carefully adjusted, no chosen gesture about her. May Heaven lead her, at last, to the full possession of her best self, in harmony with the higher laws of life!

We are not acquainted with all her works, but among those we know, mention "*La Roche Maupart*," "*André*," "*Jacques*," "*Les Sept Cordes de la Lyre*," and "*Les Maitres Mosaistes*," as representing her higher inspirations, her sincerity in expression, and her dramatic powers. They are full of faults; still they show her scope and aim with some fairness, which such of her readers as chance first on such of her books as "*Leone Leoni*" may fail to find; or even such as "*Simon*," and "*Spiridion*," though into the imperfect web of these are woven threads of pure gold. Such is the first impression made by the girl Fiamma, so noble, as she appears before us with the words "*E l'onore;*" such the thought in *Spiridion* of making the apparition the reward of virtue.

The work she is now publishing, "*Consuelo*," with its sequel, "*Baroness de Rudolstadt*," exhibits her genius poised on a firmer pedestal, breathing a serener air. Still it is faulty in conduct, and shows some obliquity of vision. She has not reached the Interpreter's house yet. But when she does, she will have clues to guide many a pilgrim, whom one less tried, less tempted than herself could not help on the way.

FROM A CRITICISM ON "CONSUELO."

* * * * * The work itself cannot fail of innumerable readers, and a great influence, for it counts many of the most significant pulse-beats of the time. Apart from its range of character and fine descriptions, it records some of the mystical apparitions, and attempts to solve some of the problems of the time. How to combine the benefits of the religious life with those of the artist-life in an existence more simple, more full, more human in short, than either of the two hitherto known by these names has been, — this problem is but poorly solved in the "Countess of Rudolstadt," the sequel to Consuelo. It is true, as the English reviewer says, that George Sand is a far better poet than philosopher, and that the chief use she can be of in these matters is, by her great range of observation and fine intuitions, to help to develop the thoughts of the time a little way further. But the sincerity, the reality of all he can obtain from this writer will be highly valued by the earnest man.

In one respect the book is entirely successful—in showing how inward purity and honor may preserve a woman from bewilderment and danger, and secure her a genuine independence. Whoever aims at this is still considered, by unthinking or prejudiced minds, as wishing to despoil the female character of its natural and peculiar loveliness.

It is·supposed that delicacy must imply weakness, and that only an Amazon can stand upright, and have sufficient command of her faculties to confront the shock of adversity, or resist the allurements of tenderness. Miss Bremer, Dumas, and the northern novelist, Andersen, make women who have a tendency to the intellectual life of an artist fail, and suffer the penalties of arrogant presumption, in the very first steps of a career to which an inward vocation called them in preference to the usual home duties. Yet nothing is more obvious than that the circumstances of the time do, more and more frequently, call women to such lives, and that, if guardianship is absolutely necessary to women, many must perish for want of it. There is, then, reason to hope that God may be a sufficient guardian to those who dare rely on him; and if the heroines of the novelists we have named ended as they did, it was for the want of the purity of ambition and simplicity of character which do not permit such as Consuelo to be either unsexed and depraved, or unresisting victims and breaking reeds, if left alone in the storm and crowd of life. To many women this picture will prove a true Consuelo (consolation), and we think even very prejudiced men will not read it without being charmed with the expansion, sweetness and genuine force, of a female character, such as they have not met, but must, when painted, recognize as possible, and may be led to review their opinions, and perhaps to elevate and enlarge their hopes, as to " Woman's sphere " and " Woman's mission." If such insist on what they have heard of the private life of this writer, and refuse to believe

that any good thing can come out of Nazareth, we reply
that we do not know the true facts as to the history of
George Sand. There has been no memoir or notice of her
published on which any one can rely, and we have seen
too much of life to accept the monsters of gossip in
reference to any one. But we know, through her works,
that, whatever the stains on her life and reputation may
have been, there is in her a soul so capable of goodness
and honor as to depict them most successfully in her
ideal forms. It is her works, and not her private life,
that we are considering. Of her works we have means
of judging; of herself, not. But among those who have
passed unblamed through the walks of life, we have not
often found a nobleness of purpose and feeling, a sincere
religious hope, to be compared with the spirit that
breathes through the pages of Consuelo.

The experiences of the artist-life, the grand and
penetrating remarks upon music, make the book a
precious acquisition to all whose hearts are fashioned to
understand such things.

We suppose that we receive here not only the mind
of the writer, but of Liszt, with whom she has publicly
corresponded in the " *Lettres d'un Voyageur.*" None
could more avail us, for " in him also is a spark of the
divine fire," as Beethoven said of Ichubert. We may
thus consider that we have in this book the benefit of the
most electric nature, the finest sensibility, and the bold-
est spirit of investigation combined, expressing themselves
in a little world of beautiful or picturesque forms.

Although there are grave problems discussed, and sad

and searching experiences described in this work, yet its spirit is, in the main, hopeful, serene, almost glad. It is the spirit inspired from a near acquaintance with the higher life of art. Seeing there something really achieved and completed, corresponding with the soul's desires, faith is enlivened as to the eventual fulfilment of those desires, and we feel a certainty that the existence which looks at present so marred and fragmentary shall yet end in harmony. The shuttle is at work, and the threads are gradually added that shall bring out the pattern, and prove that what seems at present confusion is really the way and means to order and beauty.

JENNY LIND,

THE "CONSUELO" OF GEORGE SAND.

JENNY LIND, the prima donna of Stockholm, is among the most distinguished of those geniuses who have been invited to welcome the queen to Germany. Her name has been unknown among us, as she is still young, and has not wandered much from the scene of her first triumphs; but many may have seen, last winter, in the foreign papers, an account of her entrance into Stockholm after an absence of some length. The people received her with loud cries of homage, took the horses from her carriage and drew her home; a tribute of respect often paid to conquerors and statesmen, but seldom, or, as far as we know, never to the priesthood of the muses, who have conferred the higher benefit of raising, refining and exhilarating, the popular mind.

An accomplished Swede, now in this country, communicated to a friend particulars of Jenny Lind's career, which suggested the thought that she might have given the hint for the principal figure in Sand's late famous novel, "Consuelo."

This work is at present in process of translation in "The Harbinger," a periodical published at Brook Farm, Mass.; but, as this translation has proceeded but a little way, and the book in its native tongue is not generally, though it has been extensively, circulated here, we will give a slight sketch of its plan.

It has been a work of deepest interest to those who have looked upon Sand for some years back, as one of the best exponents of the difficulties, the errors, the aspirations, the weaknesses, and the regenerative powers of the present epoch. The struggle in her mind and the experiments of her life have been laid bare to the eyes of her fellow-creatures with fearless openness — fearless not shameless. Let no man confound the bold unreserve of Sand with that of those who have lost the feeling of beauty and the love of good. With a bleeding heart and bewildered feet she sought the truth, and if she lost the way, returned as soon as convinced she had done so; but she would never hide the fact that she had lost it. " What God knows, I dare avow to man," seems to be her motto. It is impossible not to see in her, not only the distress and doubts-of the intellect, but the temptations of a sensual nature; but we see too the courage of a hero and a deep capacity for religion. This mixed nature, too, fits her peculiarly to speak to men so diseased as men are at present. They feel she knows their ailment, and if she find a cure, it will really be by a specific remedy

An upward tendency and growing light are observable in all her works for several years past, till now, in the present, she has expressed such conclusions as forty years of the most varied experience have brought to one who has shrunk from no kind of discipline, yet still cried to God amid it all; one who, whatever you may say

against her, you must feel has never accepted a word for
a thing, or worn one moment the veil of hypocrisy ; and
this person one of the most powerful nature, both as to
passion and action, and of an ardent, glowing genius.
These conclusions are sadly incomplete. There is an
amazing alloy in the last product of her crucible, but
there is also so much of pure gold that the book is
truly a cordial, as its name of Consuelo (consolation)
promises.

The young Consuelo lives as a child the life of a
beggar. Her youth is passed in the lowest circumstances
of the streets of Venice. She brings the more perti-
nacious fire of Spanish blood to be fostered by the cheerful airs of Italy. A vague sense of the benefits to be
derived, from such mingling of various influences, in the
formation of a character, is to be discerned in several
works of art now, when men are really wishing to become
citizens of the world, though old habits still interfere on
every side with so noble a development.

Nothing can be more charming than the first volume,
which describes the young girl amid the common life of
Venice. It is sunny, open, and romantic as the place.
The beauty of her voice, when a little singing-girl in the
streets, arrested the attention of a really great and
severe master, Porpora, who educated her to music. In
this she finds the vent and the echo for her higher self.
Her affections are fixed on a young companion, an
unworthy object, but she does not know him to be so.
She judges from her own candid soul, that all must be
good, and derives from the tie, for a while, the fostering

influences which love alone has for genius. Clear perception follows quickly upon her first triumphs in art. They have given her a rival, and a mean rival, in her betrothed, whose talent, though great, is of an inferior grade to hers; who is vain, every way impure. Her master, Porpora, tries to avail himself of this disappointment to convince her that the artist ought to devote himself to art alone; that private ties must interfere with his perfection and his glory. But the nature of Consuelo revolts against this doctrine, as it would against the seclusion of a convent. She feels that genius requires manifold experience for its development, and that the mind, concentrated on a single object, is likely to pay by a loss of vital energy for the economy of thoughts and time.

Driven by these circumstances into Germany, she is brought into contact with the old noblesse, a very different, but far less charming, atmosphere than that of the gondoliers of Venice. But here, too, the strong, simple character of our Consuelo is unconstrained, if not at home, and when her heart swells and needs expansion, she can sing.

Here the Count de Rudolstadt, Albert, loves Consuelo, which seems, in the conduct of the relation, a type of a religious democracy in love with the spirit of art. We do not mean that any such cold abstraction is consciously intended, but all that is said means this. It shadows forth one of the greatest desires which convulse our age.

A most noble meaning is couched in the history of Albert, and though the writer breaks down under such great attempts, and the religion and philosophy of the book are clumsily embodied compared with its poesy and rhetoric, yet great and still growing thoughts are expressed with sufficient force to make the book a companion of rare value to one in the same phase of mind.

Albert is the aristocratic democrat, such as Alfieri was; one who, in his keen perception of beauty, shares the good of that culture which ages have bestowed on the more fortunate classes, but in his large heart loves and longs for the good of all men, as if he had himself suffered in the lowest pits of human misery. He is all this and more in his transmigration, real or fancied, of soul, through many forms of heroic effort and bloody error; in his incompetency to act at the present time, his need of long silences, of the company of the dead and of fools, and eventually of a separation from all habitual ties, is expressed a great idea, which is still only in the throes of birth, yet the nature of whose life we begin to prognosticate with some clearness.

Consuelo's escape from the castle, and even from Albert, her admiration of him, and her incapacity to love him till her own character be more advanced, are told with great naturalness. Her travels with Joseph Haydn are again as charmingly told as the Venetian life. Here the author speaks from her habitual existence, and far more masterly than of those deep places of thought where she is less at home. She has lived much, discerned much, felt great need of great thoughts, but not been able to think a great way for herself. She fearlessly accompanies the spirit of the age, but she never surpasses it; *that* is the office of the great thinker.

At Vienna Consuelo is brought fully into connection with the great world as an artist. She finds that its realities, so far from being less, are even more harsh and sordid for the artist than for any other; and that with avarice, envy and falsehood, she must prepare for the fearful combat which awaits noble souls in any kind of arena, with the pain of disgust when they cannot raise themselves to patience — with the almost equal pain, when they can, of pity for those who know not what they do.

Albert is on the verge of the grave; and Consuelo, who, not being able to feel for him sufficient love to find in it compensation for the loss of that artist-life to which she feels Nature has destined her, had hitherto resisted the entreaties of his aged father, and the pleadings of her own reverential and tender sympathy with the wants of his soul, becomes his wife just before he dies.

The sequel, therefore, of this history is given under the title of Countess of Rudolstadt. Consuelo is still on the stage; she is at the Prussian court. The well-known features of this society, as given in the memoirs of the time, are put together with much grace and wit. The sketch of Frederic is excellent.

The rest of the book is devoted to expression of the author's ideas on the subject of reform, and especially of association as a means thereto. As her thoughts are yet in a very crude state, the execution of this part is equally bungling and clumsy. Worse: she falsifies the characters of both Consuelo and Albert, — who is revived again by subterfuge of trance,—and stains her best arrangements by the mixture of falsehood and intrigue.

Yet she proceeds towards, if she walks not by, the light of a great idea; and sincere democracy, universal religion, scatter from afar many seeds upon the page for a future time. The book should be, and will be, universally read. Those especially who have witnessed all Sand's doubts and sorrows on the subject of marriage, will rejoice in the clearer, purer ray which dawns upon her now. The most natural and deep part of the book, though not her main object, is what relates to the struggle between the claims of art and life, as to whether it be better for the world and one's self to develop to perfection a talent which Heaven seemed to have assigned as a special gift and vocation, or sacrifice it whenever the character seems to require this for its general development. The character of Consuelo is, throughout the first part, strong, delicate, simple, bold, and pure. The fair lines of this picture are a good deal broken in the second part; but we must remain true to the impression originally made upon us by this charming and noble creation of the soul of Sand.

It is in reference to *our* Consuelo that a correspondent * writes, as to Jenny Lind; and we are rejoiced to find that so many hints were, or might have been, furnished for the picture from real life. If Jenny Lind did not suggest it, yet she must also be, in her own sphere a Consuelo.

* We do not know how accurate is this correspondent's statement of facts. The narrative is certainly interesting. — *Ed.*

"Jenny Lind must have been born about 1822 or 1823. When a young child, she was observed, playing about and singing in the streets of Stockholm, by Mr. Berg, master of singing for the royal opera. Pleased and astonished at the purity and suavity of her voice, he inquired instantly for her family, and found her father, a poor inn-keeper, willing and glad to give up his daughter to his care, on the promise to protect her and give her an excellent musical education. He was always very careful of her, never permitting her to sing except in his presence, and never letting her appear on the stage, unless as a mute figure in some ballet, such, for instance, as Cupid and the Graces, till she was sixteen, when she at once executed her part in 'Der Freyschutz,' to the full satisfaction and surprise of the public of Stockholm. From that time she gradually became the favorite of every one. Without beauty, she seems, from her innocent and gracious manners, beautiful on the stage and charming in society. She is one of the few actresses whom no evil tongue can ever injure, and is respected and welcomed in any and all societies.

"The circumstances that reminded me of Consuelo were these: that she was a poor child, taken up by this singing-master, and educated thoroughly and severely by him; that she loved his son, who was a good-for-nothing fellow like Anzoleto, and at last discarded him; that she refuse the son of an English earl, and, when he fell sick, his father condescended to entreat for him, just as the Count of Rudolstadt did for his son; that, though plain and low in stature, when singing her best parts she appears beautiful, and awakens enthusiastic admiration ; that she is rigidly correct in her demeanor towards her numerous admirers, having even returned a present sent her by the crown-prince, Oscar, in a manner that she deemed equivocal. This last circumstance being noised abroad, the next time she appeared on the stage she was greeted with more enthusiastic plaudits than ever, and thicker showers of flowers fell upon her from the hands of her true friends, the public. She was more fortunate than Consuelo in not being compelled to sing to a public of Prussian corporals."

Indeed, the picture of Frederic's opera-audience, with the pit full of his tall grenadiers with their wives on their shoulders, never daring to applaud except when he gave the order, as if by tap of drum, opposed to the tender and expansive nature of the artist, is one of the best tragicomedies extant. In Russia, too, all is military ; as soon as a new musician arrives, he is invested with a rank in the army. Even in the church Nicholas has lately done the same. It seems as if he could not believe a man to be alive, except in the army ; could not believe the human heart could beat, except by beat of drum. But we believe in Russia there is at least a mask of gayety thrown over the chilling truth. The great Frederic wished no disguise ; everywhere he was chief corporal, and trampled with his everlasting boots the fair flowers of poesy into the dust.

The North has been generous to us of late ; she has sent us *Ole Bull.* She is about to send *Frederika Bremer.* May she add JENNY LIND !

CAROLINE.

THE other evening I heard a gentle voice reading aloud the story of Maurice, a boy who, deprived of the use of his limbs by paralysis, was sustained in comfort, and almost in cheerfulness, by the exertions of his twin sister. Left with him in orphanage, her affections were centred upon him, and, amid the difficulties his misfortunes brought upon them, grew to a fire intense and pure enough to animate her with angelic impulses and powers. As he could not move about, she drew him everywhere in a little cart; and when at last they heard that sea-bathing might accomplish his cure, conveyed him, in this way, hundreds of miles to the sea-shore. Her pious devotion and faith were rewarded by his cure, and (a French story would be entirely incomplete otherwise) with money, plaudits and garlands, from the by-standers.

Though the story ends in this vulgar manner, it is, in its conduct, extremely sweet and touching, not only as to the beautiful qualities developed by these trials in the brother and sister, but in the purifying and softening influence exerted, by the sight of his helplessness and her goodness, on all around them.

Those who are the victims of some natural blight often fulfil this important office, and bless those within their sphere more, by awakening feelings of holy tenderness and compassion, than a man healthy and strong can do by the utmost exertion of his good-will and energies. Thus, in the East, men hold sacred those in whom they find a distortion or alienation of mind which makes them unable to provide for themselves. The well and sane feel themselves the ministers of Providence to carry out a mysterious purpose, while taking care of those who are thus left incapable of taking care of themselves ; and, while fulfilling this ministry, find themselves refined and made better.

The Swiss have similar feelings as to those of their families whom cretinism has reduced to idiocy. They are attended to, fed, dressed clean, and provided with a pleasant place for the day, before doing anything else, even by very busy and poor people.

We have seen a similar instance, in this country, of voluntary care of an idiot, and the mental benefits that ensued. This idiot, like most that are called so, was not without a glimmer of mind.

His teacher was able to give him some notions, both of spiritual and mental facts; at least she thought she had given him the idea of God, and though it appeared by his gestures that to him the moon was the representative of that idea, yet he certainly did conceive of something above him, and which inspired him with reverence and delight. He knew the names of two or three persons who had done him kindness, and when they were mentioned, would point upward, as he did to the moon, showing himself susceptible, in his degree, of Mr. Carlyle's grand method of education, hero-worship. She had awakened in him a love of music, so that he could be soothed in his most violent moods by her gentle singing. It was a most touching sight to see him sitting opposite to her at such times, his wondering and lack-lustre eyes filled with childish pleasure, while in hers gleamed the same pure joy that we may suppose to animate the looks of an angel appointed by Heaven to restore a ruined world.

We knew another instance, in which a young girl became to her village a far more valuable influence than any patron saint who looks down from his stone niche, while his votaries recall the legend of his goodness in days long past.

Caroline lived in a little, quiet country village — quiet as no village can now remain, since the railroad strikes its spear through the peace of country life. She lived alone with a widowed mother, for whom, as well as for herself, her needle won bread, while the mother's strength and skill sufficed to the simple duties of their household. They lived content and hopeful, till, whether from sitting still too much, or some other cause, Caroline became ill, and soon the physician pronounced her spine to be affected, and to such a degree that she was incurable.

This news was a thunder-bolt to the poor little cottage. The mother, who had lost her elasticity of mind, wept in despair; but the young girl, who found so early all the hopes and joys of life taken from her, and that she was seemingly left without any shelter from the storm, had even at first the faith and strength to bow her head in gentleness, and say, " God will provide." She sustained and cheered her mother.

And God did provide. With simultaneous vibration

the hearts of all their circle acknowledged the divine
obligation of love and mutual aid between human beings.
Food, clothing, medicine, service, were all offered freely
to the widow and her daughter.

Caroline grew worse, and was at last in such a state
that she could only be moved upon a sheet, and by the
aid of two persons.   In this toilsome service, and every
other that she required for years, her mother never needed
to ask assistance.   The neighbors took turns in doing all
that was required, and the young girls, as they were growing up, counted it among their regular employments to
work for or read to Caroline.

Not without immediate reward was their service of
love. The mind of the girl, originally bright and pure,
was quickened and wrought up to the finest susceptibility
by the nervous exaltation that often ensues upon affection
of the spine.   The soul, which had taken an upward impulse from its first act of resignation, grew daily more
and more into communion with the higher regions of life,
permanent and pure.   Perhaps she was instructed by
spirits which, having passed through a similar trial of
pain and loneliness, had risen to see the reason why.
However that may be, she grew in nobleness of view and
purity of sentiment, and, as she received more instruction from books also than any other person in her circle,
had from many visitors abundant information as to the
events which were passing around her, and leisure to
reflect on them with a disinterested desire for truth, she
became so much wiser than her companions as to be at
last their preceptress and best friend, and her brief,

gentle comments and counsels were listened to as oracles
from one enfranchised from the films which selfishness
and passion cast over the eyes of the multitude.

The twofold blessing conferred by her presence, both
in awakening none but good feelings in the hearts of
others, and in the instruction she became able to confer,
was such, that, at the end of five years, no member of
that society would have been so generally lamented as
Caroline, had Death called her away.

But the messenger, who so often seems capricious in
his summons, took first the aged mother, and the poor
girl found that life had yet the power to bring her grief,
unexpected and severe.

And now the neighbors met in council. Caroline could
not be left quite alone in the house. Should they take
turns, and stay with her by night as well as by day?

"Not so," said the blacksmith's wife; "the house will
never seem like home to her now, poor thing! and
't would be kind of dreary for her to change about her
nusses so. I'll tell you what; all my children but one
are married and gone off; we have property enough; I
will have a good room fixed for her, and she shall live
with us. My husband wants her to, as much as me."

The council acquiesced in this truly humane arrangement, and Caroline lives there still; and we are assured
that none of her friends dread her departure so much as
the blacksmith's wife.

"'T a'n't no trouble at all to have her," she says,
"and if it was, I should n't care; she is so good and still,

and talks so pretty! It's as good bein' with her as goin' to meetin'!"

De Maistre relates some similar passages as to a sick girl in St. Petersburgh, though his mind dwelt more on the spiritual beauty evinced in her remarks, than on the good she had done to those around her. Indeed, none bless more than those who "only stand and wait." Even if their passivity be enforced by fate, it will become a spiritual activity, if accepted in a faith higher above fate than the Greek gods were supposed to sit enthroned above misfortune.

EVER-GROWING LIVES.

"Age could not wither her, nor custom stale
Her infinite variety."

So was one person described by the pen which has
made a clearer mark than any other on the history of
Man. But is it not surprising that such a description
should apply to so few?

Of two or three women we read histories that correspond with the hint given in these lines. They were
women in whom there was intellect enough to temper and
enrich, heart enough to soften and enliven the entire
being. There was soul enough to keep the body beautiful through the term of earthly existence; for while the
roundness, the pure, delicate lineaments, the flowery
bloom of youth were passing, the marks left in the course
of those years were not merely of time and care, but also
of exquisite emotions and noble thoughts. With such
chisels Time works upon his statues, tracery and fretwork,
well worth the loss of the first virgin beauty of the ala-
baster; while the fire within, growing constantly brighter
and brighter, shows all these changes in the material, as
rich and varied ornaments. The vase, at last, becomes a
lamp of beauty, fit to animate the councils of the great,
or the solitude of the altar.

Two or three women there have been, who have thus grown even more beautiful with age. We know of many more men of whom this is true. These have been heroes, or still more frequently poets and artists; with whom the habitual life tended to expand the soul, deepen and vary the experience, refine the perceptions, and immortalize the hopes and dreams of youth.

They were persons who never lost their originality of character, nor spontaneity of action. Their impulses proceeded from a fulness and certainty of character, that made it impossible they should doubt or repent, whatever the results of their actions might be.

They could not repent, in matters little or great, because they felt that their actions were a sincere exposition of the wants of their souls. Their impulsiveness was not the restless fever of one who must change his place somehow or some-whither, but the waves of a tide, which might be swelled to vehemence by the action of the winds or the influence of an attractive orb, but was none the less subject to fixed laws.

A character which does not lose its freedom of motion and impulse by contact with the world, grows with its years more richly creative, more freshly individual. It is a character governed by a principle of its own, and not by rules taken from other men's experience; and therefore it is that

> " Age cannot wither them, nor custom stale
> Their infinite variety."

Like violins, they gain by age, and the spirit of him who discourseth through them most excellent music,

"Like wine well kept and long,
Heady, nor harsh, nor strong,
With each succeeding year is quaffed
A richer, purer, mellower draught."

Our French neighbors have been the object of humorous satire for their new coinage of terms to describe the heroes of their modern romance. A hero is no hero unless he has "ravaged brows," is "blasé" or "brisé" or "fatigué." His eyes must be languid, and his cheeks hollow. Youth, health and strength, charm no more; only the tree broken by the gust of passion is beautiful, only the lamp that has burnt out the better part of its oil precious, in their eyes. This, with them, assumes the air of caricature and grimace, yet it indicates a real want of this time — a feeling that the human being ought to grow more rather than less attractive with the passage of time, and that the decrease in physical charms would, in a fair and full life, be more than compensated by an increase of those which appeal to the imagination and higher feelings.

A friend complains that, while most men are like music-boxes, which you can wind up to play their set of tunes, and then they stop, in our society the set consists of only two or three tunes at most. That is because no new melodies are added after five-and-twenty at farthest. It is the topic of jest and amazement with foreigners that what is called society is given up so much into the hands of boys and girls. Accordingly it wants spirit, variety and depth of tone, and we find there no historical presences, none of the charms, infinite in variety, of Cleopatra, no heads of Julius Cæsar, overflowing with meanings, as the sun with light:

Sometimes we hear an educated voice that shows us how these things might be altered. It has lost the fresh tone of youth, but it has gained unspeakably in depth, brilliancy, and power of expression. How exquisite its modulations, so finely shaded, showing that all the intervals are filled up with little keys of fairy delicacy and in perfect tune !

Its deeper tones sound the depth of the past ; its more thrilling notes express an awakening to the infinite, and ask a thousand questions of the spirits that are to unfold our destinies, too far-reaching to be clothed in words. Who does not feel the sway of such a voice ? It makes the whole range of our capacities resound and tremble, and, when there is positiveness enough to give an answer, calls forth most melodious echoes.

The human eye gains, in like manner, by time and experience. Its substance fades, but it is only the more filled with an ethereal lustre which penetrates the gazer till he feels as if

> " That eye were in itself a soul,"

and realizes the range of its power

> " To rouse, to win, to fascinate, to melt,
> And by its spell of undefined control
> Magnetic draw the secrets of the soul."

The eye that shone beneath the white locks of Thorwaldsen was such an one, — the eye of immortal youth, the indicator of the man's whole aspect in a future sphere

We have scanned such eyes closely; when near, we saw
that the lids were red, the corners defaced with omi-
nous marks, the orb looked faded and tear-stained; but
when we retreated far enough for its ray to reach us, it
seemed far younger than the clear and limpid gaze of
infancy, more radiant than the sweetest beam in that of
early youth. The Future and the Past met in that
glance.

O for more such eyes! The vouchers of free, of full
and ever-growing lives!

HOUSEHOLD NOBLENESS.

"Mistress of herself, though China fall."

WOMEN, in general, are indignant that the satirist should have made this the climax to his praise of a woman. And yet, we fear, he saw only too truly. What unexpected failures have we seen, literally, in this respect! How often did the Martha blur the Mary out of the face of a lovely woman at the sound of a crash amid glass and porcelain! What sad littleness in all the department thus represented! Obtrusion of the mop and duster on the tranquil meditation of a husband and brother. Impatience if the carpet be defaced by the feet even of cherished friends.

There is a beautiful side, and a good reason here; but why must the beauty degenerate, and give place to meanness?

To Woman the care of home is confided. It is the sanctuary, of which she should be the guardian angel. To all elements that are introduced there she should be the "ordering mind." She represents the spirit of beauty, and her influence should be spring-like, clothing all objects within her sphere with lively, fresh and tender hues.

She represents purity, and all that appertains to her should be kept delicately pure. She is modesty, and draperies should soften all rude lineaments, and exclude glare and dust. She is harmony, and all objects should be in their places ready for, and matched to, their uses.

We all know that there is substantial reason for the offence we feel at defect in any of these ways. A woman who wants purity, modesty and harmony, in her dress and manners, is insufferable ; one who wants them in the arrangements of her house, disagreeable to everybody. She neglects the most obvious ways of expressing what we desire to·see in her, and the inference is ready, that the inward sense is wanting.

It is with no merely gross and selfish feeling that all men commend the good housekeeper, the good nurse. Neither is it slight praise to say of a woman that she does well the honors of her house in the way of hospitality. The wisdom that can maintain serenity, cheerfulness and order, in a little world of ten or twelve persons, and keep ready the resources that are needed for their sustenance and recovery in sickness and sorrow, is the same that holds the stars in their places, and patiently prepares the precious metals in the most secret chambers of the earth. The art of exercising a refined hospitality is a fine art, and the music thus produced only differs from that of the orchestra in this, that in the former case the overture or sonata cannot be played twice in the same manner. It requires that the hostess shall combine true self-respect and repose,

"The simple art of *not too much*,"

with refined perception of individual traits and moods in

character, with variety and vivacity, an ease, grace and gentleness, that diffuse their sweetness insensibly through every nook of an assembly, and call out reciprocal sweetness wherever there is any to be found.

The only danger in all this is the same that besets us in every walk of life; to wit, that of preferring the outward sign to the inward spirit whenever there is cause to hesitate between the two.

" I admire," says Goethe, " the Chinese novels; they express so happily ease, peace and a finish unknown to other nations in the interior arrangements of their homes.

" In one of them I came upon the line, ' I heard the lovely maidens laughing, and found my way to the garden, where they were seated in their light cane-chairs.' To me this brings an immediate animation, by the images it suggests of lightness, brightness and elegance."

This is most true, but it is also most true that the garden-house would not seem thus charming unless its light cane-chairs had lovely, laughing maidens seated in them. And the lady who values her porcelain, that most exquisite product of the peace and thorough-breeding of China, so highly, should take the hint, and remember that unless the fragrant herb of wit, sweetened by kindness, and softened by the cream of affability, also crown her board, the prettiest tea-cups in the world might as well lie in fragments in the gutter, as adorn her social show. The show loses its beauty when it ceases to represent a substance.

Here, as elsewhere, it is only vanity, narrowness and self-seeking, that spoil a good thing. Women would never be too good housekeepers for their own peace and that of others, if they considered housekeeping only as a means to an end. If their object were really the peace and joy of all concerned, they could bear to have their cups and saucers broken more easily than their tempers, and to have curtains and carpets soiled, rather than their hearts by mean and small feelings. But they are brought up to think it is a disgrace to be a bad house-keeper, not because they must, by such a defect, be a cause of suffering and loss of time to all within their sphere, but because all other women will laugh at them if they are so. Here is the vice, — for want of a high motive there can be no truly good action.

We have seen a woman, otherwise noble and magnani-mous in a high degree, so insane on this point as to weep bitterly because she found a little dust on her picture-frames, and torment her guests all dinner-time with excuses for the way in which the dinner was cooked.

We have known others to join with their servants to backbite the best and noblest friends for trifling derelic-tions against the accustomed order of the house. The broom swept out the memory of much sweet counsel and loving-kindness, and spots on the table-cloth were more regarded than those they made on their own loyalty and honor in the most intimate relations.

"The worst of furies is a woman scorned," and the sex, so lively, mobile, impassioned, when passion is aroused at all, are in danger of frightful error, under great temptation. The angel can give place to a more subtle and treacherous demon, though one, generally, of less tantalizing influence, than in the breast of man. In great crises, Woman needs the highest reason to restrain her; but her besetting sin is that of littleness. Just because nature and society unite to call on her for such fineness and finish, she can be so petty, so fretful, so vain, envious and base! O, women, see your danger! See how much you need a great object in all your little actions. You cannot be fair, nor can your homes be fair, unless you are holy and noble. Will you sweep and garnish the house, only that it may be ready for a legion of evil spirits to enter in — for imps and demons of gossip, frivolity, detraction, and a restless fever about small ills? What is the house for, if good spirits cannot peacefully abide there? Lo! they are asking for the bill in more than one well-garnished mansion. They sought a home and found a work-house. Martha! it was thy fault!

"GLUMDALCLITCHES."

THIS title was wittily given by an editor of this city
to the ideal woman demanded in "Woman in the Nineteenth Century." We do not object to it, thinking it
is really desirable that women should grow beyond the
average size which has been prescribed for them. We
find in the last news from Paris these anecdotes of two
who " tower " an inch or more "above their sex," if not
yet of Glumdalclitch stature.

" *Bravissima!* — The 7th of May, at Paris, a young
girl, who was washing linen, fell into the Canal St.
Martin. Those around called out for help, but none ventured to give it. Just then a young lady elegantly
dressed came up and saw the case ; in the twinkling of
an eye she threw off her hat and shawl, threw herself in,
and succeeded in dragging the young girl to the brink,
after having sought for her in vain several times under
the water. This lady was Mlle. Adèle Chevalier, an
actress. She was carried, with the girl she had saved,
into a neighboring house, which she left, after having
received the necessary cares, in a fiacre, and amid the
plaudits of the crowd."

The second anecdote is of a different kind, but displays
a kind of magnanimity still more unusual in this poor
servile world:

" One of our (French) most distinguished painters of sea-subjects, Gudin, has married a rich young English lady, belonging to a family of high rank, and related to the Duke of Wellington. M. Gudin was lately at Berlin at the same time with K——, inspector of pictures to the King of Holland. The King of Prussia desired that both artists should be presented to him, and received Gudin in a very flattering manner; his genius being his only letter of recommendation.

"Monsieur K—— has not the same advantage; but, to make up for it, he has a wife who enjoys in Holland a great reputation for her beauty. The King of Prussia is a cavalier, who cares more for pretty ladies than for genius. So Monsieur and Madame K—— were invited to the royal table — an honor which was not accorded to Monsieur and Madame Gudin.

" Humble representations were made to the monarch, advising him not to make such a marked distinction between the French artist and the Dutch amateur. These failing, the wise counsellors went to Madame Gudin, and, intimating that they did so with the good-will of the king, said that she might be received as cousin to the Duke of Wellington, as daughter of an English general, and of a family which dates back to the thirteenth century. She could, if she wished, avail herself of her rights of birth to obtain the same honors with Madame K——. To sit at the table of the king, she need only cease for a moment to be Madame Gudin, and become once more Lady L——."

Does not all this sound like a history of the seventeenth century? Surely etiquette was never maintained in a more arrogant manner at the court of Louis XIV.

But Madame Gudin replied that her highest pride lay in the celebrated name which she bears at present; that she did not wish to rely on any other to obtain so futile a distinction, and that, in her eyes, the most noble escutcheon was the palette of her husband.

I need not say that this dignified feeling was not comprehended. Madame Gudin was not received at the table, but she had shown the nobleness of her character. For the rest, Madame K——, on arriving at Paris, had the bad taste to boast of having been distinguished above Madame Gudin, and the story reaching the Tuileries, where Monsieur and Madame Gudin are highly favored, excited no little mirth in the circle there.

"ELLEN : OR, FORGIVE AND FORGET."

WE notice this coarsely-written little fiction because it is one of a class which we see growing with pleasure. We see it with pleasure, because, in its way, it is genuine. It is a transcript of the crimes, calumnies, excitements, half-blind love of right, and honest indignation at the sort of wrong which it can discern, to be found in the class from which it emanates.

That class is a large one in our country villages, and these books reflect its thoughts and manners as half-penny ballads do the life of the streets of London. The ballads are not more true to the facts; but they give us, in a coarser form, far more of the spirit than we get from the same facts reflected in the intellect of a Dickens, for instance, or of any writer far enough above the scene to be properly its artist.

So, in this book, we find what Cooper, Miss Sedgwick and Mrs. Kirkland, might see, as the writer did, but could hardly believe in enough to speak of it with such fidelity.

It is a current superstition that country people are more pure and healthy in mind and body than those who live in cities. It may be so in countries of old-established habits, where a genuine peasantry have inherited some of the practical wisdom and loyalty of the past, with most

of its errors. We have our doubts, though, from the
stamp upon literature, always the nearest evidence of
truth we can get, whether, even there, the difference
between town and country life is as much in favor of the
latter as is generally supposed. But in our land, where
the country is at present filled with a mixed population,
who come seeking to be purified by a better life and culture from all the ills and diseases of the worst forms of
civilization, things often *look* worse than in the city;
perhaps because men have more time and room to let their
faults grow and offend the light of day.

There are exceptions, and not a few; but, in a very
great proportion of country villages, the habits of the
people, as to food, air, and even exercise, are ignorant and
unhealthy to the last degree. Their want of all pure
faith, and appetite for coarse excitement, is shown by
continued intrigues. calumnies, and crimes.

We have lived in a beautiful village, where, more favor-
ably placed than any other person in it, both as to withdrawal from bad associations and nearness to good,
we heard inevitably, from domestics, work-people, and
school-children, more ill of human nature than we could
possibly sift were we to elect such a task from all the
newspapers of this city in the same space of time.

We believe the amount of ill circulated by means of
anonymous letters, as described in this book, to be as
great as can be imported in all the French novels (and
that is a bold word). We know ourselves of two or three
cases of morbid wickedness, displayed by means of anonymous letters, that may vie with what puzzled the best wits

of France in a famous law-suit not long since. It is true,
there is, to balance all this, a healthy rebound,— a surprise and a shame; and there are heartily good people,
such as are described in this book, who, having taken a
direction upward, keep it, and cannot be bent downward
nor aside. But, then, the reverse of the picture is of a
blackness that would appall one who came to it with any
idyllic ideas of the purity and peaceful loveliness of
agricultural life.

But what does this prove? Only the need of a dis-
semination of all that is best, intellectually and morally,
through the whole people. Our groves and fields have
no good fairies or genii who teach, by legend or gentle
apparition, the truths, the principles, that can alone preserve the village, as the city, from the possession of the
fiend. Their place must be taken by the school-master,
and he must be one who knows not only "readin',
writin', and 'rithmetic," but the service of God and the
destiny of man. Our people require a thoroughly-dif-
fused intellectual life, a religious aim, such as no people
at large ever possessed before; else they must sink till
they become dregs, rather than rise to become the cream
of creation, which they are too apt to flatter themselves
with the fancy of being already.

The most interesting fiction we have ever read in this
coarse, homely, but genuine class, is one called "Metal-
lek." It may be in circulation in this city; but we
bought it in a country nook, and from a pedlar; and it
seemed to belong to the country. Had we met with it in
any other way it would probably have been to throw it

aside again directly, for the author does not know how to write English, and the first chapters give no idea of his power of apprehending the poetry of life. But happening to read on, we became fixed and charmed, and have retained from its perusal the sweetest picture of life lived in this land, ever afforded us, out of the pale of personal observation. That such things are, private observation has made us sure; but the writers of books rarely seem to have seen them; rarely to have walked alone in an untrodden path long enough to hold commune with the spirit of the scene.

In this book you find the very life; the most vulgar prose, and the most exquisite poetry. You follow the hunter in his path, walking through the noblest and fairest scenes only to shoot the poor animals that were happy there, winning from the pure atmosphere little benefit except to good appetite, sleeping at night in the dirty hovels, with people who burrow in them to lead a life but little above that of the squirrels and foxes. There is throughout that air of room-enough, and free if low forms of human nature, which, at such times, makes bearable all that would otherwise be so repulsive.

But when we come to the girl who is the presiding deity, or rather the tutelary angel of the scene, how are all discords harmonized; how all its latent music poured forth! It is a portrait from the life — it has the mystic charm of fulfilled reality, how far beyond the fairest ideals ever born of thought! Pure, and brilliantly blooming as the flower of the wilderness, she, in like manner, shares while she sublimes its nature. She plays round the most vulgar and rude beings, gentle and caressing, yet unsullied; in her wildness there is nothing cold or savage; her elevation is soft and warm. Never have we seen natural religion more beautifully expressed; never so well discerned the influence of the natural nun, who needs no veil or cloister to guard from profanation the beauty she has dedicated to God, and which only attracts human love to hallow it into the divine.

The lonely life of the girl after the death of her parents, — her fearlessness, her gay and sweet enjoyment of nature, her intercourse with the old people of the neighborhood, her sisterly conduct towards her "suitors," — all seem painted from the life; but the death-bed scene seems borrowed from some sermon, and is not in harmony with the rest.

In this connection we must try to make amends for the stupidity of an earlier notice of the novel, called "Margaret, or the Real and Ideal," &c. At the time of that notice we had only looked into it here and there, and did no justice to a work full of genius, profound in its meaning, and of admirable fidelity to nature in its details. Since then we have really read it, and appreciated the sight and representation of soul-realities; and we have lamented the long delay of so true a pleasure.

A fine critic said, "This is a Yankee novel; or rather let it be called *the* Yankee novel, as nowhere else are the thought and dialect of our villages really represented." Another discovered that it must have been written in Maine, by the perfection with which peculiar features of scenery there are described.

A young girl could not sufficiently express her delight at the simple nature with which scenes of childhood are given, and especially at Margaret's first going to meeting. She had never elsewhere found written down what she had felt.

A mature reader, one of the most spiritualized and harmonious minds we have ever met, admires the depth and fulness in which the workings of the spirit through the maiden's life are seen by the author, and shown to us; but laments the great apparatus with which the consummation of the whole is brought about, and the formation of a new church and state, before the time is yet ripe, under the banner of Mons. Christi.

But all these voices, among those most worthy to be heard, find in the book a *real presence*, and draw from it auspicious omens that an American literature is possible even in our day, because there are already in the mind here existent developments worthy to see the light, gold-fishes amid the moss in the still waters.

For ourselves, we have been most charmed with the way the Real and Ideal are made to weave and shoot rays through one another, in which Margaret bestows on external nature what she receives through books, and wins back like gifts in turn, till the pond and the mythology are alternate sections of the same chapter. We delight in the teachings she receives through Chilion and his violin, till on the grave of "one who tried to love his fellow-men" grows up the full white rose-flower of her life. The ease with which she assimilates the city

life when in it, making it a part of her imaginative tapes-
try, is a sign of the power to which she has grown.

We have much more to think and to say of the book,
as a whole, and in parts; and should the mood and
summer leisure ever permit a familiar and intimate
acquaintance with it, we trust they will be both thought
and said. For the present, we will only add that it
exhibits the same state of things, and strives to point out
such remedies as we have hinted at in speaking of the
little book which heads this notice; itself a rude char-
coal sketch, but if read as hieroglyphics are, pointing to
important meanings and results.

"COURRIER DES ETATS UNIS.

No other nation can hope to vie with the French in the talent of communicating information with ease, vivacity and consciousness. They must always be the best narrators and the best interpreters, so far as presenting a clear statement of outlines goes. Thus they are excellent in conversation, lectures, and journalizing.

After we know all the news of the day, it is still pleasant to read the bulletin of the *"Courrier des Etats Unis."* We rarely agree with the view taken; but as a summary it is so excellently well done, every topic put in its best place, with such a light and vigorous hand, that we have the same pleasure we have felt in fairy tales, when some person under trial is helped by a kind fairy to sort the silks and feathers to their different places, till the glittering confusion assumes the order. — of a kaleidoscope.

Then, what excellent correspondents they have in Paris ! What a humorous and yet clear account we have before us, now, of the Thiers game ! We have traced Guizot through every day with the utmost distinctness, and see him perfectly in the sick-room. Now, here is Thiers, playing with his chess-men, Jesuits, &c. A hundred clumsy English or American papers could not make the present crisis in Paris so clear as we see it in the glass of these nimble Frenchmen.

Certainly it is with newspaper-writing as with food; the English and Americans have as good appetites, but do not, and never will, know so well how to cook as the French. The Parisian correspondent of the *"Schnellpost"* also makes himself merry with the play of M. Thiers. Both speak with some feeling of the impressive utterance of Lamartine in the late debates. The Jesuits stand their ground, but there is a wave advancing which will not fail to wash away what ought to go, — nor are its roarings, however much in advance of the wave itself, to be misinterpreted by intelligent ears. The world is raising its sleepy lids, and soon no organization can exist which from its very nature interferes in any way with the good of the whole.

In Germany the terrors of the authorities are more and more directed against the communists. They are very anxious to know what communism really is, or means. They have almost forgotten, says the correspondent, the repression of the Jews, and like objects, in this new terror. Meanwhile, the Russian Emperor has issued an edict, commanding the Polish Jews, both men and women, to lay aside their national garb. He hopes thus to mingle them with the rest of the mass he moves. It will be seen whether such work can be done by beginning upon the outward man.

The Paris correspondent of the *"Courrier,"* who gives an account of amusements, has always many sprightly passages illustrative of the temper of the times. Horse-races are now the fashion, in which he rejoices, as being likely to give to France good horses of her own. A famous lottery is on the point of coming off.— to give an organ to the Church of St. Eustache,— on which it does not require a very high tone of morals to be severe. A public exhibition has been made of the splendid array of prizes, including every article of luxury, from jewels and cashmere shawls down to artificial flowers.

A nobleman, president of the Horticultural Society, had given an entertainment, in which the part of the different flowers was acted by beautiful women, that of fruit and vegetables by distinguished men. Such an amusement would admit of much light grace and wit, which may still be found in France, if anywhere in the world.

There is also an amusing story of the stir caused among the French political leaders by the visit of a n)ble-man of one of the great English families, to Paris. " He had had several audiences, previous to his departure from London, of Queen Victoria; he received a despatch daily from the English court. But in reply to all overtures made to induce him to open his mission, he preserved a gloomy silence. All attentions, all signs of willing confidence, are lavished on him in vain. France is troubled. ' Has England,' thought she, ' a secret from us, while we have none from her?' She was on the point of inventing one, when, lo ! the secret mission turns out to be the preparation of a ball-dress, with whose elegance, fresh from Parisian genius, her Britannic majesty wished to dazzle and surprise her native realm."

'T is a pity Americans cannot learn the grace which

decks these trifling jests with so much prettiness. Till we can import something of that, we have no right to rejoice in French fashions and French wines. Such a nervous, driving nation as we are, ought to learn to fly along gracefully, on the light, fantastic toe. Can we not learn something of the English beside the knife and fork conventionalities which, with them, express a certain solidity of fortune and resolve? Can we not get from the French something beside their worst novels?

' COURRIER DES ETATS UNIS."

OUR PROTEGEE, QUEEN VICTORIA.

THE *Courrier* laughs, though with features somewhat too disturbed for a graceful laugh, at a notice, published a few days since in the *Tribune*, of one of its jests which scandalized the American editor. It does not content itself with a slight notice, but puts forth a manifesto, in formidably large type, in reply.

With regard to the jest itself, we must remark that Mr. Greeley saw this only in a translation, where it had lost whatever of light and graceful in its manner excused a piece of raillery very coarse in its substance. We will admit that, had he seen it as it originally stood, connected with other items in the playful chronicle of Pierre Durand, it would have impressed him differently.

But the cause of irritation in the *Courrier*, and of the sharp repartees of its manifesto, is, probably, what was said of the influence among us of " French literature and French morals," to which the " organ of the French-American population " felt called on to make a spirited reply, and has done so with less of wit and courtesy than could have been expected from the organ of a people who, whatever may be their faults, are at least acknowledged in wit and courtesy preëminent. We hope that the French who come to us will not become, in these respects, Americanized, and substitute the easy sneer, and use of such terms as "ridiculous," "virtuous misanthropy," &c., for the graceful and poignant raillery of their native land, which tickles even where it wounds.

We may say, in reply to the *Courrier*, that if Fourierism "recoils towards a state of nature," it arises largely from the fact that its author lived in a country where the natural relations are, if not more cruelly, at least more lightly violated, than in any other of the civilized world. The marriage of convention has done its natural office in sapping the morals of France, till breach of the marriage vow has become one of the chief topics of its daily wit, one of the acknowledged traits of its manners, and a favorite — in these modern times we might say *the* favorite — subject of its works of fiction. From the time of Molière, himself an agonized sufferer behind his comic mask from the infidelities of a wife he was not able to cease to love, through memoirs, novels, dramas, and the volleyed squibs of the press, one fact stares us in the face as one of so common occurrence, that men, if they have not ceased to suffer in heart and morals from its poisonous action, have yet learned to bear with a shrug and a careless laugh that marks its frequency. Understand, we do not say that the French are the most deeply stained with vice of all nations. We do not think them so. There are others where there is as much, but there is none where it is so openly acknowledged in literature, and therefore there is none whose literature alone is so likely to deprave inexperienced minds, by familiarizing them with wickedness before they have known the lure and the shock of passion. And we believe that this is the very worst way for youth to be misled, since the miasma thus pervades the whole man, and he is corrupted in head and heart at once, without one strengthening effort at resistance.

Were it necessary, we might substantiate what we say by quoting from the *Courrier* within the last fortnight, jokes and stories such as are not to be found *so frequently* in the prints of any other nation. There is the story of the girl Adelaide, which, at another time, we mean to quote, for its terrible pathos. There is a man on trial for the murder of his wife, of whom the witnesses say, "he was so fond of her you would never have known she was his wife!" Here is one, only yesterday, where a man kills a woman to whom he was married by his relatives at eighteen, she being much older, and disagreeable to him, but their properties matching. After twelve years' marriage, he can no longer support the yoke, and kills both her and her father, and "his only regret is that he cannot kill all who had anything to do with the match."

Either infidelity or such crimes are the natural result of marriages made as they are in France, by agreement between the friends, without choice of the parties. It is this horrible system, and not a native incapacity for pure and permanent relations, that leads to such results.

We must observe, *en passant,* that this man was the father of five children by this hated woman — a wickedness not peculiar to France or any nation, and which cannot fail to do its work of filling the world with sickly, weak,

or depraved beings, who have reason to curse their brutal
father that he does not murder them as well as their
wretched mother, — who, more unhappy than the victim
of seduction, is made the slave of sense in the name of
religion and law.

The last steamer brings us news of the disgrace of
Victor Hugo, one of the most celebrated of the literary
men of France, and but lately created one of her peers.
The affair, however, is to be publicly " hushed up."

But we need not cite many instances to prove, what is
known to the whole world, that these wrongs are, if not
more frequent, at least more lightly treated by the
French, in literature and discourse, than by any nation
of Europe. This being the case, can an American, anxious that his country should receive, as her only safe-
guard from endless temptations, good moral instruction
and mental food, be otherwise than grieved at the pro-
miscuous introduction among us of their writings ?

We know that there are in France good men, pure books,
true wit. But there is an immensity that is bad, and
more hurtful to our farmers, clerks and country milliners,
than to those to whose tastes it was originally addressed,—
as the small-pox is most fatal among the wild men of the
woods,—and this, from the unprincipled cupidity of pub-
lishers, is broad-cast recklessly over all the land we had
hoped would become a healthy asylum for those before
crippled and tainted by hereditary abuses. This cannot
be prevented ; we can only make head against it, and
show that there is really another way of thinking and
living —ay, and another voice for it in the world. We

are naturally on the alert, and if we sometimes start too quickly, that is better than to play " *Le noir Faine-ant* " — (The Black Sluggard).

We are displeased at the unfeeling manner in which the *Courrier* speaks of those whom he calls *our models*. He did. not misunderstand us, and some things he says on this subject deserve and suggest a retort that would be bitter. But we forbear, because it would injure the innocent with the guilty. The *Courrier* ranks the editor of the *Tribune* among " the men who have undertaken an ineffectual struggle against the perversities of this lower world." By *ineffectual* we presume he means that it has never succeeded in exiling evil from this lower world. We are proud to be ranked among the band of those who at least, in the ever-memorable words of Scripture, have " done what they could " for this purpose. To this band belong all good men of all countries, and France has contributed no small contingent of those whose purpose was noble, whose lives were healthy, and whose minds, even in their lightest moods, pure. We are better pleased to act as sutler or pursuivant of this band, whose strife the *Courrier* thinks so *impuissante*, than to reap the rewards of efficiency on the other side. There is not too much of this salt, in proportion to the whole mass that needs to be salted, nor are " occasional accesses of virtuous misanthropy " the worst of maladies in a world that affords such abundant occasion for it.

In fine, we disclaim all prejudice against the French nation. We feel assured that all, or almost all, impartial minds will acquiese in what we say as to the tone of lax morality, in reference to marriage, so common in their literature. We do not like it, in joke or in earnest; neither are we of those to whom vice " loses most of its deformity by losing all its grossness." If there be a deep and ulcerated wound, we think the more " the richly-embroidered veil " is torn away the better. Such a deep social wound exists in France; we wish its cure, as we wish the health of all nations and of all men; so far indeed would we " recoil towards a state of nature." We believe that nature wills marriage and parentage to be kept sacred. The fact of their not being so is to us not a pleasant subject of jest; and we should really pity the first lady of England for injury here, though she be a queen; while the ladies of the French court, or of Parisian society, if they willingly lend themselves to be the subject of this style of jest, or find it agreeable when made, must be to us the cause both of pity and disgust. We are not unaware of the great and beautiful qualities native to the French — of their chivalry, their sweetness of temper, their rapid, brilliant and abundant genius. We would wish to see these qualities restored to their native lustre, and not receive the base alloy which has long stained the virginity of the gold.

ON BOOKS OF TRAVEL.*

* * * * * * AMONG those we have, the best, as to observation of particulars and lively expression, are by women. They are generally ill prepared as regards previous culture, and their scope is necessarily narrower than that of men, but their tact and quickness help them a great deal. You can see their minds grow by what they feed on, when they travel. There are many books of travel, by women, that are, at least, entertaining, and contain some penetrating and just observations. There has, however, been none since Lady Mary Wortley Montague, with as much talent, liveliness, and preparation to observe in various ways, as she had.

* It need not be said, probably, that Margaret Fuller did not think the fact that books of travel by women have generally been piquant and lively rather than discriminating and instructive, a result of their nature, and therefore unavoidable ; on the contrary, she regarded woman as naturally more penetrating than man, and the fact that in journeying she would see more of home-life than he, would give her a great advantage, — but she did believe woman needed a wider culture, and then she would not fail to *excel* in writing books of travels. The merits now in such works she considered striking and due to woman's natural quickness and availing herself of all her facilities, and any deficiencies simply proved the need of a broader education. — [EDIT.]

A good article appeared lately in one of the English periodicals, headed by a long list of travels by women. It was easy to observe that the personality of the writer was the most obvious thing in each and all of these books, and that, even in the best of them, you travelled with the writer as a charming or amusing companion, **rather** than as an accomplished or instructed guide.

REVIEW OF "MEMOIRS AND ESSAYS, BY MRS. JAMESON."

MRS. JAMESON appears to be growing more and more desperately modest, if we may judge from the motto:

> " What if the little rain should say,
>   ' So small a drop as I
>   Can ne'er refresh the thirsty plain,—
>   I 'll tarry in the sky ? ' "

and other superstitious doubts and disclaimers proffered in the course of the volume. We thought the time had gone by when it was necessary to plead " request of friends " for printing, and that it was understood now-a-days that, from the facility of getting thoughts into print, literature has become not merely an archive for the preservation of great thoughts, but a means of general communication between all classes of minds, and all grades of culture.

If writers write much that is good, and write it well, they are read much and long; if the reverse, people simply pass them by, and go in search of what is more interesting. There needs be no great fuss about publishing or not publishing. Those who forbear may rather be considered the vain ones, who wish to be distinguished among the crowd. Especially this extreme modesty looks superfluous in a person who knows her thoughts have been received with interest for ten or twelve years back. We do not like this from Mrs. Jameson, because we think she would be amazed if others spoke of her as this little humble flower, doubtful whether it ought to raise its head to the light. She should leave such affectations to her aunts ; they were the fashion in their day.

It is very true, however, that she should *not* have published the very first paragraph in her book, which presents an inaccuracy and shallowness of thought quite amazing in a person of her fine perceptions, talent and culture. We allude to the contrast she attempts to establish between Raphael and Titian, in placing mind in contradistinction to beauty, as if beauty were merely physical. Of course she means no such thing ; but the passage means this or nothing, and, as an opening to a paper on art, is indeed reprehensible and fallacious.

The rest of this paper, called the House of Titian, is full of pleasant chat, though some of the judgments — that passed on Canaletti's pictures, for instance — are opposed to those of persons of the purest taste ; and in other respects, such as in speaking of the railroad to Venice, Mrs. Jameson is much less wise than those over whom she assumes superiority. The railroad will destroy Venice ; the two things cannot coëxist ; and those who do not look upon that wondrous dream in this age, will, probably, find only vestiges of its existence.

The picture of Adelaide Kemble is very pretty, though there is an attempt of a sort too common with Mrs.

Jameson to make more of the subject than it deserves Adelaide Kemble was not the true artist, or she could not so soon or so lightly have stept into another sphere. It is enough to paint her as a lovely woman, and a woman-genius. The true artist cannot forswear his vocation; Heaven does not permit it; the attempt makes him too unhappy, nor will he form ties with those who can consent to such sacrilege. Adelaide Kemble loved art, but was not truly an artist.

The "Xanthian Marbles," and "Washington Allston," are very pleasing papers. The most interesting part, however, are the sentences copied from Mr. Allston. These have his chaste, superior tone. We copy some of them.

"What *light* is in the natural world, such is *fame* in the intellectual, — both requiring an *atmosphere* in order to become perceptible. Hence the fame of Michel Angelo is to some minds a nonentity; even as the Sun itself would be invisible *in vacuo.*"

(A very pregnant statement, containing the true reason why "no man is a hero to his valet de chambre.")

" Fame does not depend on the will of any man; but reputation may be given and taken away; for fame is the sympathy of kindred intellects, and sympathy is not a subject of *willing ;* while reputation, having its source in the popular voice, is a sentence which may be altered or suppressed at pleasure. Reputation, being essentially contemporaneous, is always at the mercy of the envious and ignorant. But Fame, whose very birth is posthumous, and which is only known to exist by the echoes of its footsteps through congenial minds, can neither be increased nor diminished by any degree of wilfulness."

"An original mind is rarely understood until it has been *reflected* from some half-dozen congenial with it; so averse are men to admitting the true in an unusual form; while any novelty, however fantastic, however false, is greedily swallowed. Nor is this to be wondered at, for all truth demands a response, and few people care to *think*, yet they must have something to supply the place of thought. Every mind would appear original if every man had the power of projecting his own into the minds of others."

"All effort at originality must end either in the quaint or monstrous; for no man knows himself as an original; he can only believe it on the report of others to whom he is made known, as he is by the projecting power before spoken of."

"There is an essential meanness in wishing to get the better of any one. The only competition worthy of a wise man is with himself."

"Reverence is an ennobling sentiment; it is felt to be degrading only by the vulgar mind, which would escape the sense of its own littleness by elevating itself into the antagonist of what is above it."

"He that has no pleasure in looking up is not fit to look down; of such minds are the mannerists in art, and in the world — the tyrants of all sorts."

"Make no man your idol; for the best man must have faults, and his faults will naturally become yours, in addition to your own. This is as true in art as in morals."

"The Devil s heartiest laugh is at a detracting witti-
cism. Hence the phrase 'devilish good' has sometimes a
literal meaning."

"Woman's Mission and Woman's Position" is an excellent paper, in which plain truths are spoken with an
honorable straight-forwardness, and a great deal of good
feeling. We despise the woman who, knowing such
facts, is afraid to speak of them; yet we honor one, too,
who does the plain right thing, for she exposes herself to
the assaults of vulgarity, in a way painful to a person who
has not strength to find shelter and repose in her motives.
We recommend this paper to the consideration of all
those, the unthinking, wilfully unseeing million, who are
in the habit of talking of "Woman's sphere," as if it
really were, at present, for the majority, one of protection, and the gentle offices of home. The rhetorical
gentlemen and silken dames, who, quite forgetting their
washerwomen, their seamstresses, and the poor hirelings
for the sensual pleasures of Man, that jostle them daily in
the streets, talk as if women need be fitted for no other
chance than that of growing like cherished flowers in the
garden of domestic love, are requested to look at this
paper, in which the state of women, both in the manufacturing and agricultural districts of England, is exposed
with eloquence, and just inferences drawn.

"This, then, is what I mean when I speak of the
anomalous condition of women in these days. I would
point out, as a primary source of incalculable mischief, the
contradiction between her assumed and her real position;
between what is called her proper sphere by the laws of

God and Nature, and what has become her real sphere by the laws of necessity, and through the complex relations of artificial existence. In the strong language of Carlyle, I would say that ' Here is a lie standing up in the midst of society.' I would say 'Down with it, even to the ground ; ' for while this perplexing and barbarous anomaly exists, fretting like an ulcer at the very heart of society, all new specifics and palliatives are in vain. The question must be settled one way or another ; either let the man in all the relations of life be held the natural guardian of the woman, constrained to fulfil that trust, responsible in society for her well-being and her maintenance ; or, if she be liable to be thrust from the sanctuary of home, to provide for herself through the exercise of such faculties as God has given her, let her at least have fair play ; let it not be avowed in the same breath that protection is necessary to her, and that it is refused her ; and while we send her forth into the desert, and bind the burthen on her back, and put the staff in her hand, let not her steps be beset, her limbs fettered, and her eyes blindfolded." Amen.

The sixth and last of these papers, on the relative social position of " mothers and governesses," exhibits in true and full colors a state of things in England, beside which the custom in some parts of China of drowning female infants looks mild, generous, and refined ; — an accursed state of things, beneath whose influence nothing can, and nothing ought to thrive. Though this paper, of which we have not patience to speak further at this moment, is valuable from putting the facts into due relief, it is very inferior to the other, and shows the want of thoroughness and depth in Mrs. Jameson's intellect. She has taste, feeling and knowledge, but she cannot think out a subject thoroughly, and is unconsciously tainted and hampered by conventionalities. Her advice to the governesses reads like a piece of irony, but we believe it was not meant as such. Advise them to be burnt at the stake at once, rather than submit to this slow process of petrifaction. She is as bad as the Reports of the "Society for the relief of distressed and dilapidated Governesses." We have no more patience. We must go to England ourselves, and see these victims under the water torture. Till then, à Dieu !

WOMAN'S INFLUENCE OVER THE INSANE.

In reference to what is said of entrusting an infant to the insane, we must relate a little tale which touched the heart in childhood from the eloquent lips of the mother.

The minister of the village had a son of such uncommon powers that the slender means on which the large family lived were strained to the utmost to send him to college. The boy prized the means of study as only those under such circumstances know how to prize them ; indeed.far beyond their real worth ; since, by excessive study, prolonged often at the expense of sleep, he made himself insane.

All may conceive the feelings of the family when their star returned to them again, shorn of its beams; their pride, their hard-earned hope, sunk to a thing so hopeless, so helpless, that there could be none so poor to do him reverence. But they loved him, and did what the ignorance of the time permitted. There was little provision then for the treatment of such cases, and what there was was of a kind that they shrunk from resorting to, if it could be avoided. They kept him at home, giving him, during the first months, the freedom of the house ; but on his making an attempt to kill his father, and confessing afterwards that his old veneration had, as is so often the case in these affections, reäcted morbidly to its opposite, so that he never saw a once-loved parent turn his back without thinking how he could rush upon him and do him an injury, they felt obliged to use harsher measures, and chained him to a post in one room of the house.

There, so restrained, without exercise or proper medicine, the fever of insanity came upon him in its wildest form. He raved, shrieked, struck about him, and tore off all the raiment that was put upon him.

One of his sisters, named Lucy, whom he had most loved when well, had now power to soothe him. He would listen to her voice, and give way to a milder mood when she talked or sang. But this favorite sister married, went to her rew home, and the maniac became wilder, more violent than ever.

After two or three years, she returned, bringing with her an infant. She went into the room where the naked, blaspheming, raging object was confined. He knew her instantly, and felt joy at seeing her.

"But, Lucy," said he, suddenly, " is that your baby you have in your arms? Give it to me, I want to hold it !"

A pang of dread and suspicion shot through the young mother's heart, — she turned pale and faint. Her brother was not at that moment so mad that he could not understand her fears.

"Lucy," said he, "do you suppose I would hurt *your* child?"

His sister had strength of mind and of heart; she could not resist the appeal, and hastily placed the child in his arms. Poor fellow ! he held it awhile, stroked its little face, and melted into tears, the first he had shed since his insanity.

For some time after that he was better, and probably, had he been under such intelligent care as may be had at present, the crisis might have been followed up, and a favorable direction given to his disease. But the subject was not understood then, and, having once fallen mad, he was doomed to live and die a madman.

POCAHONTAS.*

YESTERDAY, the 4th July, we passed in looking through this interesting work. The feelings and reflections it induced were in harmony with the aspect of the day, a day of gloom, of searching chill and dripping skies. We were very sorry for all the poor laborers and children whom the weather deprived of pleasure on the pleasantest occasion of their year — most of all for those poor children of the Farm Schools on this, perhaps, the first holiday of their dull, narrow little lives. But the mourning aspect of the day seemed to us most appropriate. The boys and boyish young men were letting off their crackers and revelling in smoke and hubbub all day long; a din not more musical, of empty panegyric and gratulation, was going on within the halls of oratory; the military were parading our profaned banners. But the sweet heavens, conscious of the list of wrongs by which this nation, in its now more than threescore years and ten of independent existence, has abused the boon, veiled themselves in crape and wept.

---

* Memoirs, Official and Personal; with Sketches of Travel among the Northern and Southern Indians. By Thomas L. M'Kenney, late Chief of the Bureau of Indian Affairs.

The nation may wrap itself in callousness and stop its ears to every cry except that of profit or loss; it may build its temples of wood and stone, and hope, by formal service of the lips, to make up for that paid to Mammon in the spirit, but God is not mocked; it is all recorded, all known. The want of honor and even honorable sentiment shown by this people in the day of repudiation; the sin of slavery and the conduct of the slaveholder, who, at first pretending that he wished, if possible, to put an end to this curse of unlawful bondage, has now unveiled his falsehood by the contrivance and consummation of a plan to perpetuate it, if possible, through all ages; the intolerance and bigotry which disgrace a country whose fundamental idea affords them no excuse, shown in a thousand ways and on every side, but, of late, in a most flagrant form, through the murder of the Mormon leader, the expulsion of his followers, and their persecution even while passing out of these borders, persecution of precisely the same kind, excused on the same grounds, as that with which the Egyptians pursued the Hebrews; these things must make every thoughtful spirit sad. And to these must be added the war which at present engages us, at whose very triumphs those who have steady intellect or steady principle must look with an aching heart, and which the Louisiana *Marseillaise* is fain to celebrate in such terms as these:

> "Levez vous! fils de l'Amerique,
> La patrie invoque vos bras,

Verrez vous le *faible Mexique,*
Ravager, piller vos Etats! "

" Rise, sons of America, your country demands your aid, will you see
feeble Mexico ravage, pillage your States! "

And even in this city they were not ashamed to
pen and sing verses calling on the citizens to fight in
defence of " liberty," as if it were not the Mexicans
alone, the *feeble* Mexicans, that were fighting in defence of their rights, and we for liberty to do our
pleasure.

But of all these plague-spots there is none from
which we feel such burning pain of shame and indignation, as from the conduct of this nation toward the
Indians. Spoliation, aggression, falsehood of the blackest character, a hundred times repeated, each time with
increased shamelessness, mark every step of this intercourse. If good men have sometimes interposed, it is
but as a single human arm might strive to stay the
torrent. The sense of the nation has been throughout, " Might makes Right ; we will get what we
want at any rate. What does it signify what becomes
of the Indians ? They are red. They are unlike us
in character and person. Let them save themselves
if they can, the Indian dogs." During the last twenty-five years these proceedings have assumed a still
darker shade, and it has been the effort of public and
private avarice alike to drive the Indians beyond the
Mississippi. Treaties have been made by treachery,
signed only by a minority of the tribes, then en-

forced by our Government so long as they served its
purpose, broken then and new ones made and adhered
to with the same fidelity. How bitter is the satire
of the Indian phrase, "*A White Man's Treaty!*"
How just and natural the reply to the missionary who
urged upon them the religious benefit of becoming
Christians. "Christians! — Why, the white men are
Christians!"

Most of the facts on these subjects contained in
Colonel M'Kenney's book we knew before; but they
are here detailed in their full force by one intimately
connected, often an eye-witness, and whose benevolence, liberal views, and manly sympathy had made
him a "beloved brother" to the red man. He can
conclusively show the falsehood of the pretext that the
Indians are incapable of civilization, a pretext, indeed,
refuted by all who please to look at it, and by the prospects of the Cherokees, if they had not been so wick-
edly arrested in their progress. He can show how
open they are to the advice of any friend who they
think has judgment combined with sympathy for their
sad and difficult position. This reliance is expressed
toward Colonel M'Kenney with the most touching
simplicity by these stalwart men, childlike because
representing a race reduced to the weakness of childhood.

"Brother: We have opened our ears wide to your
talk; we have not lost a word of it. We were happy
and our hearts grew big, when we heard you had come

to our country. We have always thought of you **as**
our friend ; we have confidence in you ; we have listened more close, because we think so much of you;
we know well you would not deceive us, and we believe you know what is best for us and for our children. Brother, do not you forsake us. Our friends,
as you told us, are few — we have none to spare —
we know that."

How deeply affecting are the images in the following magnificent speech of the Choctaw chief!

SPEECH OF COLONEL COBB,

*Head Mingo of the Choctaws, East of the Mississippi, in reply to
the Agent of the United States.*

" Brother — We have heard your talk as from the
lips of our father, the great white chief at Washington,
and my people have called upon me to speak to you.
The red man has no books, and when he wishes to
make known his views, like his father before him, he
speaks from his mouth. He is afraid of writing.
When he speaks he knows what he says ; the Great
Spirit hears him. Writing is the invention of the
pale-faces ; it gives birth to error and to feuds. The
Great Spirit talks — we hear him in the thunder —
in the rushing winds and the mighty waters — but
he never writes.

" Brother — When you were young we were strong,

we fought by your side; but our arms are now broken. You have grown large : my people have become small.

"Brother — My voice is weak ; you can scarcely hear me ; it is not the shout of a warrior, but the wail of an infant. I have lost it in wailing over the misfortunes of my people. These are their graves, and in those aged pines you hear the ghosts of the departed. Their ashes are here, and we have been left to protect them. Our warriors are nearly all gone to the far country west ; but here are our dead. Shall we go, too, and give their bones to the wolves ?

"Brother — Two sleeps have passed since we heard you talk. We have thought upon it. You ask us to leave our country, and tell us it is our father's wish. We would not desire to displease our father. We respect him, and you his child. But the Choctaw always thinks. We want time to answer.

"Brother — Our hearts are full. Twelve winters ago our chiefs sold our country. Every warrior that you see here was opposed to the treaty. If the dead could have been counted, it could never have been made; but, alas! though they stood around, they could not be seen or heard. Their tears came in the raindrops, and their voices in the wailing wind, but the pale-faces knew it not, and our land was taken away.

"Brother — We do not now complain. The Choctaw suffers, but never weeps. You have the strong arm, and we cannot resist : but the pale-face worships the Great Spirit. So does the red man. The Great Spirit loves truth. When you took our country you promised us land. There is your promise in the book. Twelve times have the trees dropped their leaves, yet we have received no land. Our houses have been taken from us. The white man's plough turns up the bones of our fathers. We dare not kindle our fires; and yet you said we might remain, and you would give us land.

" Brother — Is this *truth?* But we believe now our great father knows our condition, he will listen to us. We are as mourning orphans in our country ; but our father will take us by the hand. When he fulfils his promise, we will answer his talk. He means well. We know it. But we cannot think now. Grief has made children of us. When our business is settled, we shall be men again, and talk to our great father about what he has proposed.

" Brother — You stand in the moccasons of a great chief, you speak the words of a mighty nation, and your talk was long. My people are small, their shadow scarcely reaches to your knee ; they are scattered and gone ; when I shout, I hear my voice in the depth of the woods, but no answering shout comes back. My words, therefore, are few. I have nothing more to say, but to request you to tell what I have said to the tall chief of the pale-faces."

Still more affecting, however, is the address of

Lowrey, the now acting chief of the Cherokees, to the Christian community of the United States, published in our papers a few days since. It is affecting, not from its eloquence, like the preceding, but from its broken-hearted, subdued tone as overpoweringly pathetic, from this once great, strong, seemingly indomitable race, as when the perishing Cæsar cries, "Give me some drink, Titinius, — like a sick girl." He appeals to the Christian community, which to-day has been dozing in the churches over texts of Scripture which they apply only to the by-gone day, while there is before them at this moment such a mighty appeal for sympathy, for justice, such wrong to be set right, such service to be done in obedience to the gospel, "Love one another!" — "Feed my lambs!" — "Go forth to the Gentile!" O Jesus! how dare we say to thee, "Lord, Lord"? Can there be hope of avoiding the repulse — "Depart from me, I never knew ye."

Colonel M'Kenney, in showing the mistakes that have been made, and the precious opportunities lost of doing right and good to the Indians, shows also that, at this very moment, another such opportunity is presented, probably the last. We bespeak attention to this plan. We do not restate it here, preferring the public should be led to it by gradual steps, through his own book, which we hope to see in general circulation. We shall content ourselves with repeating that the time to attend to the subject, get information and act, is NOW, or never. A very short time and it will be

too late to release ourselves, in any measure, from the
weight of ill-doing, or preserve any vestiges of a race,
one large portion of the creation of God, and whose
life and capacities ought by all enlightened and honest, not to say religious, minds to be held infinitely
precious, if only as a part of the history of the human
family.

The details of conduct in General Jackson are very
characteristic. That a man so incompetent should
have been placed in so responsible a position at such
a crisis, merely because he had a ray of genius, some
fine instincts, and represented the war spirit in the
country, was very sad and fatal. Happy those who opposed it, vanquished though they were! The account
of Osceola's and the Agent's conduct relatively at the
time when the Indian thrust his knife into the treaty,
on being urged, as if he had been a sullen school-boy,
to make his mark, is a history in little of the whole relation between the two races. No wonder Osceola, on
his death-bed, painted his face red, in token of eternal
enmity to the whites.

This work is embellished with many appropriate designs, and, as frontispiece to the second volume, boasts
a colored lithograph portrait of POCAHONTAS, from an
undoubted original, painted in London in 1616.* The

* A copy of this portrait, of a larger size than that in the volume, was
presented to my sister by Colonel M'Kenney as a token of his appreciation
of her sympathy for the Indian race. This portrait was much valued by
Margaret, and is now carefully preserved by me. — ED.

face is extremely lovely, the eye has the wild, sweet look of the Indian women, with more fulness of soul than they usually possess; the lips, too, are full, the upper one too much so for regular beauty, but very expressive of tenderness and generosity. The skin has that golden lustre which makes the Indian complexion as beautiful, compared with the swarthy or dingy red, as the softest blonde is, compared to the coarse or tarnished skins so common among Europeans. The hair is flowing and slightly curled; the dress, a rich green, lined and faced with white, leaving bare the neck and the lower part of the arms, is very beautiful and no less becoming. The possession of so fair a copy of a beloved original would, of itself, alone, make the book a desirable possession to many.

All men love Pocahontas for the angelic impulse of tenderness and pity that impelled her to the rescue of Smith. We love her for a sympathy with our race which seemed instinctive and marked her as an instrument of Destiny. Yet we pity her, too, for being thus made a main agent in the destruction of her own people, and sympathize much with Philip, Pontiac, Tecumseh, Nappier, who died in defence of the stock from which they sprang. Of the tender mercies which were to be the reward of every kindness conferred by the red upon the white man, we have a sample in the way in which Smith meets, in *his* native land, the lovely heroine who had saved his life. She, alone, among strangers, rushes to him, calls him *father*, secure of a kind welcome to his heart. He, entrenched in cold conventional restraints, takes her hand and leads her to a chair, addresses her as Miss or Madam, and freezes back at once the warm, gushing stream of her affections with the ice of civic life.

A comment upon this is found in the position of the Indian boys brought up by Colonel M'Kenney, and especially in the catastrophe of McDonald.

The book, adorned with the portrait of Pocahontas, is enriched by many traits especially calculated to interest women. Among these is the punishment of an Indian for ill-treatment of his mother-in-law, received with acclamation by the women of the tribe, as bringing a new era in their destiny. We could have wished, however, that the punishment had been something else than the degradation of the brave to the position of a woman. The Indian custom to that effect being the most powerful expression of the contempt in which they hold the sex, ought not to have been countenanced in an attempt to rectify this way of thinking. The book is appropriately dedicated to two women. The first volume, with a portrait of the author for its frontispiece beneath which might have been inscribed as a proud title which few can boast, " The Indian's Friend," is dedicated to Mrs. Madison, and an autograph letter from her in reply, forms an interesting prefix to its pages. The second, with the portrait of Pocahontas, is dedicated to Mrs. Saunders, of Salem, Mass., as having also shown herself with talents, time, and money, a friend to the Indians, a happiness which we envy her, and must wish her many competitors more powerful and leisurely than ourselves in its enjoyment.

Honors are paid to the character of John Ross, which it gives us great pleasure to see, as confirmation of what we have always felt. There is a tone not to be mistaken in the papers which Ross has addressed to the public — a grave, majestic sorrow, a resolute honor, justice, and courage to act as love and duty prompt in a losing cause to the last, an excellent discernment, and a serenely tempered wisdom. We have often wished to extend the hand of friendship to this man, and assure him that there was one pale-face who, not having seen, yet knows him, and prizes his efforts as they deserve. We may name, in the late Dr. Channing, another who felt thus toward Ross from the perusal of his writings.

We solicit an extensive perusal of this book; the interest of its contents will repay the money and trouble that may be thus expended. We scarcely dare hope that anything righteous will be done in consequence, for our hopes as to National honor and goodness are almost wearied out, and we feel obliged to turn to the Individual and to the Future for consolation. Yet, oh Father! might we pray that thou wouldst grant a ray of pure light in this direction, and grant us to help let it in! It were a blessed com-

pensation for many sorrows, many disappointments.
At all events, none who have leisure and heart to
feel on these subjects may stand excused from bearing open testimony to the truth, whether it avail
or no.

CHILDREN'S BOOKS.

THERE is no branch of literature that better deserves cultivation, and none that so little obtains it from worthy hands, as this of Children's Books. It requires a peculiar development of the genius and sympathies, rare among men of factitious life, who are not men enough to revive with force and beauty the thoughts and scenes of childhood.

It is all idle to talk baby-talk, and give shallow accounts of deep things, thinking thereby to interest the child. He does not like to be too much puzzled; but it is simplicity he wants, not silliness. We fancy their angels, who are always waiting in the courts of our Father, smile somewhat sadly on the ignorance of those who would feed them on milk and water too long, and think it would be quite as well to give them a stone.

There is too much amongst us of the French way of palming off false accounts of things on children, "to do them good," and showing nature to them in a magic lantern "purified for the use of childhood," and telling stories of sweet little girls and brave little boys,— O, all so good or so bad! and above all, so *little*, and everything about them so little! Children accustomed to move in full-sized apartments, and converse with full-grown men and women, do not need so much of this baby-house style in their literature. They like, or would like if they could get them, better things much more. They like the *Arabian Nights*, and *Pilgrim's Progress*, and *Bunyan's Emblems*, and *Shakspeare*, and the *Iliad* and *Odyssey*,— at least, they used to like them; and if they do not now, it is because their taste has been injured by so many sugar-plums. The books that were written in the childhood of nations suit an uncorrupted childhood now. They are simple, picturesque, robust. Their moral is not forced, nor is the truth veiled with a well-meant but sure-to-fail hypocrisy. Sometimes they are not moral at all,— only free plays of the fancy and intellect. These, also, the child needs, just as the infant needs to stretch its limbs, and grasp at objects it cannot hold. We have become so fond of the moral, that we forget the nature in which it must find its root; so fond of instruction, that we forget development.

Where ballads, legends, fairy-tales, *are* moral, the morality is heart-felt; if instructive, it is from the healthy common sense of mankind, and not for the convenience of nursery rule, nor the " peace of schools and families."

O, that winter, freezing, snow-laden winter, which ushered in our eighth birthday ! There, in the lonely farm-house, the day's work done, and the bright wood-fire all in a glow, we were permitted to slide back the panel of the cupboard in the wall,— most fascinating object still in our eyes, with which no stateliest alcoved library can vie,— and there saw, neatly ranged on its two shelves, not — praised be our natal star ! — *Peter Parley*, nor a

History of the Good Little Boy who never took anything that did not belong to him; but the *Spectator, Telemachus, Goldsmith's Animated Nature*, and the *Iliad*.

Forms of gods and heroes more distinctly seen, and with eyes of nearer love then than now! — our true uncle, Sir Roger de Coverley, and ye, fair realms of Nature's history, whose pictures we tormented all grown persons to illustrate with more knowledge, still more, — how we bless the chance that gave to us your great realities, which life has daily helped us, helps us still, to interpret, instead of thin and baseless fictions that would all this time have hampered us, though with only cobwebs!

Children need some childish talk, some childish play, some childish books. But they also need, and need more, difficulties to overcome, and a sense of the vast mysteries which the progress of their intelligence shall aid them to unravel. This sense is naturally their delight, as it is their religion, and it must not be dulled by premature explanations or subterfuges of any kind. There has been too much of this lately.

Miss Edgeworth is an excellent writer for children. She is a child herself, as she writes, nursed anew by her own genius. It is not by imitating, but by reproducing childhood, that the writer becomes its companion. Then, indeed, we have something especially good, for,

> " Like wine, well-kept and long,
> Heady, nor harsh, nor strong,
> With each succeeding year is quaffed,
> A richer, purer, mellower draught."

Miss Edgeworth's grown people live naturally with the children; they do not talk to them continually about angels or flowers, but about the things that interest themselves. They do not force them forward, nor keep them back. The relations are simple and honorable; all ages in the family seem at home under one roof and sheltered by one care.

The *Juvenile Miscellany*, formerly published by Mrs. Child, was much and deservedly esteemed by children. It was a healthy, cheerful, natural and entertaining companion to them.

We should censure too monotonously tender a manner in what is written for children, and too constant an attention to moral influence. We should prefer a larger proportion of the facts of natural or human history, and that they should speak for themselves.

* * * * * *

WOMAN IN POVERTY.

WOMAN, even less than Man, is what she should be as a whole. She is not that self-centred being, full of profound intuitions, angelic love, and flowing poesy, that she should be. Yet there are circumstances in which the native force and purity of her being teach her how to conquer where the restless impatience of Man brings defeat, and leaves him crushed and bleeding on the field.

Images rise to mind of calm strength, of gentle wisdom learning from every turn of adverse fate,— of youthful tenderness and faith undimmed to the close of life, which redeem humanity and make the heart glow with fresh courage as we write. They are mostly from obscure corners and very private walks. There was nothing shining, nothing of an obvious and sounding heroism to make their conduct doubtful, by tainting their motives with vanity. Unknown they lived, untrumpeted they died. Many hearts were warmed and fed by them, but perhaps no mind but our own ever consciously took account of their virtues.

Had Art but the power adequately to tell their simple virtues, and to cast upon them the light which, shining through those marked and faded faces, foretold the glories of a second spring! The tears of holy emotion which fell from those eyes have seemed to us pearls beyond all price; or rather, whose price will be paid only when, beyond the grave, they enter those better spheres in whose faith they felt and acted here.

From this private gallery we will, for the present, bring forth but one picture. That of a Black Nun was wont to fetter the eyes of visitors in the royal galleries of France, and my Sister of Mercy, too, is of that complexion. The old woman was recommended as a laundress by my friend, who had long prized her. I was immediately struck with the dignity and propriety of her manner. In the depth of winter she brought herself the heavy baskets through the slippery streets; and, when I asked her why she did not employ some younger person to do what was so entirely disproportioned to her strength, simply said, "she lived alone, and could not afford to hire an errand-boy." "It was hard for her?" "No, she was fortunate in being able to get work at her age, when others could do it better. Her friends were very good to procure it for her." "Had she a comfortable home?" "Tolerably so, — she should not need one long." "Was that a thought of joy to her?" "Yes, for she hoped to see again the husband and children from whom she had long been separated."

Thus much in answer to the questions, but at other times the little she said was on general topics. It was not from her that I learnt how the great idea of Duty had held her upright through a life of incessant toil, sorrow, bereavement; and that not only she had remained upright, but that her character had been constantly pro-

gressive. Her latest act had been to take home a poor
sick girl who had no home of her own, and could not
bear the idea of dying in a hospital, and maintain and
nurse her through the last weeks of her life. " Her eyesight was failing, and she should not be able to work
much longer, — but, then, God would provide. *Somebody* ought to see to the poor, motherless girl."

It was not merely the greatness of the act, for one in
such circumstances, but the quiet matter-of-course way
in which it was done, that showed the habitual tone of
the mind, and made us feel that life could hardly do
more for a human being than to make him or her the
somebody that is daily so deeply needed, to represent the
right, to do the plain right thing.

" God will provide." Yes, it is the poor who feel
themselves near to the God of love. Though he slay
them, still do they trust him.

" I hope," said I to a poor apple-woman, who had
been drawn on to disclose a tale of distress that, almost
in the mere hearing, made me weary of life, " I hope I
may yet see you in a happier condition." " With God's
help," she replied, with a smile that Raphael would have
delighted to transfer to his canvas ; a Mozart, to strains
of angelic sweetness. All her life she had seemed an
outcast child ; still she leaned upon a Father's love.

The dignity of a state like this may vary its form in
more or less richness and beauty of detail. but here is the
focus of what makes life valuable. It is this spirit which
makes poverty the best servant to the ideal of human
nature. I am content with this type, and will only

quote, in addition, a ballad I found in a foreign periodical, translated from Chamisso, and which forcibly recalled
my own laundress as an equally admirable sample of the
same class, the Ideal Poor, which we need for our consolation, so long as there must be real poverty.

"THE OLD WASHERWOMAN.

" Among yon lines her hands have laden,
    A laundress with white hair appears,
Alert as many a youthful maiden,
    Spite of her five-and-seventy years ;
Bravely she won those white hairs, still
    Eating the bread hard toil obtained her,
And laboring truly to fulfil
    The duties to which God ordained her.

" Once she was young and full of gladness,
    She loved and hoped, — was wooed and won ;
Then came the matron's cares, — the sadness
    No loving heart on earth may shun.
Three babes she bore her mate ; she prayed
    Beside his sick-bed, — he was taken ;
She saw him in the church-yard laid,
    Yet kept her faith and hope unshaken.

" The task her little ones of feeding
    She met unfaltering from that hour ;
She taught them thrift and honest breeding,
    Her virtues were their worldly dower.
To seek employment, one by one,
    Forth with her blessing they departed,
And she was in the world alone—
    Alone and old, but still high-hearted.

" With frugal forethought, self-denying,
    She gathered coin, and flax she bought,

And many a night her spindle plying,
Good store of fine-spun thread she wrought.
The thread was fashioned in the loom ;
She brought it home, and calmly seated
To work, with not a thought of gloom,
Her decent grave-clothes she completed.

"She looks on them with fond elation ;
They are her wealth, her treasure rare,
Her age's pride and consolation,
Hoarded with all a miser's care.
She dons the sark each Sabbath day,
To hear the Word that faileth never ;
Well-pleased she lays it then away
Till she shall sleep in it forever !

" Would that my spirit witness bore me
That, like this woman, I had done
The work my Master put before me
Duly from morn till set of sun !
Would that life's cup had been by me
Quaffed in such wise and happy measure,
And that I too might finally
Look on my shroud with such meek pleasure ! "

Such are the noble of the earth. They do not repine,
they do not chafe, even in the inmost heart. They
feel that, whatever else may be denied or withdrawn,
there remains the better part, which cannot be taken
from them. This line exactly expresses the woman I
knew : —

" Alone and old, but still high-hearted."

Will any, poor or rich, fail to feel that the children
of such a parent were rich when

" Her virtues were their worldly dower " ?

Will any fail to bow the heart in assent to the aspiration,

> " Would that my spirit witness bore me
> That, like this woman, I had done
> The work my Maker put before me
> Duly from morn till set of sun " ?

May not that suffice to any man's ambition?

[Perhaps one of the most perplexing problems which beset Woman in her domestic sphere relates to the proper care and influence which she should exert over the domestic aids she employs. As these are, and long must be, taken chiefly from one nation, the following pages treating of the Irish Character, and the true relation between Employer and Employed, can hardly fail to be of interest. They contain, too, some considerations which Woman as well as Man is too much in danger of overlooking, and which seem, even more than when first urged, to be timely in this reäctionary to-day. — Ed]

THE IRISH CHARACTER.

In one of the eloquent passages quoted in the " *Tribune* " of Wednesday, under the head, "Spirit of the Irish Press," we find these words :

"Domestic love, almost morbid from external suffering, prevents him (the Irishman) from becoming a fanatic and a misanthrope, and reconciles him to life."

This recalled to our mind the many touching instances known to us of such traits among the Irish we have seen here. We have known instances of morbidness like this. A girl sent "home," after she was well established herself, for a young brother, of whom she was particularly fond. He came, and shortly after died. She was so overcome by his loss that she took poison. The great poet of serious England says, and we believe it to be his serious thought though laughingly said, "Men have died, and worms have eaten them, but not for love."

Whether or not death may follow from the loss of a lover or child, we believe that among no people but the Irish would it be upon the loss of a young brother.

Another poor young woman, in the flower of her youth, denied herself, not only every pleasure, but almost the necessaries of life to save the sum she thought ought to be hers before sending to Ireland for a widowed mother. Just as she was on the point of doing so she heard that her mother had died fifteen months before. The keenness and persistence of her grief defy description. With a delicacy of feeling which showed the native poetry of the Irish mind, she dwelt, most of all, upon the thought that while she was working, and pinching, and dreaming of happiness with her mother, it was indeed but a dream, and that cherished parent lay still and cold beneath the ground. She felt fully the cruel cheat of Fate. " Och ! and she was dead all those times I was thinking of her ! " was the deepest note of her lament.

They are able, however, to make the sacrifice of even these intense family affections in a worthy cause. We knew a woman who postponed sending for her only child, whom she had left in Ireland, for years, while she maintained a sick friend who had no one else to help her.

The poetry of which I have spoken shows itself even here, where they are separated from old romantic associations, and begin the new life in the New World by doing all its drudgery. We know flights of poetry repeated to us by those present at their wakes, — passages of natural eloquence, from the lamentations for the dead, more beautiful than those recorded in the annals of Brittany or Roumelia.

It is the same genius, so exquisitely mournful, tender, and glowing, too, with the finest enthusiasm, that makes their national music, in these respects, the finest in the world. It is the music of the harp ; its tones are deep and thrilling. It is the harp so beautifully described in " The Harp of Tara's Halls," a song whose simple pathos is unsurpassed. A feeling was never more adequately embodied.

It is the genius which will enable Emmet's appeal to draw tears from the remotest generations, however much they may be strangers to the circumstances which called it forth. It is the genius which beamed in chivalrous loveliness through each act of Lord Edward Fitzgerald, — the genius which, ripened by English culture, favored by suitable occasions, has shed such glory on the land which has done all it could to quench it on the parent hearth.

When we consider all the fire which glows so untamably in Irish veins, the character of her people, considering the circumstances, almost miraculous in its goodness, we cannot forbear, notwithstanding all the temporary ills they aid in here, to give them a welcome to our shores. Those ills we need not enumerate ; they are known to all, and we rank among them, what others would not, that by their ready service to do all the hard work, they make it easier for the rest of the population to grow effeminate, and help the country to grow too fast. But that is her destiny, to grow too fast : there is no use

talking against it. Their extreme ignorance, their blind
devotion to their priesthood, their pliancy in the hands
of demagogues, threaten continuance of these ills   yet,
on the other hand, we must regard them as most valuable elements in the new race. They are looked upon
with contempt for their want of aptitude in learning new
things; their ready and ingenious lying; their eye-ser-
vice. These are the faults of an oppressed race, which
must require the aid of better circumstances through two
or three generations to eradicate. Their virtues are their
own ; they are many, genuine, and deeply-rooted. Can
an impartial observer fail to admire their truth to domestic ties, their power of generous bounty, and more
generous gratitude, their indefatigable good-humor (for
ages of wrong which have driven them to so many acts
of desperation, could never sour their blood at its source),
their ready wit, their elasticity of nature? They are
fundamentally one of the best nations of the world.
Would they were welcomed here, not to work merely,
but to intelligent sympathy, and efforts, both patient and
ardent, for the education of their children! No sympathy
could be better deserved, no efforts wiselier timed. Future
Burkes and Currans would know how to give thanks
for them, and Fitzgeralds rise upon the soil — which
boasts the magnolia with its kingly stature and majestical
white blossoms, — to the same lofty and pure beauty.
Will you not believe it, merely because that bog-bred
youth you placed in the mud-hole tells you lies, and
drinks to cheer himself in those endless diggings ? You
are short-sighted, my friend ; you do not look to the

future; you will not turn your head to see what may have been the influences of the past. You have not examined your own breast to see whether the moniton there has not commanded you to do your part to counteract these influences; and yet the Irishman appeals to you, eye to eye. He is very personal himself, — he expects a personal interest from you. Nothing has been able to destroy this hope, which was the fruit of his nature. We were much touched by O'Connell's direct appeal to the queen, as "Lady!" But she did not listen, — and we fear few ladies and gentlemen will till the progress of Destiny compels them.

THE IRISH CHARACTER.

SINCE the publication of a short notice under this head in the "*Tribune*," several persons have expressed to us that their feelings were awakened on the subject, especially as to their intercourse with the lower Irish. Most persons have an opportunity of becoming acquainted, if they will, with the lower classes of Irish, as they are so much employed among us in domestic service, and other kinds of labor.

We feel, say these persons, the justice of what has been said as to the duty and importance of improving these people. We have sometimes tried; but the want of real gratitude which, in them, is associated with such warm and wordy expressions of regard, with their incorrigible habits of falsehood and evasion, have baffled and discouraged us. You say their children ought to be educated; but how can this be effected when the all but omnipotent sway of the Catholic religion and the example of parents are both opposed to the formation of such views and habits as we think desirable to the citizen of the New World?

We answer first with regard to those who have grown up in another land, and who, soon after arriving here, are engaged in our service.

First, as to ingratitude. We cannot but sadly smile on the remarks we hear so often on this subject.

Just Heaven! — and to us how liberal! which has given those who speak thus an unfettered existence, free from religious or political oppression; which has given them the education of intellectual and refined intercourse with men to develop those talents which make them rich in thoughts and enjoyment, perhaps in money, too, certainly rich in comparison with the poor immigrants they employ, — what is thought in thy clear light of those who expect in exchange for a few shillings spent in presents or medicines, a few kind words, a little casual thought or care, such a mighty payment of gratitude? Gratitude! Under the weight of old feudalism their minds were padlocked by habit against the light; they might be grateful then, for they thought their lords were as gods, of another frame and spirit than theirs, and that they had no right to have the same hopes and wants, scarcely to suffer from the same maladies, with those creatures of silk, and velvet, and cloth of gold. Then, the crumbs which fell from the rich man's table might be received with gratitude, and, if any but the dogs came to tend the beggar's sores, such might be received as angels. But the institutions which sustained such ideas have fallen to pieces. It is understood, even in Europe, that

> "The rank is but the guinea's stamp,
> The man 's the gowd for a' that,
> A man 's a man for a' that."

And being such, has a claim on this earth for some-

thing better than the nettles of which the French peasantry made their soup, and with which the persecuted
Irish, "under hiding," turned to green the lips white
before with famine.

And if this begins to be understood in Europe, can
you suppose it is not by those who, hearing that America
opens a mother's arms with the cry, "All men are born
free and equal," rush to her bosom to be consoled for
centuries of woe, for their ignorance, their hereditary
degradation, their long memories of black bread and
stripes? However little else they may understand,
believe they understand well *this much*. Such inequal-
ities of privilege, among men all born of one blood,
should not exist. They darkly feel that those to whom
much has been given owe to the Master an account of
stewardship. They know now that your gift is but a
small portion of their right.

And you, O giver! how did you give? With religious
joy, as one who knows that he who loves God cannot fail
to love his neighbor as himself? with joy and freedom, as
one who feels that it is the highest happiness of gift to us
that we have something to give again? Didst thou put
thyself into the position of the poor man, and do for him
what thou wouldst have had one who was able to do for
thee? Or, with affability and condescending sweetness,
made easy by internal delight at thine own wondrous virtue, didst thou give five dollars to balance five hundred
spent on thyself? Did you say, "James, I shall expect
you to do right in everything, and to attend to my concerns as I should myself; and, at the end of the quarter,

I will give you my old clothes and a new pocket-handker-
chief, besides seeing that your mother is provided with
fuel against Christmas ? "

Line upon line, and precept upon precept, the tender
parent expects from the teacher to whom he confides his
child; vigilance unwearied, day and night, through long
years. But he expects the raw Irish girl or boy to correct, at a single exhortation, the habit of deceiving those
above them, which the expectation of being tyrannized
over has rooted in their race for ages. If we look fairly
into the history of their people, and the circumstances
under which their own youth was trained, we cannot
expect that anything short of the most steadfast patience
and love can enlighten them as to the beauty and value of
implicit truth, and, having done so, fortify and refine them
in the practice of it.

This we admit at the outset : First, You must be prepared for a religious and patient treatment of these people,
not merely *un*educated, but *ill*-educated ; a treatment far
more religious and patient than is demanded by your own
children, if they were born and bred under circumstances
at all favorable.

Second, Dismiss from your minds all thought of gratitude. Do what you do for them for God's sake, and as
a debt to humanity — interest to the common creditor upon
principal left in your care. Then insensibility, forgetful-
ness, or relapse, will not discourage you, and you will
welcome proofs of genuine attachment to yourself chiefly
as tokens that your charge has risen into a higher state of
thought and feeling, so as to be enabled to value the bene-

fits conferred through you. Could we begin so, there
would be hope of our really becoming the instructors and
guardians of this swarm of souls which come from their
regions of torment to us, hoping, at least, the benefits of
purgatory.

The influence of the Catholic priesthood must continue
very great till there is a complete transfusion of character
in the minds of their charge. But as the Irishman, or
any other foreigner, becomes Americanized, he will demand
a new form of religion to suit his new wants. The priest,
too, will have to learn the duties of an American citizen;
he will live less and less for the church, and more for the
people, till at last, if there be Catholicism still, it will be
under Protestant influences, as begins to be the case in
Germany. It will be, not Roman, but American Catholicism; a form of worship which relies much, perhaps, on
external means and the authority of the clergy,— for such
will always be the case with religion while there are
crowds of men still living an external life, and who have
not learned to make full use of their own faculties,— but
where a belief in the benefits of confession and the power
of the church, as church, to bind and loose, atone for or
decide upon sin, with similar corruptions, must vanish in
the free and searching air of a new era.

*   *   *   *   *

Between employer and employed there is not sufficient
pains taken on the part of the former to establish a
mutual understanding. People meet, in the relations of
master and servant, who have lived in two different worlds.
In this respect we are much worse situated than the same

parties have been in Europe. There is less previous acquaintance between the upper and lower classes. (We must, though unwillingly, use these terms to designate the state of things as at present existing.) Meals are taken separately; work is seldom shared; there is very little to bring the parties together, except sometimes the farmer works with his hired Irish laborer in the fields, or the mother keeps the nurse-maid of her baby in the room with her.

In this state of things the chances for instruction, which come every day of themselves where parties share a common life instead of its results merely, do not occur. Neither is there opportunity to administer instruction in the best manner, nor to understand when and where it is needed.

The farmer who works with his men in the field, the farmer's wife who attends with her women to the churn and the oven, may, with ease, be true father and mother to all who are in their employ, and enjoy health of conscience in the relation, secure that, if they find cause for blame, it is not from faults induced by their own negligence. The merchant who is from home all day, the lady receiving visitors or working slippers in her nicely-furnished parlor, cannot be quite so sure that their demands, or the duties involved in them, are clearly understood, nor estimate the temptations to prevarication.

It is shocking to think to what falsehoods human beings like ourselves will resort, to excuse a love of amusement, to hide ill-health, while they see us indulging freely in the one, yielding lightly to the other; and yet we have, or ought to have, far more resources in either temptation than they. For us it is hard to resist, to give up going to the places where we should meet our most interesting companions, or do our work with an aching brow. But we have not people over us whose careless, hasty anger drives us to seek excuses for our failures; if so, perhaps, — perhaps; who knows? — we, the better-educated, rigidly, immaculately true as we are at present, *might* tell falsehoods. Perhaps we might, if things were given us to do which we had never seen done, if we were surrounded by new arrangements in the nature of which no one instructed us. All this we must think of before we can be of much use.

We have spoken of the nursery-maid as *the* hired domestic with whom her mistress, or even the master, is likely to become acquainted. But, only a day or two since, we saw, what we see so often, a nursery-maid with the family to which she belonged, in a public conveyance. They were having a pleasant time; but in it she had no part, except to hold a hot, heavy baby, and receive frequent admonitions to keep *it* comfortable. No inquiry was made as to *her* comfort; no entertaining remark, no information of interest as to the places we passed, was addressed to her. Had she been in that way with that family ten years she might have known *them* well enough, for their characters lay only too bare to a careless scrutiny; but her joys, her sorrows, her few thoughts, her almost buried capacities, would have been as unknown to them, and they as little likely to benefit her, as the Emperor of China.

Let the employer place the employed first in good physical circumstances, so as to promote the formation of different habits from those of the Irish hovel, or illicit still-house. Having thus induced feelings of self-respect, he has opened the door for a new set of notions. Then let him become acquainted with the family circumstances and history of his new pupil. He has now got some ground on which to stand for intercourse. Let instruction follow for the mind, not merely by having the youngest daughter set, now and then, copies in the writing-book, or by hearing read aloud a few verses in the Bible, but by putting good books in their way, if able to read, and by intelligent conversation when there is a chance,— the master with the man who is driving him, the lady with the woman who is making her bed. Explain to them the relations of objects around them; teach them to compare the old with the new life. If you show a better way than theirs of doing work, teach them, too, *why* it is better. Thus will the mind be prepared by development for a moral reformation; there will be some soil fitted to receive the seed.

When the time is come,— and will you think a poor, uneducated person, in whose mind the sense of right and wrong is confused, the sense of honor blunted, easier of access than one refined and thoughtful? Surely you will not, if you yourself are refined and thoughtful, but rather that the case requires far more care in the choice of a favorable opportunity,— when, then, the good time is come, perhaps it will be best to do what you do in a way that will make a permanent impression. Show the Irishman that a vice not indigenous to his nation — for the rich and noble who are not so tempted are chivalrous to an uncommon degree in their openness, bold sincerity, and adherence to their word — has crept over and become deeply rooted in the poorer people from the long oppressions they have undergone. Show them what efforts and care will be needed to wash out the taint. Offer your aid, as a faithful friend, to watch their lapses, and refine their sense of truth. You will not speak in vain. If they never mend, if habit is too powerful, still, their nobler nature will not have been addressed in vain. They will not forget the counsels they have not strength to follow, and the benefits will be seen in their children or children's children.

Many say, "Well, suppose we do all this; what then? They are so fond of change, they will leave us." What then? Why, let them go and carry the good seed elsewhere. Will you be as selfish and short-sighted as those who never plant trees to shade a hired house, lest some one else should be blest by their shade?

It is a simple duty we ask you to engage in; it is, also, a great patriotic work. You are asked to engage in the great work of mutual education, which must be for this country the system of mutual insurance.

We have some hints upon this subject, drawn from the experience of the wise and good, some encouragement to offer from that experience, that the fruits of a wise planting sometimes ripen sooner than we could dare to expect But this must be for another day.

One word as to this love of change. We hear people

blaming it in their servants, who can and do go to Niagara, to the South, to the Springs, to Europe, to the sea-
side; in short, who are always on the move whenever
they feel the need of variety to reänimate mind, health,
or spirits. Change of place, as to family employment, is
the only way domestics have of " seeing life " — the only
way immigrants have of getting thoroughly acquainted
with the new society into which they have entered. How
natural that they should incline to it ! Once more; put
yourself in their places, and then judge them gently from
your own, if you would be just to them if you would be
of any use.

EDUCATE MEN AND WOMEN AS SOULS.

HAD Christendom but been true to its standard, while accommodating its modes of operation to the calls of successive times, Woman would now have not only equal *power* with Man, — for of that omnipotent nature will never suffer her to be defrauded, — but a *chartered* power, too fully recognized to be abused. Indeed, all that is wanting is, that Man should prove his own freedom by making her free. Let him abandon conventional restriction, as a vestige of that Oriental barbarity which confined Woman to a seraglio. Let him trust her entirely, and give her every privilege already acquired for himself, — elective franchise, tenure of property, liberty to speak in public assemblies, &c.

Nature has pointed out her ordinary sphere by the circumstances of her physical existence. She cannot wander far. If here and there the gods send their missives through women as through men, let them speak without remonstrance. In no age have men been able wholly to hinder them. A Deborah must always be a spiritual mother in Israel. A Corinna may be excluded from the Olympic games, yet all men will hear her song, and a Pindar sit at her feet. It is Man's fault that there ever were Aspasias and Ninons. These exquisite forms were intended for the shrines of virtue.

Neither need men fear to lose their domestic deities. Woman is born for love, and it is impossible to turn her from seeking it. Men should deserve her love as an inheritance, rather than seize and guard it like a prey. Were they noble, they would strive rather not to be loved too much, and to turn her from idolatry to the true, the only Love. Then, children of one Father, they could not err nor misconceive one another.

Society is now so complex, that it is no longer possible to educate Woman merely as Woman; the tasks which come to her hand are so various, and so large a proportion of women are thrown entirely upon their own resources. I admit that this is not their state of perfect development; but it seems as if Heaven, having so long issued its edict in poetry and religion without securing intelligent obedience, now commanded the world in prose to take a high and rational view. The lesson reads to me thus : —

Sex, like rank, wealth, beauty, or talent, is but an accident of birth. As you would not educate a soul to be an aristocrat, so do not to be a woman. A general regard to her usual sphere is dictated in the economy of nature. You need never enforce these provisions rigorously. Achilles had long plied the distaff as a princess; yet, at first sight of a sword, he seized it. So with Woman; one hour of love would teach her more of her proper relations than all your formulas and conventions. Express your views, men, of what you *seek* in women; thus best do you give them laws. Learn, women, what you should *demand* of men; thus only can they become themselves. Turn both from the contemplation of what is merely phenomenal in your existence, to your permanent life as souls. Man, do not prescribe how the Divine shall display itself in Woman. Woman, do not expect to see all of God in Man. Fellow-pilgrims and helpmeets are ye, Apollo and Diana, twins of one heavenly birth, both beneficent, and both armed. Man, fear not to yield to Woman's hand both the quiver and the lyre; for if her urn be filled with light, she will use both to the glory of God. There is but one doctrine for ye both, and that is the doctrine of the SOUL.

PART III.

EXTRACTS FROM JOURNALS AND LETTERS

[The following extract from Margaret's Journal will be read with a degree of melancholy interest when connected with the eventful end of her eventful life. It was written many years before her journey to Europe, and rings in our ears now almost with the tones of prophecy. — ED.]

I LIKE to listen to the soliloquies of a bright child. In this microcosm the philosophical observer may trace the natural progression of the mind of mankind. I often silently observe L——, with this view. He is generally imitative and dramatic; the day-school, the singing-school or the evening party, are acted out with admirable variety in the humors of the scene, and great discrimination of character in its broader features. What is chiefly remarkable is his unconsciousness of his mental processes, and how thoughts it would be impossible for him to recall spring up in his mind like flowers and weeds in the soil But to-night he was truly in a state of lyrical inspiration, his eyes flashing, his face glowing, and his whole composition chanted out in an almost metrical form. He began by mourning the death of a certain Harriet whom he had let go to foreign parts, and who had died at sea. He described her as having "blue, sparkling eyes, and a sweet smile," and lamented that he could never kiss her cold lips again. This part, which he continued for some time, was in prolonged cadences, and a low, mournful tone, with a frequently recurring burden of "O, my Harriet, shall I never see thee more!"

EXTRACT FROM JOURNAL.

*   *   *   *   *   *

IT is so true that a woman may be in love with a woman, and a man with a man. It is pleasant to be sure of it, because it is undoubtedly the same love that we shall feel when we are angels, when we ascend to the only fit place for the Mignons, where

"Sie fragen nicht nach Mann und Weib."

It is regulated by the same law as that of love between persons of different sexes, only it is purely intellectual and spiritual, unprofaned by any mixture of lower instincts, undisturbed by any need of consulting temporal interests; its law is the desire of the spirit to realize a whole, which makes it seek in another being that which it finds not in itself.

Thus the beautiful seek the strong; the mute seek the eloquent; the butterfly settles on the dark flower. Why did Socrates so love Alcibiades? Why did Körner so love Schneider? How natural is the love of Wallenstein for Max, that of Madame de Stael for de Recamier, mine for ——! I loved —— for a time with as much passion as I was then strong enough to feel. Her face was always gleaming before me; her voice was echoing in my ear; all poetic thoughts clustered round the dear image.

This love was for me a key which unlocked many a treasure which I still possess; it was the carbuncle (emblematic gem!) which cast light into many of the darkest corners of human nature. She loved me, too, though not so much, because her nature was "less high, less grave, less large, less deep;" but she loved more tenderly, less passionately. She loved me, for I well remember her suffering when she first could feel my faults, and knew one part of the exquisite veil rent away — how she wished to stay apart and weep the whole day.

These thoughts were suggested by a large engraving representing Madame Recamier in her boudoir. I have so often thought over the intimacy between her and Madame de Stael.

Madame Recamier is half-reclining on a sofa; she is clad in white drapery, which clings very gracefully to her round, but elegantly-slender form; her beautiful neck and arms are bare; her hair knotted up so as to show the contour of her truly-feminine head to great advantage. A book lies carelessly on her lap; one hand yet holds it at the place where she left off reading; her lovely face is turned towards us; she appears to muse on what she has been reading. When we see a woman in a picture with a book, she seems to be doing precisely that for which she was born; the book gives such an expression of purity to the female figure. A large window, partially veiled by a white curtain, gives a view of a city at some little distance. On one side stand the harp and piano; there are just books enough for a lady's boudoir. There is no picture, except one of De Recamier herself, as

Corinne. This is absurd; but the absurdity is interesting, as recalling the connection. You imagine her to have been reading one of De Stael's books, and to be now pondering what those brilliant words of her gifted friend can mean.

Everything in the room is in keeping. Nothing appears to have been put there because other people have it; but there is nothing which shows a taste more noble and refined than you would expect from the fair Frenchwoman. All is elegant, modern, in harmony with the delicate habits and superficial culture which you would look for in its occupant.

TO HER MOTHER.

Sept. 5, 1837.

* * * * If I stay in Providence, and more money is wanting than can otherwise be furnished, I will take a private class, which is ready for me, and by which, even if I reduced my terms to suit the place, I can earn the four hundred dollars that —— will need. If I do not stay, I will let her have my portion of our income, with her own, or even capital which I have a right to take up, and come into this or some other economical place, and live at the cheapest rate. It will not be even a sacrifice to me to do so, for I am weary of society, and long for the opportunity for solitary concentration of thought. I know what I say; if I live, you may rely upon me.

God be with you, my dear mother! I am sure he will prosper the doings of so excellent a woman if you will only keep your mind calm and be firm. Trust your daughter too. I feel increasing trust in mine own good mind. We will take good care of the children and of one another. Never fear to trouble me with your perplexities. I can never be so situated that I do not earnestly wish to know them. Besides, things do not trouble me as they did, for I feel within myself the power to aid, to serve.

Most affectionately,
Your daughter, M.

PART OF LETTER TO M.

Providence, Oct. 7, 1838.

* * * For yourself, dear ——, you have attained an important age. No plan is desirable for you which is to be pursued with precision. The world, the events of every day, which no one can predict, are to be your teachers, and you must, in some degree, give yourself up, and submit to be led captive, if you would learn from them. Principle must be at the helm, but thought must shift its direction with the winds and waves.

Happy as you are thus far in worthy friends, you are not in much danger of rash intimacies or great errors. I think, upon the whole, quite highly of your judgment about people and conduct; for, though your first feelings are often extravagant, they are soon balanced.

I do not know other faults in you beside that want of retirement of mind which I have before spoken of. If M—— and A—— want too much seclusion, and are too severe in their views of life and man, I think you are too little so. There is nothing so fatal to the finer faculties as too ready or too extended a publicity. There is some danger lest there be no real religion in the heart which craves too much of daily sympathy. Through your mind the stream of life has coursed with such rapidity that it has often swept away the seed or loosened the roots of the young plants before they had ripened any fruit.

I should think writing would be very good for you. A journal of your life, and analyses of your thoughts, would teach you how to generalize, and give firmness to your conclusions. Do not write down merely that things are beautiful, or the reverse; but *what* they are, and *why* they are beautiful or otherwise; and show these papers, at least at present, to nobody. Be your own judge and your own helper. Do not go too soon to any one with your difficulties, but try to clear them up for yourself.

I think the course of reading you have fallen upon, of late, will be better for you than such books as you formerly read, addressed rather to the taste and imagination than the judgment. The love of beauty has rather an undue development in your mind. See now what it is, and what it has been. Leave for a time the Ideal, and return to the Real.

I should think two or three hours a day would be quite enough, at present, for you to give to books. Now learn buying and selling, keeping the house, directing the servants; all that will bring you worlds of wisdom if you keep it subordinate to the one grand aim of perfecting the whole being. And let your self-respect forbid you to do imperfectly anything that you do at all.

I always feel ashamed when I write with this air of wisdom; but you will see, by my hints, what I mean. Your mind wants depth and precision; your character condensation. Keep your high aim steadily in view; life will open the path to reach it. I think ———, even if she be in excess, is an excellent friend for you; her character seems to have what yours wants, whether she has or has not found the right way.

TO HER BROTHER, A. B. F.

Providence, Feb. 19, 1838

MY DEAR A. :

*   *   *   *   *

I wish you could see the journals of two dear little girls, eleven years old, in my school. They love one another like Bessie Bell and Mary Gray in the ballad. They are just of a size, both lively as birds, affectionate, gentle, ambitious in good works and knowledge. They encourage one another constantly to do right; they are rivals, but never jealous of one another. One has the quicker intellect, the other is the prettier. I have never had occasion to find fault with either, and the forwardness of their minds has induced me to take both into my reading-class, where they are associated with girls many years their elders. Particular pains do they take with their journals. These are written daily, in a beautiful, fair, round hand, well-composed, showing attention, and memory well-trained, with many pleasing sallies of playfulness, and some very interesting thoughts.

TO THE SAME.

Jamaica Plain, Dec. 20, 1840.

* * * * ABOUT your school I do not think I could give you much advice which would be of value, unless I could know your position more in detail. The most important rule is, in all relations with our fellow-creatures, never forget that, if they are imperfect persons, they are immortal souls, and treat them as you would wish to be treated by the light of that thought.

As to the application of means, abstain from punishment as much as possible, and use encouragement as far as you can *without flattery.* But be even more careful as to strict truth in this regard, towards children, than to persons of your own age ; for, to the child, the parent or teacher is the representative of *justice ;* and as that of life is severe, an education which, in any degree, excites vanity, is the very worst preparation for that general and crowded school.

I doubt not you will teach grammar well, as I saw you aimed at principles in your practice.

In geography, try to make pictures of the scenes, that they may be present to their imaginations, and the nobler faculties be brought into action, as well as memory.

In history, try to study and paint the characters of *great men;* they best interpret the leadings of events amid the nations.

I am pleased with your way of speaking of both people and pupils ; your view seems from the right point. Yet beware of over great pleasure in being popular, or even beloved. As far as an amiable disposition and powers of entertainment make you so, it is a happiness; but if there is one grain of plausibility, it is poison.

But I will not play Mentor too much, lest I make you averse to write to your very affectionate sister, M.

TO HER BROTHER, R.

I ENTIRELY agree in what you say of *tuition* and *intui-tion ;* the two must act and react upon one another, to make a man, to form a mind. Drudgery is as necessary, to call out the treasures of the mind, as harrowing and planting those of the earth. And besides, the growths of literature and art are as much nature as the trees in Concord woods ; but nature idealized and perfected.

TO THE SAME.

1841.

I TAKE great pleasure in that feeling of the living pres-ence of beauty in nature which your letters show. But you, who have now lived long enough to see some of my prophecies fulfilled, will not deny, though you may not yet believe the truth of my words when I say you go to an extreme in your denunciations of cities and the social institutions. *These* are a growth also, and, as well as the diseases which come upon them, under the control of the one spirit as much as the great tree on which the insects prey, and in whose bark the busy bird has made many a wound.

When we get the proper perspective of these things we shall find man, however artificial, still a part of nature. Meanwhile, let us trust; and while it is the soul's duty ever to bear witness to the best it knows, let us not be hasty to conclude that in what suits us not there can be no good. Let us be sure there *must* be eventual good, could we but see far enough to discern it. In maintaining perfect truth to ourselves and choosing that mode of being which suits us, we had best leave others alone as much as may be. You prefer the country, and I doubt not it is on the whole a better condition of life to live there; but at the country party you have mentioned you saw that no circumstances will keep people from being frivolous. One may be gossipping, and vulgar, and idle in the country,— earnest, noble and wise, in the city. Nature cannot be kept from us while there is a sky above, with so much as one star to remind us of prayer in the silent night.

As I walked home this evening at sunset, over the Mill-Dam, towards the city, I saw very distinctly that the city also is a bed in God's garden. More of this some other time.

TO A YOUNG FRIEND.

Concord, May 2, 1837.

MY DEAR: I am passing happy here, except that I am not well,—so unwell that I fear I must go home and ask my good mother to let me rest and vegetate beneath her sunny kindness for a while. The excitement of conversation prevents my sleeping. The drive here with Mr. E—— was delightful. Dear Nature and Time, so often calumniated, will take excellent care of us if we will let them. The wisdom lies in schooling the heart not to expect too much. I did that good thing when I came here, and I am rich. On Sunday I drove to Watertown with the author of "Nature." The trees were still bare, but the little birds care not for that; they revel, and carol, and wildly tell their hopes, while the gentle, "voluble" south wind plays with the dry leaves, and the pine-trees sigh with their soul-like sounds for June. It was beauteous; and care and routine fled away, and I was as if they had never been, except that I vaguely whispered to myself that all had been well with me.

*　　*　　*　　*　　*　　*

The baby here is beautiful. He looks like his father, and smiles so sweetly on all hearty, good people. I play with him a good deal, and he comes so *natural* after Dante and other poets.

Ever faithfully your friend.

TO THE SAME.

1837.

My beloved Child: I was very glad to get your note. Do not think you must only write to your friends when you can tell them you are happy; they will not misunderstand you in the dark hour, nor think you *forsaken*, if cast down. Though your letter of Wednesday was very sweet to me, yet I knew it could not last as it was then. These hours of heavenly, heroic strength leave us, but they come again : their memory is with us amid after-trials, and gives us a foretaste of that era when the steadfast soul shall be the only reality.

My dearest, you must suffer, but you will always be growing stronger, and with every trial nobly met, you will feel a growing assurance that nobleness is not a mere *sentiment* with you. I sympathize deeply in your anxiety about your mother; yet I cannot but remember the bootless fear and agitation about my mother, and how strangely our destinies were guided. Take refuge in prayer when you are most troubled; the door of the sanctuary will never be shut against you. I send you a paper which is very sacred to me. Bless Heaven that your heart is awakened to sacred duties before any kind of gentle ministering has become impossible, before any relation has been broken.*

---

* It has always been my desire to find appropriate time and place to correct an erroneous impression which has gained currency in regard to my father, and which does injustice to his memory. That impression is that he was exceedingly stern and exacting in the parental relation, and especially in regard to my sister ; that he forbid or

LINES WRITTEN IN MARCH, 1836.

"I will not leave you comfortless."

O, Friend divine ! this promise dear
Falls sweetly on the weary ear !
Often, in hours of sickening pain,
It soothes me to thy rest again.

frowned upon her sports ; — excluded her from intercourse with other children when she, a child, needed such companionship, and required her to bend almost unceasingly over her books. This impression has, certainly in part, arisen from an autobiographical sketch, never written for publication nor intended for a literal or complete statement of her father's educational method, or the relation which existed between them, which was most loving and true on both sides. While the narrative is true, it is not the all she would have said, and, therefore, taken alone, conveys an impression which misleads those who did not know our father well. Perhaps no better opportunity or place than this may ever arise to correct this impression so far as it is wrong. It is true that my father had a very high standard of scholarship, and did expect conformity to it in his children. He was not stern toward them.

It is doubtless true, also, that he did not perfectly comprehend the rare mind of his daughter, or see for some years that she required no stimulating to intellectual effort, as do most children, but rather the reverse. But how many fathers are there who would have understood at once such a child as Margaret Fuller was, or would have done even as wisely as he ? And how long is it since a wiser era has dawned upon the world (its light not yet fully welcomed), in which attention first to physical development to the exclusion of the mental, is an axiom in education ? Was it so deemed forty years ago ? Nor has it been considered that so gifted a child would naturally, as she did, *seek* the companionship of those older than herself, and not of children who had little in unison with her. She needed, doubtless, to be *urged* into the usual sports of children, and the company of those of her own age ; if *not*

Might I a true disciple be,
Following thy footsteps faithfully,
Then should I still the succor prove
Of him who gave his life for love.

When this fond heart would vainly beat
For bliss that ne'er on earth we meet,
For perfect sympathy of soul,
From those such heavy laws control ;

When, roused from passion's ecstasy,
I see the dreams that filled it fly,
Amid my bitter tears and sighs
Those gentle words before me rise.

urged to enter these she was never excluded from either. She needed
to be kept from books for a period, or to be led to those of a lighter
cast than such as she read, and which usually task the thoughts
of mature men. This simply was not done, and the error arose from
no lack of tenderness, or consideration, from no lack of the wisdom of
those times, but from the simple fact that the laws of physiology as
connected with those of mind were not understood then as now, nor
was attention so much directed to physical culture as of the primary
importance it is now regarded. Our father was indeed exact and
strict with himself and others ; but none has ever been more devoted to
his children than he, or more painstaking with their education, nor
more fondly loved them ; and in later life they have ever been more
and more impressed with the conviction of his fidelity and wisdom.
That Margaret venerated her father, and that his love was returned, is
abundantly evidenced in her poem which accompanies this letter. This,
too, was not written for the public eye, but it is too noble a tribute,
too honorable both to father and daughter, to be suppressed. I trust
that none, passing from one extreme to the other, will infer from the
natural self-reproach and upbraiding because of short-comings, felt by
every true mind when an honored and loved parent departs, that she
lacked fidelity in the relation of daughter. She agreed not always
with his views and methods, but this diversity of mind never affected
their mutual respect and love. — [ED.]

With aching brows and feverish brain
The founts of intellect I drain,
And con with over-anxious thought
What poets sung and heroes wrought.

Enchanted with their deeds and lays,
I with like gems would deck my days ;
No fires creative in me burn,
And, humbled, I to Thee return ;

When blackest clouds around me rolled
Of scepticism drear and cold,
When love, and hope, and joy and pride,
Forsook a spirit deeply tried ;

My reason wavered in that hour,
Prayer, too impatient, lost its power ;
From thy benignity a ray
I caught, and found the perfect day.

A head revered in dust was laid ;
For the first time I watched my dead ;
The widow's sobs were checked in vain,
And childhood's tears poured down like rain.

In awe I gaze on that dear face,
In sorrow, years gone by retrace,
When, nearest duties most forgot,
I might have blessed, and did it not !

Ignorant, his wisdom I reproved,
Heedless, passed by what most he loved,
Knew not a life like his to prize,
Of ceaseless toil and sacrifice.

No tears can now that hushed heart move,
No cares display a daughter's love,

The fair occasion lost, no more
Can thoughts more just to thee restore.

What can I do ?   And how atone
For all I 've done, and left undone ?
Tearful I search the parting words
Which the beloved John records.

" Not comfortless ! "   I dry my eyes,
My duties clear before me rise, —
Before thou think'st of taste or pride,
See home-affections satisfied !

Be not with generous *thoughts* content,
But on well-doing constant bent :
When self seems dear, self-seeking fair,
Remember this sad hour in prayer !

Though all thou wishest fly thy touch,
Much can one do who loveth much.
More of thy spirit, Jesus give,
Not comfortless, though sad, to live.

And yet not sad, if I can know
To copy Him who here below
Sought but to do his Father's will,
Though from such sweet composure still

My heart be far.   Wilt thou not aid
One whose best hopes on thee are stayed?
Breathe into me thy perfect love,
And guide me to thy rest above !

TO HER BROTHER, R——.

*   *   *   MR. KEATS, Emma's father, is dead.   To
me this brings unusual sorrow, though I have never yet

seen him; but I thought of him as one of the very few persons known to me by reputation, whose acquaintance might enrich me. His character was a sufficient answer to the doubt, whether a merchant can be a man of honor. He was, like your father, a man all whose virtues had stood the test. He was no word-hero.

*   *   *   *

TO A YOUNG FRIEND.

Providence, June 16, 1837.

My dear ——: I pray you, amid all your duties, to keep some hours to yourself. Do not let my example lead you into excessive exertions. I pay dear for extravagance of this sort; five years ago I had no idea of the languor and want of animal spirits which torment me now. Animal spirits are not to be despised. An earnest mind and seeking heart will not often be troubled by despondency; but unless the blood can dance at proper times, the lighter passages of life lose all their refreshment and suggestion.

I wish you and —— had been here last Saturday. Our school-house was dedicated, and Mr. Emerson made the address; it was a noble appeal in behalf of the best interests of culture, and seemingly here was fit occasion. The building was beautiful, and furnished with an even elegant propriety.

I am at perfect liberty to do what I please, and there are apparently the best dispositions, if not the best preparation, on the part of the hundred and fifty young minds with whom I am to be brought in contact.

I sigh for the country; trees, birds and flowers, assure me that June is here, but I must walk through streets many and long, to get sight of any expanse of green. I had no fine weather while at home, though the quiet and rest were delightful to me; the sun did not shine once really warmly, nor did the apple-trees put on their blossoms until the very day I came away.

SONNET.

TO THE SAME.

ALTHOUGH the sweet, still watches of the night
Find me all lonely now, yet the delight
Hath not quite gone, which from thy presence flows.
The love, the joy that in thy bosom glows,
Lingers to cheer thy friend.   From thy fresh dawn
Some golden exhalations have I drawn
To make less dim my dusty noon.   Thy tones
Are with me still; some plaintive as the moans
Of Dryads, when their native groves must fall,
Some wildly wailing, like the clarion-call
On battle-field, strewn with the noble dead.
Some in soft romance, like the echoes bred
In the most secret groves of Arcady;
    Yet all, wild, sad, or soft, how steeped in poesy!
Providence, April, 1838.

TO THE SAME.

Providence, Oct. 21, 1838.
*   *   *   *   I AM reminded by what you say, of an era in my own existence; it is seven years bygone.   For

bitter months a heavy weight had been pressing'on me,—
the weight of deceived friendship. I could not be much
alone,— a great burden of family cares pressed upon me;
I was in the midst of society, and obliged to act my part
there as well as I could. At that time I took up the
study of German, and my progress was like the rebound
of a string pressed almost to bursting. My mind being
then in the highest state of action, heightened, by intellectual appreciation, every pang; and imagination, by
prophetic power, gave to the painful present all the
weight of as painful a future.

At this time I never had any consolation, except in
long solitary walks, and my meditations then were so far
aloof from common life, that on my return my fall was
like that of the eagle, which the sportsman's hand calls
bleeding from his lofty flight, to stain the earth with his
blood.

In such hours we feel so noble, so full of love and
bounty, that we cannot conceive how any pain should
have been needed to teach us. It then seems we are so
born for good, that such means of leading us to it were
wholly unnecessary. But I have lived to know that the
secret of all things is pain, and that nature travaileth
most painfully with her noblest product. I was not without hours of deep spiritual insight, and consciousness of
the inheritance of vast powers. I touched the secret of
the universe, and by that touch was invested with talis-
manic power which has never left me, though it sometimes lies dormant for a long time.

One day lives always in my memory; one chastest,

heavenliest day of communion with the soul of things. It was Thanksgiving-day. I was free to be alone ; in the meditative woods, by the choked-up fountain, I passed its hours, each of which contained ages of thought and emotion. I saw, then, how idle were my griefs; that I had acquired *the thought* of each object which had been taken from me; that more extended personal relations would only have given me pleasures which then seemed not worth my care, and which would surely have dimmed my sense of the spiritual meaning of all which had passed. I felt how true it was that nothing in any being which was fit for me, could long be kept from me ; and that, if separation could be, real intimacy had never been. All the films seemed to drop from my existence, and I was sure that I should never starve in this desert world, but that manna would drop from Heaven, if I would but rise with every rising sun to gather it.

In the evening I went to the church-yard; the moon sailed above the rosy clouds,— the crescent moon rose above the heavenward-pointing spire. At that hour a vision came upon my soul, whose final scene last month interpreted. The rosy clouds of illusion are all vanished ; the moon has waxed to full. May my life be a church, full of devout thoughts and solemn music. I pray thus, my dearest child! "Our Father! let not the heaviest shower be spared; let not the gardener forbear his knife till the fair, hopeful tree of existence be brought to its fullest blossom and fruit!"

TO THE SAME.

Jamaica Plain, June, 1839.

* * * I HAVE had a pleasant visit at Nahant, but was no sooner there than the air braced me so violently as to drive all the blood to my head. I had headache two of the three days we were there, and yet I enjoyed my stay very much. We had the rocks and piazzas to ourselves, and were on sufficiently good terms not to destroy, if we could not enhance, one another's pleasure.

The first night we had a storm, and the wind roared and wailed round the house that Ossianic poetry of which you hear so many strains. Next day was clear and brilliant, with a high north-west wind. I went out about six o'clock, and had a two hours' scramble before breakfast. I do not like to sit still in this air, which exasperates all my nervous feelings; but when I can exhaust myself in climbing, I feel delightfully,— the eye is so sharpened, and the mind so full of thought. The outlines of all objects, the rocks, the distant sails, even the rippling of the ocean, were so sharp that they seemed to press themselves into the brain. When I see a natural scene by such a light it stays in my memory always as a picture; on milder days it influences me more in the way of reverie. After breakfast, we walked on the beaches. It was quite low tide, no waves, and the fine sand eddying wildly about. I came home with that frenzied headache which you are so unlucky as to know, covered my head with wet towels, and went to bed. **After** dinner I was better, and we went to the Spou'...ng-horn. C—— was perched close to the fissure, far above me and, in a pale green dress, she looked like the nymph of the place. I lay down on a rock, low in the water, where I could hear the twin harmonies of the sucking of the water into the spout, and the washing of the surge on the foot of the rock. I never passed a more delightful afternoon. Clouds of pearl and amber were slowly drifting across the sky, or resting a while to dream, like me, near the water. Opposite me, at considerable distance, was a line of rock, along which the billows of the advancing tide chased one another, and leaped up exultingly as they were about to break. That night we had a sunset of the gorgeous, autumnal kind, and in the evening very brilliant moonlight; but the air was so cold I could enjoy it but a few minutes. Next day, which was warm and soft, I was out on the rocks all day. In the afternoon I was out alone, and had an admirable place, a cleft between two vast towers of rock with turret-shaped tops. I got on a ledge of rock at their foot, where I could lie and let the waves wash up around me, and look up at the proud turrets rising into the prismatic light. This evening was very fine; all the sky covered with crowding clouds, profound, but not sullen of mood, the moon wading, the stars peeping, the wind sighing very softly. We lay on the high rocks and listened to the plashing of the waves. The next day was good, but the keen light was too much for my eyes and brain; and, though I am glad to have been there, I am as glad to get back to our garlanded rocks, and richly-green

fields and groves. I wish you could come to me now;
we have such wealth of roses.

TO THE SAME.

Jamaica Plain, Aug., 1839.

* * * * I RETURNED home well, full of earnestness; yet, I know not why, with the sullen, boding sky
came a mood of sadness, nay, of gloom, black as Hades,
which I have vainly striven to fend off by work, by exercise, by high memories. Very glad was I of a painful
piece of intelligence, which came the same day with your
letter, to bring me an excuse for tears. That was a black
Friday, both above and within. What demon resists our
good angel, and seems at such times to have the mastery?
Only *seems*, I say to myself; it is but the sickness of
the immortal soul, and shall by-and-by be cast aside
like a film. I think this is the great step of our life,—
to change the *nature* of our self-reliance. We find that
the will cannot conquer circumstances, and that our temporal nature must vary its hue here with the food that is
given it. Only out of mulberry leaves will the silk-worm
spin its thread fine and durable. The mode of our existence is not in our own power; but behind it is the
immutable essence that cannot be tarnished; and to hold
fast to this conviction, to live as far as possible by its
light, cannot be denied us if we elect this kind of self-
trust. Yet is sickness wearisome; and I rejoice to say
that my demon seems to have been frightened away by

this day's sun. But, conscious of these diseases of the mind, believe that I can sympathize with a friend when subject to the same. Do not fail to go and stay with —————— ; few live so penetrating and yet so kind, so true, so sensitive. She is the spirit of love as well as of intellect. * * * *

TO THE SAME.

My beloved Child: I confess I was much disappointed when I first received your letter this evening. I have been quite ill for two or three days, and looked forward to your presence as a restorative. But think not I would have had you act differently; far better is it for me to have my child faithful to duty than even to have her with me. Such was the lesson I taught her in a better hour. I am abashed to think how often lately I have found excuses for indolence in the weakness of my body; while now, after solitary communion with my better nature, I feel it was weakness of mind, weak fear of depression and conflict. But the Father of our spirits will not long permit a heart fit for worship

> " —————— to seek
> From weak recoils, exemptions weak,
> After false gods to go astray,
> Deck altars vile with garlands gay," etc.

His voice has reached me; and I trust the postponement of your visit will give me space to nerve myself to what strength I should, so that, when we do meet, I shall rejoice that you did not come to help or soothe me ; for I shall have helped and soothed myself. Indeed, I would not so willingly that you should see my short-comings as know that they exist. Pray that I may never lose sight of my vocation; that I may not make ill-health a plea for sloth and cowardice; pray that, whenever I do, I may be punished more swiftly than this time, by a sadness as deep as now.

TO HER BROTHER, R.

Cambridge, August 5, 1842.

My dear R. : I want to hear how you enjoyed your journey, and what you think of the world as surveyed from mountain-tops. I enjoy exceedingly staying among the mountains. I am satisfied with reading these bolder lines in the manuscript of Nature. Merely gentle and winning scenes are not enough for me. I wish my lot had been cast amid the sources of the streams, where the voice of the hidden torrent is heard by night, where the eagle soars, and the thunder resounds in long peals from side to side; where the grasp of a more powerful emotion has rent asunder the rocks, and the long purple shadows fall like a broad wing upon the valley. All places, like all persons, I know, have beauty; but only in some scenes, and with some people, can I expand and feel myself at home. I feel all this the more for having passed my earlier life in such a place as Cambridgeport. There I had nothing except the little flower-garden behind the house, and the elms before the door. I used to long and sigh for beautiful places such as I read of. There was

not one walk for me, except over the bridge. I liked
that very much, — the river, and the city glittering in
sunset, and the lovely undulating line all round, and the
light smokes, seen in some weather.

LETTER TO THE SAME.

Milwaukie, July 29, 1843.

DEAR R.: * * * Daily I thought of you during my
visit to the Rock-river territory. It is only five years
since the poor Indians have been dispossessed of this
region of sumptuous loveliness, such as can hardly be
paralleled in the world. No wonder they poured out
their blood freely before they would go. On one island,
belonging to a Mr. H., with whom we stayed, are still to
be found their "caches" for secreting provisions, — the
wooden troughs in which they pounded their corn, the
marks of their tomahawks upon felled trees. When he
first came, he found the body of an Indian woman, in a
canoe, elevated on high poles, with all her ornaments on.
This island is a spot, where Nature seems to have exhausted her invention in crowding it with all kinds of
growths, from the richest trees down to the most delicate
plants. It divides the river which there sweeps along in
clear and glittering current, between noble parks, richest
green lawns, pictured rocks crowned with old hemlocks,
or smooth bluffs, three hundred feet high, the most beautiful of all. Two of these, — the Eagle's Nest, and the
Deer's Walk, still the resort of the grand and beautiful
creature from which they are named, — were the scene of

some of the happiest hours of my life. I had no idea, from verbal description, of the beauty of these bluffs, nor can I hope to give any to others. They lie so magnificently bathed in sunlight, they touch the heavens with so sharp and fair a line. This is one of the finest parts of the river; but it seems beautiful enough to fill any heart and eye all along its course, nowhere broken or injured by the hand of man. And there, I thought, if we two could live, and you could have a farm which would not cost a twentieth part the labor of a New England farm, and would pay twenty times as much for the labor, and have our books and our pens and a little boat on the river, how happy we might be for four or five years, — at least, *as* happy as Fate permits mortals to be. For we, I think, are congenial, and if I could hope permanent peace on the earth, I might hope it with you.

You will be glad to hear that I feel overpaid for coming here. Much is my life enriched by the images of the great Niagara, of the vast lakes, of the heavenly sweetness of the prairie scenes, and, above all, by the heavenly region where I would so gladly have lived. My health, too, is materially benefited. I hope to come back better fitted for toil and care, as well as with beauteous memories to sustain me in them.

Affectionately always, &c.

TO MISS R.

Chicago, August 4, 1843.

I HAVE hoped from time to time, dear ——, that I should receive a few lines from you, apprizing me how you are this summer, but a letter from Mrs. F—— lately comes to tell me that you are not better, but, at least when at Saratoga, worse.

So writing is of course fatiguing, and I must not expect letters any more. To that I could make up my mind if I could hear that you were well again. I fear, if your malady disturbs you as much as it did, it must wear on your strength very much, and it seems in itself dangerous. However, it is good to think that your composure is such that disease can only do its legitimate work, and not undermine two ways, — the body with its pains, and the body through the mind with thoughts and fears of pains.

I should have written to you long ago except that I find little to communicate this summer, and little inclination to communicate that little; so what letters I have sent, have been chiefly to beg some from my friends. I have had home-sickness sometimes here, as do children for the home where they are even little indulged, in the boarding-school where they are only tolerated. This has been in the town, where I have felt the want of companionship, because the dissipation of fatigue, or expecting soon to move again, has prevented my employing myself *for* myself; and yet there was nothing well worth looking at without. When in the country I have enjoyed myself highly, and my health has improved day by day. The characters of persons are brought out by the little wants and adventures of country life as you see it in this region ; so that each one awakens a healthy interest ; and the same persons who, if I saw them at these hotels, would no; have a word to say that could fix the attention, become most plea;ing companions; their topics are before them, and they take the hint. You feel so grateful, too, for the hospitality of the log-cabin ; such gratitude as the hospitality of the rich, however generous, cannot inspire ; for these wait on you with their domestics and money, and give of their superfluity only ; but here the Master gives you his bed, his horse, his lamp, his grain from the field, his all, in short; and you see that he enjoys doing so thoroughly, and takes no thought for the morrow ; so that you seem in fields full of lilies perfumed with pure kindness; and feel, verily, that Solomon in all his glory could not have entertained you so much to the purpose. Travelling, too, through the wide green woods and prairies, gives a feeling both of luxury and repose that the sight of highly-cultivated country never can. There seems to be room enough for labor to pause and man to fold his arms and gaze, forgetting poverty, and care, and the thousand walls and fences that in the cultivated region must be built and daily repaired both for mind and body. Nature seems to have poured forth her riches so without calculation, merely to mark the fulness of her joy ; to swell in larger strains the hymn, "the one Spirit doeth all things well, for its life is love."

I will not ask you to write to me now, as I shall so soon be at home. Probably, too, I shall reserve a visit to B—— for another summer ; I have been so much a rover that when once on the ¬oad I shall wish to hasten home.

Ever yours, M.

TO THE SAME.

Cambridge, January 21, 1844.

MY DEAR —— : I am anxious to get a letter, telling me how you fare this winter in the cottage. Your neighbors who come this way do not give very favorable accounts of your looks ; and, if you are well enough, I should like to see a few of those firm, well-shaped characters from your own hand. Is there no chance of your coming to Boston all this winter? I had hoped to see you for a few hours at least.

I wrote you one letter while at the West : I know not if it was ever received; it was sent by a private opportunity, one of those "traps to catch the unwary," as they have been called. It was no great loss, if lost. I did not feel like writing letters while travelling. It took all my strength of mind to keep moving and to receive so many new impressions. Surely I never had so clear an idea before of the capacity to bless, of mere *Earth*, when fresh from the original breath of the creative spirit. To have this impression, one must see large tracts of wild country, where the traces of man's inventions are too few and slight to break the harmony of the first design. It will not be so, long, even where I have been now ; in three or four years those vast flowery plains will be broken up for tillage, — those shapely groves converted into logs and boards. I wished I could have kept on now, for two or three years, while yet the first spell rested on the scene. I feel much refreshed, even by this brief intimacy with Nature, in an aspect of large and unbroken lineaments.

I came home with a treasure of bright pictures and suggestions, and seemingly well. But my strength, which had been sustained by a free, careless life in the open air, has yielded to the chills of winter, and a very little work, with an ease that is not encouraging. However, I have had the influenza, and that has been about as bad as fever to everybody. *Now* I am pretty well, but much writing does not agree with me.

* * * I wish you were near enough for me to go in and see you now and then. I know that, sick or well, you are always serene, and sufficient to yourself; but now you are so much shut up, it might animate existence agreeably to hear some things I might have to tell. * * *

TO THE SAME.

* * * 1844.

JUST as I was beginning to visit the institutions here, of a remedial and benevolent kind, I was stopped by influenza. So soon as I am quite well I shall resume the survey. I do not expect to do much, practically, for the suffering, but having such an organ of expression as the *Tribune*, any suggestions that are well grounded may be of use. I have always felt great interest for those women who are trampled in the mud to gratify the brute appetites of men, and I wished I might be brought, naturally, into contact with them. Now I am so, and I think I shall have much that is interesting to tell you when we meet.

I go on very moderately, for my strength is not great; but I am now connected with a person who is anxious I should not overtask it. I hope to do more for the paper by-and-by. At present, besides the time I spend in looking round and examining my new field, I am publishing a volume, of which you will receive a copy, called "Woman in the Nineteenth Century." A part of my available time is spent in attending to it as it goes through the press; for, really, the work seems but half done when your book is *written*. I like being here; the streams of life flow free, and I learn much. I feel so far satisfied as to have laid my plans to stay a year and a half, if not longer, and to have told Mr. G—— that I probably shall do so. That is long enough for a mortal to look forward, and not too long, as I must look forward in order to get what I want from Europe.

Mr. Greeley is a man of genuine excellence, honorable, benevolent, of an uncorrupted disposition, and of great abilities. In modes of life and manners he is the man of the people, and of the *American* people. * * *

I rejoice to hear that your situation is improved. I hope to pass a day or two with you next summer, if you can receive me when I can come. I want to hear from you now and then, if it be only a line to let me know the state of your health. Love to Miss G——, and tell her I have the cologne-bottle on my mantle-piece now. I sent home for all the little gifts I had from friends, that my room might look more homelike. My window commands a most beautiful view, for we are quite out of the town, in a lovely place on the East River. I like this, as I can be in town when I will, and here have much retirement. You were right in supposing my signature is the star.   Ever affectionately yours.

TO HER BROTHER, R.

Fishkill-Landing, Nov 23, 1844.

DEAR R. :

* * * * * *

The seven weeks of proposed abode here draw to a close, and have brought what is rarest,—fruition, of the sort proposed from them. I have been here all the time, except that three weeks since I went down to New York, and with —— visited the prison at Sing-Sing. On Saturday we went up to Sing-Sing in a little way-boat, thus seeing that side of the river to much greater advantage than we can in the mammoth boats. We arrived in resplendent moonlight, by which we might have supposed the prisons palaces, if we had not known too well what was within.

On Sunday —— addressed the male convicts in a strain of most noble and pathetic eloquence. They listened with earnest attention : many were moved to tears, — some, I doubt not, to a better life. I never felt such sympathy with an audience ; — as I looked over that sea of faces marked with the traces of every ill, I felt that at least heavenly truth would not be kept out by self-complacency and a dependence on good appearances.

I talked with a circle of women, and they showed the natural aptitude of the sex for refinement. These women — some black, and all from the lowest haunts of vice — showed a sensibility and a sense of propriety which would not have disgraced any place.

Returning, we had a fine storm on the river, clearing up with strong winds.

TO HER BROTHER, A. B. F.

Rome, Jan. 20, 1849.

MY DEAR A.: Your letter and mother's gave me the first account of your illness. Some letters were lost during the summer, I do not know how. It did seem very hard upon you to have that illness just after your settlement; but it is to be hoped we shall some time know a good reason for all that seems so strange. I trust you are now becoming fortified in your health, and if this could only be, feel as if things would go well with you in this difficult world. I trust you are on the threshold of an honorable and sometimes happy career. From many pains, many dark hours, let none of the progeny of Eve hope to escape ! * * * *

Meantime, I hope to find you in your home, and make you a good visit there. Your invitation is sweet in its tone, and rouses a vision of summer woods and New England Sunday-morning bells.

It seems to me that mother is at last truly in her sphere, living with one of her children. Watch over her carefully, and don't let her do too much. Her spirit is only all too willing, — but the flesh is weak, and her life so precious to us all ! * * * *

TO MAZZINI.

"Al Cittadino Reppresentante del Popolo Romano."

Rome, March 3, 1849.

DEAR MAZZINI: Though knowing you occupied by the most important affairs, I again feel impelled to write

a few lines. What emboldens me is the persuasion that
the best friends, in point of sympathy and intelligence,—
the only friends of a man of ideas and of marked character, — must be women. You have your mother; no
doubt you have others, perhaps many. Of that I know
nothing; only I like to offer also my tribute of affection.

When I think that only two years ago you thought
of coming into Italy with us in disguise, it seems very
glorious that you are about to enter republican Rome as
a Roman citizen. It seems almost the most sublime and
poetical fact of history. Yet, even in the first thrill of
joy, I felt "he will think his work but beginning,
now."

When I read from your hand these words, " Il lungo
esilio testè ricominciato, la vita non confortata, fuorchè
d'affetti lontani e contesi, e la speranza lungamente pro-
trata, e il desiderio che comincia a farmi si supremo, di
dormire finalmente in pace, da chè non ho potuto, vivere
in terra mia," — when I read these words they made me
weep bitterly, and I thought of them always with a
great pang at the heart. But it is not so, dear Mazzini,
— you do not return to sleep under the sod of Italy, but
to see your thought springing up all over the soil. The
gardeners seem to me, in point of instinctive wisdom or
deep thought, mostly incompetent to the care of the
garden; but an idea like this will be able to make use
of any implements. The necessity, it is to be hoped, will
educate the men, by making them work. It is not this,
I believe, which still keeps your heart so melancholy;
for I seem to read the same melancholy in your answer

to the Roman assembly. You speak of "few and late years," but some full ones still remain. A century is not needed, nor should the same man, in the same form of thought, work too long on an age. He would mould and bind it too much to himself. Better for him to die and return incarnated to give the same truth on yet another side. Jesus of Nazareth died young; but had he not spoken and acted as much truth as the world could bear in his time? A frailty, a perpetual short-coming, motion in a curve-line, seems the destiny of this earth.

The excuse awaits us elsewhere; there must be one, — for it is true, as said Goethe, "care is taken that the tree grow not up into the heavens." Men like you, appointed ministers, must not be less earnest in their work; yet to the greatest, the day, the moment is all their kingdom. God takes care of the increase.

Farewell! For your sake I could wish at this moment to be an Italian and a man of action; but though I am an *American*, I am not even *a woman of action ;* so the best I can do is to pray with the whole heart, "Heaven bless dear Mazzini! — cheer his heart, and give him worthy helpers to carry out his holy purposes."

TO MR. AND MRS. SPRING.

Florence, Dec. 12, 1849.

DEAR M. AND R.: * * * Your letter, dear R., was written in your noblest and most womanly spirit. I thank you warmly for your sympathy about my little boy. What he is to me, even you can hardly dream; you that have three, in whom the natural thirst of the heart was earlier satisfied, can scarcely know what my one ewe-lamb is to me. That he may live, that I may find bread for him, that I may not spoil him by over-weening love, that I may grow daily better for his sake, are the ever-recurring thoughts,— say prayers,— that give their hue to all the current of my life.

But, in answer to what you say, that it is still better to give the world a living soul than a portion of my life in a printed book, it is true ; and yet, of my book I could know whether it would be of some worth or not; of my child, I must wait to see what his worth will be. I play with him, my ever-growing mystery ! but from the solemnity of the thoughts he brings is refuge only in God. Was I worthy to be parent of a soul, with its eternal, immense capacity for weal and woe ? " God be merciful to me a sinner ! " comes so naturally to a mother's heart !

* * * * * * *

What you say about the Peace way is deeply true; if any one see clearly how to work in that way, let him, in God's name ! Only, if he abstain from fighting against giant wrongs, let him be sure he is really and ardently at work undermining them, or, better still, sustaining the rights that are to supplant them. Meanwhile, I am not sure that I can keep my hands free from blood. Cobden is good ; but if he had stood in Kossuth's place, would he not have drawn his sword against the Austrian ? You, could you let a Croat insult your wife, carry off your son to be an Austrian serf, and leave your daughter bleeding in the dust?   Yet it is true that while Moses slew the Egyptian, Christ stood still to be spit upon; and it is true that death to man could do him no harm.   You have the truth, you have the right, but could you act up to it in all circumstances?   Stifled under the Roman priesthood, would you not have thrown it off with all your force? Would you have waited unknown centuries, hoping for the moment when you could see another method?

Yet the agonies of that baptism of blood I feel, O how deeply! in the golden June days of Rome.   Consistent no way, I felt I should have shrunk back,—I could not have had it shed.   Christ did not have to see his dear ones pass the dark river; he could go alone, however, in prophetic spirit.   No doubt he foresaw the crusades.

In answer to what you say of ———, I wish the little effort I made for him had been wiselier applied.   Yet these are not the things one regrets.   It does not do to calculate too closely with the affectionate human impulse. We must be content to make many mistakes, or we should move too slowly to help our brothers much.

TO HER BROTHER, R.

Florence, Jan. 8, 1850.

My dear R : * * * * The way in which you speak of my marriage is such as I expected from you.   Now that we have once exchanged words on these important changes in our lives, it matters little to write letters, so much has happened, and the changes are too great to be

made clear in wri;ing.   It would not be worth while to
keep the family thinking of me.   I cannot fix precisely the
period of my return, though at present it seems to me
probable we may make the voyage in May or June.   At
first we should wish to go and make a little visit to mother.
I should take counsel with various friends before fixing
myself in any place; see what openings there are for me,
&c.   I cannot judge at all before I am personally in the
United States, and wish to engage myself no way.   Should
I finally decide on the neighborhood of New York, I
should see you all, often.   I wish, however, to live with
mother, if possible.   We will discuss it on all sides when
I come.   Climate is one thing I must think of.   The
change from the Roman winter to that of New England
might be very trying for Ossoli.   In New York he would
see Italians often, hear his native tongue, and feel less
exiled.   If we had our affairs in New York and lived in
the neighboring country, we could find places as quiet as
C——, more beautiful, and from which access to a city
would be as easy by means of steam.

On the other hand, my family and most cherished
friends are in New England.   I shall weigh all advantages at the time, and choose as may then seem best.

I feel also the great responsibility about a child, and
the mixture of solemn feeling with the joy its sweet ways
and caresses give; yet this is only different in degree,
not in kind, from what we should feel in other relations.
We may more or less impede or brighten the destiny of
all with whom we come in contact.   Much as the child
lies in our power, still God and Nature are there, fur-

nishing a thousand masters to correct our erroneous and fill up our imperfect, teachings. I feel impelled to try for good, for the sake of my child, most powerfully; but if I fail, I trust help will be tendered to him from some other quarter. I do not wish to trouble myself more than is inevitable, or lose the simple, innocent pleasure of watching his growth from day to day, by thinking of his future. At present my care of him is to keep him pure, in body and mind, to give for body and mind simple nutriment when he requires it, and to play with him. Now he learns, playing, as we all shall when we enter a higher existence. With him my intercourse thus far has been precious, and if I do not well for *him*, he at least has taught *me* a great deal.

I may say of Ossoli, it would be difficult to help liking him, so sweet is his disposition, so disinterested without effort, so simply wise his daily conduct, so harmonious his whole nature. And he is a perfectly unconscious character, and never dreams that he does well. He is studying English, but makes little progress. For a good while you may not be able to talk freely with him, but you will like showing him your favorite haunts,— he is so happy in nature, so sweet in tranquil places.

TO ———.

WHAT a difference it makes to come home to a child! How it fills up all the gaps of life just in the way that is most consoling, most refreshing! Formerly I used to feel sad at that hour; the day had not been nobly spent,

— I had not done my duty to myself or others, and I felt so lonely! Now I never feel lonely; for, even if my little boy dies, our souls will remain eternally united. And I feel *infinite* hope for him,— hope that he will serve God and man more loyally than I have done; and seeing how full he is of life, how much he can afford to throw away, I feel the inexhaustibleness of nature, and console myself for my own incapacities.

Madame Arconati is near me. We have had some hours of great content together, but in the last weeks her only child has been dangerously ill. I have no other acquaintance except in the American circle, and should not care to make any unless singularly desirable; for I want all my time for the care of my child, for my walks, and visits to objects of art, in which again I can find pleasure, and in the evening for study and writing. Ossoli is forming some taste for books; he is also studying English; he learns of Horace Sumner, to whom he teaches Italian in turn.

TO MR. AND MRS. S.

Florence, Feb. 5, 1850.

MY DEAR M. AND R.: You have no doubt ere this received a letter written, I think, in December, but I must suddenly write again to thank you for the New-Year's letter. It was a sweet impulse that led you all to write together, and had its full reward in the pleasure you gave. I have said as little as possible about Ossoli and our relation, wishing my old friends to form their own impressions naturally, when they see us together. I have faith that all who ever knew me will feel that I have become somewhat milder, kinder, and more worthy to serve all who need, for my new relations. I have expected that those who have cared for me chiefly for my activity of intellect, would not care for him; but that those in whom the moral nature predominates would gradually learn to love and admire him, and see what a treasure his affection must be to me. But even that would be only gradually; for it is by acts, not by words, that one so simple, true, delicate and retiring, can be known. For me, while some of my friends have thought me exacting, I may say Ossoli has always outgone my expectations in the disinterestedness, the uncompromising bounty, of his every act.

He was the same to his father as to me. His affections are few, but profound, and thoroughly acted out. His permanent affections are few, but his heart is always open to the humble, suffering, heavy-laden. His mind has little habitual action, except in a simple, natural poetry, that one not very intimate with him would never know anything about. But once opened to a great impulse, as it was to the hope of freeing his country, it rises to the height of the occasion, and stays there. His enthusiasm is quiet, but unsleeping. He is very unlike most Italians, but very unlike most Americans, too. I do not expect all who cared for me to care for him, nor is it of importance to him that they should. He is wholly without vanity. He is too truly the gentleman not to be respected by all persons of refinement. For the rest, if

my life is free, and not too much troubled, if he can
enjoy his domestic affections, and fulfil his duties in his
own way, he will be content.   Can we find this much for
ourselves in bustling America the next three or four
years?   I know not, but think we shall come and try.
I wish much to see you all, and exchange the kiss of
peace.   There will, I trust, be peace within, if not without.   I thank you most warmly for your gift.   Be
assured it will turn to great profit.   I have learned to
be a great adept in economy, by looking at my little
boy.   I cannot bear to spend a cent for fear he may
come to want.   I understand now how the family-men
get so mean, and shall have to begin soon to pray
against that danger.   My little Nino, as we call him
for house and pet name, is in perfect health.   I wash,
and dress, and sew for him; and think I see a great
deal of promise in his little ways, and shall know him
better for doing all for him, though it is fatiguing and
inconvenient at times.   He is very gay and laughing,
sometimes violent, — for he is come to the age when he
wants everything in his own hands, — but, on the whole,
sweet as yet, and very fond of me.   He often calls me to
kiss him.   He says, "kiss," in preference to the Italian
word bàcio.   I do not cherish sanguine visions about
him, but try to do my best by him, and enjoy the present moment.

It was a nice account you gave of Miss Bremer.   She
found some "neighbors" as good as her own.   You say
she was much pleased by ———; could she know her,
she might enrich the world with a portrait as full of

little delicate traits as any in her gallery, and of a higher
class than any in which she has been successful.   I would
give much that a competent person should paint ———.
It is a shame she should die and leave the world no
copy.

*   *   *   *   *   *

TO MR. CASS, CHARGE D'AFFAIRES DES ETATS UNIS D'AMERIQUE.

Florence, May 2, 1850.

DEAR MR. CASS: I shall most probably leave Florence and Italy the 8th or 10th of this month, and am
not willing to depart without saying adieu to yourself.
I wanted to write the 30th of April, but a succession of
petty interruptions prevented.   That was the day I saw
you first, and the day the French first assailed Rome.
What a crowded day that was!   I had been to visit
Ossoli. in the morning, in the garden of the Vatican
Just after my return you entered.   I then went to the
hospital, and there passed the night amid the groans of
many suffering and some dying men.   What a strange
first of May it was, as I walked the streets of Rome by
the early sunlight of the next day!   Those were to me
grand and impassioned hours.   Deep sorrow followed, —
many embarrassments, many pains!   Let me once more,
at parting, thank you for the sympathy you showed me
amid many of these.   A thousand years might pass, and
you would find it unforgotten by me.

I leave Italy with profound regret, and with only a
vague hope of returning.   I could have lived here

always, full of bright visions, and expanding in my faculties, had destiny permitted. May you be happy who remain here! It would be well worth while to be happy in Italy!

I had hoped to enjoy some of the last days, but the weather has been steadily bad since you left Florence. Since the 4th of April we have not had a fine day, and all our little plans for visits to favorite spots and beautiful objects, from which we have long been separated, have been marred!

I sail in the barque Elizabeth for New York. She is laden with marble and rags — a very appropriate companionship for wares of Italy! She carries Powers' statue of Calhoun. Adieu! Remember that we look to you to keep up the dignity of our country. Many important occasions are now likely to offer for the American (I wish I could write the Columbian) man to advocate, — more, to *represent* the cause of Truth and Freedom in the face of their foes. Remember me as their lover, and your friend,   M. O.

———

TO ———.

Florence, April 16, 1850.

* * * There is a bark at Leghorn, highly spoken of, which sails at the end of this month, and we shall very likely take that. I find it imperatively necessary to go to the United States to make arrangements that may free me from care. Shall I be more fortunate if I go in person? I do not know. I am ill adapted to push my

claims and pretensions; but, at least, it will not be such slow work as passing from disappointment to disappointment here, where I wait upon the post-office, and must wait two or three months, to know the fate of any proposition.

I go home prepared to expect all that is painful and difficult. It will be a consolation to see my dear mother; and my dear brother E., whom I have not seen for ten years, is coming to New England this summer. On that account I wish to go *this* year.

* * * * * *

May 10. — My head is full of boxes, bundles, phials of medicine, and pots of jelly. I never thought much about a journey for myself, except to try and return all the things, books especially, which I had been borrowing; but about my child I feel anxious lest I should not take what is necessary for his health and comfort on so long a voyage, where omissions are irreparable. The unpropitious, rainy weather delays us now from day to day, as our ship, the Elizabeth, — (look out for news of shipwreck !) cannot finish taking in her cargo till come one or two good days.

I leave Italy with most sad and unsatisfied heart, — hoping, indeed, to return, but fearing that may not be permitted in my "cross-biased" life, till strength of feeling and keenness of perception be less than during these bygone rich, if troubled, years.

I can say least to those whom I prize most. I am so sad and weary, leaving Italy, that I seem paralyzed.

* * * * * *

TO THE SAME.

Ship Elizabeth, off Gibraltar, June 3, 1850.

MY DEAR M——: You will, I trust, long ere receiving this, have read my letter from Florence, enclosing one to my mother, informing her under what circumstances I had drawn on you through ————, and mentioning how I wished the bill to be met in case of any accident to me on my homeward course. That course, as respects weather, has been thus far not unpleasant; but the disaster that has befallen us is such as I never dreamed of. I had taken passage with Captain Hasty — one who seemed to me one of the best and most high-minded of our American men. He showed the kindest interest in us. His wife, an excellent woman, was with him. I thought, during the voyage, if safe and my child well, to have as much respite from care and pain as sea-sickness would permit. But scarcely was that enemy in some measure quelled, when the captain fell sick. At first his disease presented the appearance of nervous fever. I was with him a great deal; indeed, whenever I could relieve his wife from a ministry softened by great love and the courage of womanly heroism. The last days were truly terrible with disgusts and fatigues; for he died, we suppose,— no physician has been allowed to come on board to see the body,— of confluent small-pox. I have seen, since we parted, great suffering, but nothing physical to be compared to this, where the once fair and expressive mould of man is thus lost in corruption before life has fled. He died yesterday morning, and was buried in deep water, the American Consul's barge towing out one from this ship which bore the body, about six o'clock. It was Sunday. A divinely calm, glowing afternoon had succeeded a morning of bleak, cold wind. You cannot think how beautiful the whole thing was : — the decent array and sad reverence of the sailors; the many ships with their banners flying; the stern pillar of Hercules all bathed in roseate vapor; the little white sails diving into the blue depths with that solemn spoil of the good man, so still, when he had been so agonized and gasping as the last sun stooped. Yes, it was beautiful; but how dear a price we pay for the poems of this world! We shall now be in quarantine a week; no person permitted to come on board until it be seen whether disease break out in other cases. I have no good reason to think it will *not ;* yet I do not feel afraid. Ossoli has had it; so he is safe. The baby is, of course, subject to injury. In the earlier days, before I suspected small-pox, I carried him twice into the sick-room, at the request of the captain, who was becoming fond of him. He laughed and pointed; he did not discern danger, but only thought it odd to see the old friend there in bed. It is vain by prudence to seek to evade the stern assaults of destiny. I submit. Should all end well, we shall be in New York later than I expected; but keep a look-out. Should we arrive safely, I should like to see a friendly face. Commend me to my dear friends; and, with most affectionate wishes that joy and peace may continue to dwell in your house, adieu, and love as you can,

Your friend,   MARGARET.

LETTER FROM HON. LEWIS CASS, JR., UNITED STATES CHARGE D'AFFAIRES AT ROME, TO MRS. E. K. CHANNING.

Legation des Etats Unis d'Amerique,
Rome, May 10, 1851.

MADAME : I beg leave to acknowledge the receipt of your letter of the — ult., and to express my regret that the weak state of my eyesight has prevented me from giving it an earlier reply.

In compliance with your request, I have the honor to state, succinctly, the circumstances connected with my acquaintance with the late Madame Ossoli, your deceased sister, during her residence in Rome.

In the month of April, 1849, Rome, as you are no doubt aware, was placed in a state of siege by the approach of the French army.   It was filled at that time with exiles and fugitives who had been contending for years, from Milan in the north to Palermo in the south, for the republican cause; and when the gates were closed, it was computed that there were, of Italians alone, thirteen thousand refugees within the walls of the city, all of whom had been expelled from adjacent states, till Rome became their last rallying-point, and, to many, their final resting-place.   Among these was to be seen every variety of age, sentiment, and condition,— striplings and blanched heads; wild, visionary enthusiasts; grave, heroic men, who, in the struggle for freedom, had ventured all, and lost all; nobles and beggars; bandits, felons and brigands.   Great excitement naturally existed ; and, in the general apprehension which pervaded all classes, that

acts of personal violence and outrage would soon be committed, the foreign residents, especially, found themselves
placed in an alarming situation.

On the 30th of April the first engagement took place
between the French and Roman troops, and in a few days
subsequently I visited several of my countrymen, at their
request, to concert measures for their safety. Hearing,
on that occasion, and for the first time, of Miss Fuller's
presence in Rome, and of her solitary mode of life, I
ventured to call upon her, and offer my services in any
manner that might conduce to her comfort and security.
She received me with much kindness, and thus an acquaintance commenced. Her residence on the Piazzi
Barberini being considered an insecure abode, she removed to the Casa Dies, which was occupied by several
American families.

In the engagements which succeeded between the
Roman and French troops, the wounded of the former
were brought into the city, and disposed throughout the
different hospitals, which were under the superintendence
of several ladies of high rank, who had formed themselves
into associations, the better to ensure care and attention
to those unfortunate men. Miss Fuller took an active
part in this noble work; and the greater portion of her
time, during the entire siege, was passed in the hospital
of the Trinity of the Pilgrims, which was placed under
her direction, in attendance upon its inmates.

The weather was intensely hot; her health was feeble
and delicate; the dead and dying were around her in
every stage of pain and horror; but she never shrank

from the duty she had assumed. Her heart and soul
were in the cause for which these men had fought, and
all was done that Woman could do to comfort them in
their sufferings. I have seen the eyes of the dying,
as she moved among them, extended on opposite beds,
meet in commendation of her universal kindness; and the
friends of those who then passed away may derive consolation from the assurance that nothing of tenderness and
attention was wanting to soothe their last moments. And
I have heard many of those who recovered speak with all
the passionate fervor of the Italian nature, of her whose
sympathy and compassion, throughout their long illness,
fulfilled all the offices of love and affection. Mazzini, the
chief of the Triumvirate, who, better than any man in
Rome, knew her worth, often expressed to me his admiration of her high character; and the Princess Bel-
giojoso, to whom was assigned the charge of the Papal
Palace, on the Quirinal, which was converted on this
occasion into a hospital, was enthusiastic in her praise.
And in a letter which I received not long since from this
lady, who was gaining the bread of an exile by teaching
languages in Constantinople, she alludes with much feeling
to the support afforded by Miss Fuller to the republican
party in Italy. Here, in Rome, she is still spoken of in
terms of regard and endearment, and the announcement
of her death was received with a degree of sorrow not
often bestowed upon a foreigner, especially one of a different faith.

On the 29th of June, the bombardment from the
French camp was very heavy, shells and grenades fall-

ing in every part of the city. In the afternoon of the 30th, I received a brief note from Miss Fuller, requesting me to call at her residence. I did so without delay, and found her lying on a sofa, pale and trembling, evidently much exhausted. She informed me that she had sent for me to place in my hand a packet of important papers, which she wished me to keep for the present, and, in the event of her death, to transmit it to her friends in the United States. She then stated that she was married to Marquis Ossoli, who was in command of a battery on the Pincian Hill, — that being the highest and most exposed position in Rome, and directly in the line of bombs from the French camp. It was not to be expected, she said, that he could escape the dangers of another night, such as the last; and therefore it was her intention to remain with him, and share his fate. At the Ave Maria, she added, he would come for her, and they would proceed together to his post. The packet which she placed in my possession, contained, she said, the certificates of her marriage, and of the birth and baptism of her child. After a few words more, I took my departure, the hour she named having nearly arrived. At the porter's lodge I met the Marquis Ossoli, and a few moments afterward I saw them walking toward the Pincian Hill.

Happily, the cannonading was not renewed that night, and at dawn of day she returned to her apartments, with her husband by her side. On that day the French army entered Rome, and, the gates being opened, Madame Ossoli, accompanied by the Marquis, immediately proceeded to Rieti, where she had left her child in the charge of a confidential nurse, formerly in the service of the Ossoli family.

She remained, as you are no doubt aware, some months at Rieti, whence she removed to Florence, where she resided until her ill-fated departure for the United States. During this period I received several letters from her, all of which, though reluctant to part with them, I enclose to your address in compliance with your request.

I am, Madame, very respectfully,

Your obedient servant,

LEWIS CASS, JR.

PART IV.

MEMORIALS OF MARGARET FULLER OSSOLI.

[In place of the Appendix to this volume, which appeared in the previous editions, and which contained only extracts from other writers than my sister Margaret, I have inserted the following memorials and critiques upon her writings, believing them of more interest to the public. The first memorial, by her constant friend, Horace Greeley, deserves a permanent record, as does all which appears from his pen. It is alike generous and discriminating. The second, by Mrs. A. A. Livermore, and the third, by Mrs. Hanaford, are valuable for themselves, and as indicating how my sister's views and character are regarded by her own sex. The entire articles are not inserted, but most which pertains to these points. Excellent articles by Mrs. Crosland, in her "Memorable Women," and Mrs. Dall, in "Historical Pictures," are not inserted here, because easily accessible to the public elsewhere. — Ed.]

MARGARET FULLER OSSOLI

BY HON. HORACE GREELEY.

TEN years ago — on the 19th of July, 1850 — Margaret Fuller Ossoli, with her husband and child, was lost to her mortal friends and kindred, in the wreck of the bark Elizabeth, from Leghorn to New York, on Fire Island Beach, Long Island, just as she came within sight of her native shores, after a most eventful absence of more than four years ; and her printed works * — all that the general public can ever know

---

* "Memoirs and Complete Works of Margaret Fuller Ossoli," 6 vols., edited by her brother, Rev. Arthur B. Fuller. Published by Brown and Taggard, 29 Cornhill, Boston.

of her genius and her character — have only been given complete to the reading world within the last few weeks. This delay, though not calculated, has not been unfortunate. Their preparation has been thorough and conscientious ; time has been gained for inquiry, for reflection, for comparison of recollections and impressions, and for unlocking the private cabinets wherein some of her choicest thoughts lay hidden, under garb of casual letters to valued friends ; so that these six volumes afford a clearer and deeper insight into the mind and heart of Margaret Fuller than any number could have done if issued in the hot haste which the interests of "the trade" are supposed to require. Could they have been put forth within the year of her startling and widely-lamented decease, they would probably have been more generally, but less usefully, less satisfactorily read, than now. Yet meantime the public appreciation of their author-subject has been steadily broadening ; and the full series will be welcomed and treasured by many who had never heard of her while she lived. Then the new and brighter page opened in the history of Italy — that sunny land of classic memories, for whose redemption she dared and did all of which a high-souled woman is capable — will necessarily win fresh regard for her who was one of the earliest, most enthusiastic, most devoted, American champions of Italian liberty and unity.

But who was Margaret Fuller Ossoli ?

Hon. Timothy Fuller, of the fourth generation from

Thomas Fuller, a Puritan who migrated from Old to New England in 1638, was born in the Island of Martha's Vineyard, Massachusetts, in 1778, and in 1809 married Margaret, daughter of Major Peter Crane, of Canton, Mass. Of the seven children born of this union, Margaret, our subject, was the first. The father was an industrious, energetic, painstaking lawyer, with some solid but no shining qualities, who began life in very straitened circumstances, but, early attaching himself to the old Jeffersonian Republican party, rose with its rising fortunes, and became in 1815 a state senator, thence in 1817 a representative in Congress, where he served till 1825, resisting the Missouri Compromise and efficiently contributing to the election of John Quincy Adams to the Presidency. He served afterward in the Executive Council, and died suddenly of cholera in 1835, leaving his widow and six surviving children in very moderate circumstances. The mother was a woman of modest intellectual attainments, but of rare mental as well as personal loveliness, who survived her husband twenty-four years, dying on the 31st of July, 1859. The oldest daughter gave very early indications of rare intellectual force, and her mental vivacity and love of acquisition were rather stimulated than judiciously restrained by the father, not through vanity or mistaken pride, but simply because in his day the laws of life and health, and their rigorous exactions of a due proportion between mental and physical exertion, were not under-

stood as they now are. At eight years of age, we
have heard, the child was required by him, as a part
of her daily tasks, to compose a number of Latin
verses ; at fourteen, she had probably made larger
and more various intellectual acquisitions, whether of
words, of facts, or of ideas, than any other person of
like years in the world. But these treasures had been
won at a serious cost to a physical frame naturally vigorous and robust, and she endured much in after-life,
and was often disabled for days by sick headaches and
spinal sufferings resulting from these youthful excesses
in study. Her education mainly proceeded under her
father's immediate guidance and his roof; but she
spent some time at a boarding-school, and some years
afterward became principal teacher in a seminary for
young women in Providence, R. I., where her rare
intellectual powers were evinced and acknowledged.
Returning to Massachusetts, she, in 1839, commenced
in Boston a series of " Conversations " for women,
which were continued through the two or three succeeding winters. Her first book — a translation of Eck-
erman's Conversations with Goethe — was published
about this time. In 1841 she partly translated the
letters of Günderode and Bettine. " The Dial," a
quarterly serial of eminent originality and force, was
commenced in 1840, edited by Margaret Fuller, as-
sisted by R. W. Emerson, and others ; and she gave
to it some of her best days and energies throughout
the four years of its existence, though lacking ⹀ne

stimulus and almost the hope of pecuniary recompense. The essays on Goethe, Haydn, Mozart, Handel, Bach, Beethoven, the two Herberts, and some others reprinted in these volumes, first appeared in "The Dial," and so replete are they with fresh, vigorous thoughts that they will yet be read with interest and profit by thousands.

In 1843 she made a summer excursion with some friends to Niagara and the (then) Far West, — that is, the prairies surrounding the head of Lake Michigan, — journeying so far west as Rock River. Her pictures of that region, then just beginning to resound to the hum of civilized industry, are at once graceful and vivid, truthful and poetic, and may still be read with pleasure as enduring records of a state of things which will seem stranger to none than to those who now inhabit those regions, and who reflect that the villages of Chicago and Milwaukie, described by her, are separated by barely seventeen years from the cities now covering their sites. The Indians who then camped beside them, the prairies which stretched, vast and in virgin solitude, beyond them, have seldom or never been gazed on with more discerning, sympathizing eyes.

Toward the close of 1844, she removed to New York, the better to fulfil an engagement then formed to contribute to the literary department of "THE TRIBUNE." Here she remained till the August of 1846, and about one fourth of the contents of the four volumes of her writings now before us first appeared in our columns, distinguished by the * signature so welcome to our more cultivated readers of fifteen years ago. Thomas Hood — Edgar A. Poe — Frederick Douglass — Festus — Emerson's Essays — Capital Punishment — Cassius M. Clay — New Year's Day — St. Valentine's — Fourth of July — First of August — Thanksgiving — Christmas — Grace Church — The Rich Poor Man — The Poor Rich Man — Farewell to New York, — such are the titles of a few of the essays which many readers who " were younger once than they are now," will be glad to greet again in these fair volumes.

In 1846, Margaret found herself able to fulfil her long-cherished, reluctantly postponed desire to visit Europe. Accompanying a family of beloved and loving friends, she traversed England, Scotland, France, thence proceeding to Italy, and finding at length a resting-place in Rome, that " city of the soul," wherewith her name and fortunes were destined to be henceforth blended. Entering its walls almost simultaneously with the dawn of the new hopes for Italy and for Man based on the accession of Pius IX. " the Reform Pope," she flung her whole soul into the struggle then initiated, never blinded by the glare of present unbounded and almost unresisted triumph to the black thunder-clouds gathering and muttering in the distance; honoring the Pope for his kindly feelings and good intentions, she was yet

never oblivious of the weakness of his character, the
infirmity of his purpose, and the unchangeable hos-
tility of the influences surrounding the institutions
enshrouding him, to that development of popular intelligence, freedom of discussion, and independence of
judgment which is the essential basis of republican
liberty.   While others, more sanguine, less far-see-
ing, were dancing in exultation over the grave of
civil and religious despotism, she was appealing to
her countrymen at home for sympathy, arms, material aid, in view of the deadly struggle inevitably
approaching.   Hence the hour of overwhelming reaction, of deadly perils, of priestly maledictions and
popular consternation, of mustering legions and gleaming bayonets converging from France, from Austria,
from Naples, to quench the beacon-fires of liberty
still burning brightly if not cheerily on the ramparts
of the seven-hilled city, found her calm, resolute,
tearless, leaving her young babe in its rural nest to
stand through the night-watches beside her husband
in the batteries on the ramparts of the beleaguered
city, and give her days to sympathizing labors in the
hospitals where the wounded soldiers of the Republic,
torn with cannon-shot and parched with fever, were
breathing their last in the bitter consciousness that
they had poured out their life-blood in behalf of a
hopeless, ruined cause.

The triumph of despotism, though nobly resisted,
was inevitable.   The defence of Rome, hopeless from

the first, was yet necessary and beneficent. It arrested and fixed the gaze of the civilized world, compelling millions to perceive and realize the ready, instinctive union of all the powers of darkness and despotism to quench the flame of liberty, — the readiness alike of sacerdotal and political oligarchies to shed torrents of blood for the retention or recovery of justly forfeited power. Rome fell; but nations saw and comprehended the catastrophe; and the seed watered by the blood of her martyred defenders already throbs with the new life quickening in its bosom. Yet a little while, and the upspringing tree of liberty will overspread the sunny land of the Gracchi and of Rienzi, and twenty-five millions of happy people will exult in its protecting shade.

After the fall of Rome, Margaret lingered some months in Italy, mainly in Florence, devoting her time and energies to a history of the uprising of 1848, and the disastrous overthrow of 1849. That history, still in manuscript, was irrecoverably lost with her in the shipwreck of July 19, 1850. The lovers of freedom throughout the world have reason to lament this loss. No one else could have set forth so clearly, so forcibly, so movingly, that magnificent uprising of a nation; no one could have more effectively aroused and diffused indignation at the manifold treacheries and crimes which quenched the hopes of Italy in a sea of her own blood.

Aside from that lost history, all of her writings that

were not in their nature special and temporary will be found collected and fitly presented in the volumes before us. We believe them surpassed in value and suggestiveness by those of no other American woman. They combine richness and ripeness of culture with vigorous independence of thought and absolute fearlessness of utterance. No human being ever lived whose mental habitudes were more thoroughly self-centred and self-reliant than those of Margaret Fuller. No one ever wrote in more perfect and pure unconsciousness of the dictates of "Society" — of Mrs. Potiphar and Mrs. Grundy. Hence she sometimes gave expression to what scarcely another woman would have said, yet what, once uttered, many felt grateful to her for saying. Her "Woman in the Nineteenth Century," especially in its avowals of sympathy for the debased and scorned outcasts of her own sex, and in its stinging rebukes of those fashionable butterflies who loathe the thought of speaking to one of these, yet associate freely and smilingly with those whom they well know to be the authors of their ruin, the partners of their guilt, could hardly have been more direct and unsparing.

We consider this the most original and effective of her works; and yet, regarded from a strictly literary stand-point, it is not entirely satisfactory. It convinces you, if you need to be convinced, that the position, the consideration, the education of Woman, are not what they should be; it does not so clearly

point out, to the general mind, the practical reforms
whereby these are to be rectified. No woman, no
man, ever read it without profit; but many have
closed it with but vague and dim ideas of what ought
to be done. And this resulted inevitably from the
structure of the author's mind. She was a philanthro-
pist, preëminently a critic, a relentless destroyer of
shams and outworn traditions; not a creator, a legislator, a builder. No book was ever better calculated
to arouse and quicken intellect; none has more clearly
demonstrated that something should and must be done;
but just what should be done was left to be devised
and indicated by others, whom this living word should
awaken to a consciousness of wrong, of necessity, and
of duty. Hence many abuses have been and will be
corrected, many wise and humane modifications of
our laws affecting Woman have been and will be
enacted, in consequence of this book, by persons who
have scarcely heard the name, and know nothing of
the works, of Margaret Fuller.

How large a proportion of our young women, now
acquiring an education, are qualified to read the
writings of Margaret Fuller with interest and appreciation, we will not judge; but for all who can
thus read them, we are sure that the possession of
these volumes will prove of greater value and profit
than an additional quarter at the most expensive or
the most famous seminary.

·Those who would know Margaret Fuller as a

Woman as well as a Thinker, will find her faithfully and vividly depicted in these volumes, especially in those which constitute her Memoirs, being in good part the personal recollections of her near and true friends, Ralph Waldo Emerson, James Freeman Clarke, and William Henry Channing. Some further revelations of the reverent admiration and fervent affection wherewith she was justly regarded as a daughter, sister, and family counsellor and guide, will be found in the brief but fit prefaces to the several volumes of her works by her brother, Rev. Arthur B. Fuller. How truly and deeply she was loved by the members of her home-circle, — by the child barely old enough to climb to her knee, — the humble, illiterate servant who was encouraged by her kindness to make her a confidant, and who found in her a true friend, — by the unfortunate, the destitute, the despairing, — can never be fully set forth, yet is sufficiently indicated in these volumes. No one in limited circumstances ever dealt more generously with those whose needs were more pressing than her own; few have oftener found in others a more ready and sympathetic response to the liberality of her own large nature. Misconceived and disparaged by many of her contemporaries, whom sectarian prejudice or dread of her reformatory tendencies made her enemies, she has, since her death, grown steadily and visibly in the regard of the high-souled and philanthropic in either hemisphere, and generations yet unborn will honor

the genius and intrepidity, the labors and achieve-
ments of MARGARET FULLER OSSOLI. — *New York
Tribune.*

MARGARET FULLER OSSOLI,

A REPRESENTATIVE WOMAN.

BY MRS. A. A. LIVERMORE.

WE have but lately received the Memoirs and
Works of Margaret Fuller Ossoli ; and we have only
waited to reperuse thoughts which have always been
full of suggestion to us, before we give our latest impressions of one who, for want of a better term, we
denominate a *representative woman.*

In doing this, we will endeavor to express what we
mean by it, as applied to one who, by her native talent
and acquired culture, and through authorship, stands
prominent before the American public. If we mistake
not, she was the first who raised a clear note, so as to
command attention, in behalf of a *higher culture, greater
privilege,* and a *rightful sphere of activity* for the women
of her country.

It is curious to note the result, through an overrul-
ing Providence, of the intention of her father to give
her what is called a masculine education, (though he
evidently meant only to properly unfold her uncom-

mon powers,) by which she rose to the point of most thoroughly appreciating what is peculiarly feminine in woman, and by her advocacy of its worth, to open a way for its needed influence.

That she did not create the desire for a better culture, privilege, and sphere of activity, is manifest by the almost simultaneous rising of persons in different localities in favor of the same, which has resulted in what is called the "Woman's Rights Movement." She but expressed in strong and definite terms the promptings of her own full nature, and therefore stands as the representative of a general want.

It is not necessary to suppose that she suffered peculiar disabilities in any form of her outward lot ; on the contrary, she was unusually favored with affection, respect, and opportunities of mental acquisition. But she was one of the disinterested few, who, through warm sympathy and a keen sensibility, gather into themselves the woes of their race, suffering their evils, and lacking their needed good.

For this large-hearted, this magnetic and electrifying life, even more than for her uncommon attainments, do we place her foremost of all who have plead for their sex, and we cannot but regard the full publication of her writings as an important era in the movement, and as giving a fit opportunity to say a few words upon the same.

To the unobservant and unthinking, it must seem revolutionary for a class who from nature and custom seem to love and to rest in dependence, to ask and even demand the enjoyment of rights and the performance of duties which in the past have been confined to the masculine minds of the community.

But we must consider the different position woman at once assumed in the emancipation of our country from British rule. The commencement of our hostilities with England, which gave her a share of the responsibilities and dangers of that struggle, was the true date of her resistance to the established order of things, and essentially instituted her equal freedom by its success. Ever since that time her way of life has been one specially suited to develop her energies and increase her self-respect. In pioneering, planting, and building, she has had her full share of incidental privations and toils ; while, in her desire to aid the common cause, she has seldom paused to think whether her helping hand stopped short or went beyond the employments usually assigned her. Added to this, since education has become the ruling passion of our people, her brain has been stimulated to incessant activity, while the very air she breathes, filled as it is with the life of unprecedented action, compels her, as a matter of course, to new uses of her powers. As the pressure of business keeps the head of the family much from home, and its weight of care returns him to it wearied and oppressed, longing for rest and recreation rathe1 than to enter it as a scene of discipline and correction, the government of its younger members devolves much upon herself, which, when added to the experimental character which our republican principles give to our whole domestic *menage*, no less than to our social life, taxes her faculties to an uncommon degree. So when, as often occurs, he whose protection she would gladly shelter herself under, falters through manifold worldly temptations, and falls by the way-side helpless and burdensome, or worse still, comes home to heap upon her abuse, and those to whom she has given life return, it may be, from its snares, marred and spoiled, to mock her best endeavors in their nurture, it is but a natural and slightly forward step for her to seek to bring more within her own power the hoarded means of the family, by calling for a change of law to aid her, and to ask to share in devising social and public restraints to save her own from moral and physical ruin. Or, if this is impossible, that the prohibitions of society, or the selfish rivalry of the more fortunate, may not prevent her seeking in some sphere a little aside from the common one that support denied her by her appointed guardian. This, in simple terms, is what we understand by the plea for woman's rights. It is for this that Margaret Fuller entreated ; and when she said, " Let her be a sea-captain if she will," she but expressed in strong and somewhat exaggerated terms her wish for them to be allowed to prepare for any emergency. Singularly enough, this duty has since devolved upon a lady through pressing necessity, and was performed, as is well known, with such success as to win unmingled approbation.*

That there has been heat and passion in the discussion, is but the necessary accompaniment of the introduction of a new subject for public attention. It seems as if it were necessary that the human mind should thrust itself beyond the boundaries of reason and thorough judgment, that it may obtain a vantage ground from which to overlook a subject, before it settles down into that medium position safe alike from the degradation of servitude and the dangers of license.

It is for the restrained tone of feeling with which she advocates her cause, for its mingled womanly earnestness and lady-like reserve, that we turn to Margaret Fuller's pages with satisfaction and hope. Through her own example and precepts she shows that an increase of benefit is to come to us chiefly by the culture of a higher tone of thought, a truer life, and a more faithful employment of time and talent. For this end she was ever ready to help and encourage both the older and the younger. To her inspiration as a teacher many must date the upward tendencies of their lives. Her keen discernment of their qualities of mind, her ready perception of character, and her generous sympathy, must have had an untold force upon those whom she taught, and made her their truest benefactor.

The rapid and intense working of her mind, con-

* Mrs. Patten.

nected with its uncommon grasp, caused her to include within the moderate term of her one life the thoughts, feelings, and experiences of many, while the necessity there was for busy action gave it a practical and wise direction. This told, also, upon her natural temper, being one to seek the original right and reason of things, rather than to walk unreflectingly in the beaten way, which, in itself, creating for her a loneliness of spirit, might, but for industry, have degenerated into morbidness and misanthropy.

Though at times, through her thoughtful far-sightedness, her native idealism, and inherent energy, she becomes impatient of the slow unfolding of events, and forgetful of life's limitations, — feels herself, as it were, withheld by fate, — yet she never abates her labors, or loses her faith in the final triumph of good.

For her wonderful combination of natural talent for study, genius for colloquial expression, ability to use her varied gifts for her wide-spread philanthropy and domestic virtues, and especially for her power of moral inspiration, we might challenge the world to produce her equal. As critic, narrator, essayist, journalist, and historian, this woman of a century, who never wrote a sentence which her own conscience did not sanction, and which was not the fruit of rigid self-culture, may well stand for us as a symbol of woman's capabilities.

Her poems, as she says, were but the attempt tc

vary for herself her mode of expression, and do not reveal her full power. Had she stopped to muse until the fire burned in that direction, she might have become a lyrist of no mean stamp. Her " Farewell to Summer " shows a thirst for harmony, and a sense of melody which, when worked and waited for patiently, flows out into verse. But then she might not have been our representative woman. As it was, her poetic feeling heightened for her the value of life and its opportunities ; it exalted her conceptions of duty, opened her eyes to the worth of humanity, and made her eloquent in behalf of the suffering. It cleared from her vision the false illusions which often surround the most applauded, and ennobled for her the least virtues of the lowly. It made her country's interests her own, and induced her to share in the sufferings of Italy, and rejoice in its every gleam of success. It nerved her to moral courage when painful truths were to be uttered, and gave to her presence a dignity from which the selfish coxcomb retired, thanking her for a rebuke, and melted to tears the murderous brigands who, with a strong arm, at the risk of her life, she divided from their strife. It drew to her the young maiden in loving and wholesome confidence ; it sent from her the young man with the dawn of new and better purposes in his breast, and softened the prejudices of the older and more cautious who had been slow to approach her.

It is for this unfaltering poetic spirit, an essentially

religious one as it is, which ever points to higher and
more refined excellence, and infuses itself through
every page of her works, for which more than anything else we cordially hope they may find a place
in every woman's library. It is not that she is faultless, a model woman, a pattern for all, — far from it.
She had quick impulses and a spirit of sarcasm which
she found hard to train, prejudices which were with
difficulty corrected, the imperiousness of a strong mind,
which knows its power, and is determined to use it
for her own good and others' welfare, and which is
slow to mellow into that just and graceful influence
which in the end is most effective.   There was in her
the visible self-consciousness of a nature continually
pressing upon itself from its abundant fulness, and at
times an abandonment to self-laudation, which were
absurd did we not see in it a recognition of the value
of our common humanity; and an assertion of her
influence over other minds simply amusing were it
not in spirit so true.   But with all her idealism, her
love of progress, and intensity of interior life, she was
yet eminently conservative, and self-denying for herself and others in the application of means to ends.
While she demands privilege for her sex, she incul-
cates the idea, and sets herself to work to secure
their proportionate culture.   While she asks for them
a healthful sphere of activity, and aspires after a wider
range for her own faculties, she is yet chary of at-
tempting what she fears not to achieve, and in ad-

vocating the cause of woman she never forgets the self-restraint appropriate to the lady.

For this mingling of reserve and frankness in writing of woman's disabilities and needs, for her energy of character and general grasp of mind, we have been accustomed to place Margaret Fuller at the head of the ameliorating movement for woman ; and though others may have done much, we consider her its greatest representative.

And as we turn from the mists and mazes of transcendentalism and rationalism to the clear teachings of DR. CHANNING, in which he points to the pure theism of the Scriptures, and to the value of our common nature, as is shown in the Gospels, so do we turn with equal satisfaction from the extravagances of womanly conventions to the books before us, and give our assent to her definition of what is peculiar to woman, in words somewhat enigmatical, it is true, in which she speaks of their quickness of perception, their promptness in action, and their religious desires. Add to these the patience which, through much pondering, becomes, so to speak, an *intellectual* virtue, and the tact which, through a never-sleeping sense of responsibility, becomes a *moral* one, and the circle of traits which enable her to act most beneficently may be considered complete.

If it should be said that our notice of Margaret Fuller bears a tone of exaggerated praise, it is from no personal friendship for her. We knew her not, and were but seldom in the way of hearing of her. Once only we took a glance at her as she walked with stately step through the hall of the White Mountain Hotel, (in familiar conversation with a friend,) where for an hour our ways chanced to meet. We have but taken these books, read and re-read them, and what we have written of her is the spirit of their teaching, and the summary of our study of her character and life.

It was in Italy, now so present to our interests and hopes, that she found a second home, and the companion of her life. Shipwrecked in their worldly fortunes by the disasters of his country, she sought in her own a support for her beloved ones, and the sympathies of her friends. There were hearts waiting to claim her again as their own, minds whose opening genius mothers desired to consign to her direction, and eyes to see how the muse and the authoress would act the part of the mother and the wife. But the waves closed over her and she was no more. But not so; for a soul so living can never die; and that among the many mansions where her spirit has found a home, must ever be a beneficent element in creation. Peace to her *memory* we cannot say to what will be more and more a *presence* among us, but rather joy to her re-awakening; henceforth go on rejoicing!

In conclusion we must be allowed to thank the devoted brother who, through years of patient labor, has gathered up these literary remains of a sister so revered, and given them to the public in so readable and worthy a form. Wherever Margaret Fuller Ossoli is known, he will be named with her as one who appreciated her genius, venerated her worth, and did what he could to make them known to the world. — *New York Christian Inquirer.*

MARGARET FULLER OSSOLI.

BY MRS. J. H. HANAFORD.

WHEN a true and noble soul passes from earth, it is wise to preserve some memorial of its excellence, some record of the circumstances which surrounded it, some delineation of its personal peculiarities and description of character, while fighting the battles of life, and winning, eventually, the victory. Such a memorial may prove as a way-mark to some one of similar habits, pursuits, and character, who desires to tread a similar pathway tending upward toward celestial heights of excellence.

This desirable result has been the aim of the biographers of Margaret Fuller, Marchioness Ossoli, whose published works and tragic death must be familiar to many readers. Her Memoirs, by W. H. Channing, R. W. Emerson, and J. Freeman Clarke, have been for several years before the public. They have recently been republished, edited by her brother, Rev. Arthur B. Fuller, in connection with her complete works, and with the addition of a genealogical sketch of the Fuller family, and a touching tribute, by her son, to the memory of Margaret's mother. Having read them with deep and absorbing interest myself, I am anxious that others may share in my delight; and should any, by this brief sketch, be inspired, as I was by the Memoirs, with more earnest intellectual aspirations, and a deeper consciousness of the power which lies in true nobility of soul, I shall not have written in vain.

* * * * * *

As an author Margaret Fuller will never be forgotten. Many of the ideas contained in her writings are those that succeeding generations will see developed into harmonious existence, and their early advocate must be held in remembrance.

In this brief sketch, opportunity is not afforded for presenting an extended account of her life and writings. But it may serve to induce the young women of our country, especially, to seek a further acquaintance with its noble and pure-minded subject, that they may imitate her virtues. Faults she undoubtedly had, for she was human; and it is only in a future state that we are to realize the bliss intimated in Jude's ascription of praise. " Now unto him that is able . . . . . to present you *faultless* before the presence of his glory with exceeding joy . . . . . be glory and majesty, dominion and power, both now and ever!"

In many a loving heart is the memory of Margaret fondly cherished, and long after her bereaved friends and relatives shall follow her to the tearless land, will she be proudly numbered among the most gifted and highly cultured daughters of America; while the historian of Italy, in coming days, shall write no name upon his list of freedom's friends, which shall shine brighter, or be dearer to Italian hearts, than that of Margaret Fuller Ossoli. — *New York Life Illustrated.*